Specifying Software

This innovative volume provides a hands-on introducti the behavior of software components. Featured topics programmer-friendly assertional notations to specify, (nontrivial algorithms and data representations and for using state diagrams, grammars, and regular expressions to specify and develop recognizers for formal languages.

The presentation is based on numerous examples and case studies. It is appropriate for second- and third-year computer science and computer engineering students familiar with basic concepts of discrete mathematics and logic. Using this book will help readers improve their programming skills and develop a solid foundation for subsequent courses in advanced algorithms and data structures, software design, formal methods, compilers, programming languages, and theory.

R. D. Tennent is Professor of Computing and Information Science at Queen's University in Kingston, Canada, where he has been teaching since 1971. He has also held visiting positions at the University of Grenoble, Oxford University, and the University of Edinburgh. He has published three other books – *Principles of Programming Languages* (1981), *Semantics of Programming Languages* (1991), and *Algol-like Languages* (1997, co-edited with Peter O'Hearn) as well as more than 25 articles in scientific journals. His research interests encompass the design, description, and effective implementation and use of programming languages including: denotational semantics; applications of formal semantics to language design; formal systems for specifying, developing, and verifying programs; advanced type systems and their description; integration of functional and procedural programming; and programming methodology.

Specifying Software

A HANDS–ON INTRODUCTION

R. D. Tennent
Queen's University, Kingston, Canada

CAMBRIDGE
UNIVERSITY PRESS

CAMBRIDGE UNIVERSITY PRESS
Cambridge, New York, Melbourne, Madrid, Cape Town, Singapore,
São Paulo, Delhi, Dubai, Tokyo, Mexico City

Cambridge University Press
The Edinburgh Building, Cambridge CB2 8RU, UK

Published in the United States of America by Cambridge University Press, New York

www.cambridge.org
Information on this title: www.cambridge.org/9780521004015

© R. D. Tennent 2002

This publication is in copyright. Subject to statutory exception
and to the provisions of relevant collective licensing agreements,
no reproduction of any part may take place without the written
permission of Cambridge University Press.

First published 2002

A catalogue record for this publication is available from the British Library

Library of Congress Cataloguing in Publication data

Tennent, R. D., 1944 –
    Specifying software : a hands-on introduction / R. D. Tennent.
        p. cm.
    Includes bibliographical references.
    ISBN 0-521-80814-6 – ISBN 0-521-00401-2 (pb.)
    1. Computer programming. 2. Computer software – Specifications. I. Title.

    QA76.6 .T4416 2001
    005.1–dc21   2001037939

ISBN 978-0-521-80814-9 Hardback
ISBN 978-0-521-00401-5 Paperback

Cambridge University Press has no responsibility for the persistence or
accuracy of URLs for external or third-party Internet Web sites referred to in
this publication, and does not guarantee that any content on such Web sites is,
or will remain, accurate or appropriate. Information regarding prices, travel
timetables, and other factual information given in this work are correct at
the time of first printing but Cambridge University Press does not guarantee
the accuracy of such information thereafter.

Contents

C Language Recognizers

D   Unimplementable Specifications   243

Appendices   255

Preface

This book was written to support a short course in the second or third year of an undergraduate computer science, software engineering, or software design program. The prerequisites are fairly modest: some programming experience (ideally in C or C++ or a related language such as JAVA) and some exposure to the most basic concepts of discrete mathematics (sets, functions, binary relations, sequences) and to the language of elementary logic (connectives and quantifiers). It is intended to be only an *introduction* to software specifications, *not* a systematic survey of requirements engineering, formal methods, compilers, or computation theory suitable for a senior or graduate-level course. A course based on this book would provide a good foundation for such courses but should not replace them.

The contents may be summarized briefly as follows:

- specification, verification, and development of simple algorithms using pre- and post-conditions and loop invariants;

- specification, verification, and development of simple data representations using abstract models and representation invariants; and

- specification and systematic development of recognizers for formal languages using regular expressions, grammars, and automata.

These techniques have been well studied and are sound and useful. They may be presented to and immediately used by undergraduate students on simple but nontrivial examples. They may be taught without requiring upper-level prerequisites or major investments of time to teach complex notations or computer-based tools. But such material is not often presented at this level, nor in this combination. To explain why I have written this book, I will briefly describe its origins. Perhaps readers will recognize some similarities with the situations at their institutions.

At Queens's University, the undergraduate program in computer science has for many years included the following final-year courses:

- a "theory" course: formal languages, automata, and elementary complexity and computability theory;

- a "compilers" course: aspects of formal languages and automata relevant to development of scanners and parsers, as well as other topics on compilers such as symbol tables, code generation, and optimization;

- a "formal methods" course: various notations and tools for software specification and validation.

But a few years ago a controversy arose about whether such courses should be *required* of every graduating student. Some argued that every graduate of our degree programs should know *basic* material on computability and complexity, syntax analysis, and specification methods. But the instructors of the courses complained that there was not enough time available to treat all the material they thought should be covered and that many of the students were ill prepared for material involving mathematical formalism. On the other hand, many students were of the opinion that much of the material in these courses, which they called "abstract theory," had no practical relevance.

These issues were addressed by creating a new course. It was to be taken in the second or third year of our program and was to cover "basic" material formerly in the three final-year courses. The new course is now a prerequisite to these three courses and also to a variety of other courses in our program, including software engineering and foundations of programming languages. The final-year courses are now selected as *options* by students who are interested in those particular subjects (subject to some "breadth" constraints).

This approach to curriculum design has had several benefits. The basic material previously covered in the final-year courses is now required for almost all graduating students, without forcing every student to study advanced specialized material in areas of little interest to them. The duplication of material on formal languages and automata in the theory and compiler courses has been avoided by moving basic material into the new course. The final-year courses now have time to do advanced material, and the students in those courses are better prepared and more motivated. Perhaps the most important benefit has been that many students discover early in their programs that "theory" is actually *useful* because they now have an opportunity to apply mathematical rigor to programming problems at their level of expertise.

The main difficulty in presenting a "nonstandard" course is in finding a suitable text. Material on program and data specifications may be supported by a number of specialized texts [Rey81, Bac86, Gor88, Dro89, LG00], and a few books give an applications-oriented introductory presentation of formal-language material [Gou88, AU92], in addition to many specialized books on compilers; however, many of these books are now out of print, and a *unified* treatment of the two bodies of material is clearly preferable. Also, students are unhappy if less than half of the material is covered from each of *two* expensive texts.

The present book, based on my lecture notes for the new course, addresses these problems. The main pedagogical novelties would seem to be the following:

- the hands-on and pragmatic approach to what is usually taught as theory, or as abstract discussion of "large complex systems";

- the way the material on formal languages has been integrated into a specification-oriented framework by treating state diagrams, regular expressions, and context-free grammars as specialized specification languages: formalisms for specifying language recognizers.

Students seem to find this approach far more relevant and convincing than traditional approaches to formal methods and formal languages. It must be emphasized, however, that the material presented here is intended to be only a *prelude* to, and not a *replacement* for, conventional compiler, theory-of-computation, and software-engineering courses.

I have *not* provided an introductory survey of discrete mathematics and logic on the assumption that students studying this material have recently taken or are concurrently taking a course in basic concepts of discrete mathematics and logic and have available a suitable textbook that they will be able to use as a reference. Some of the notation used here is superficially nonstandard, such as the "C-like" bounded quantifiers described in Section 1.3.2, but the concepts should be familiar.

The choice of a programming language to use for the examples was difficult. Java has become the most popular introductory language in computer science programs, despite some rather serious deficiencies in this role [BT97, AB+98, Gre]. But Java seems even less well suited to *this* material: it uses reference assignment and reference equality for = and == on objects, it lacks enum and (assignable) struct types, its scope rules and exception handling are complex and intrusive, it lacks a standard library for straightforward textual input, and simple algorithmic code doesn't fit easily into its object-oriented framework. Pascal and similar languages such as Modula, Ada, and Turing might be the most appropriate for the material, but students these days find the syntax strange and do not perceive them as being "practical" languages.

I decided to use a small fragment of C, with some simple use of C++ classes when information hiding is needed. Students who have programmed in Java or in another imperative language have very little difficulty reading and adapting simple C programs when unfamiliar idioms such as pointer arithmetic are avoided, as they have been here.

I am grateful to Michael Norrish (University of Cambridge), David Gries (University of Georgia), several anonymous reviewers, my Ph.D. student Dan Ghica, and my colleagues Jürgen Dingel and David Skillicorn for comments on draft versions of the material and to Tim Marchen and Tran Pham for programming assistance. Any remaining errors are my responsibility.

I would be pleased to receive comments and corrections; these may be sent to me at rdt@cs.queensu.ca. Errata will be posted here:

    http://www.cs.queensu.ca/home/specsoft

                                                                                        R. D. T.
                                                                                  January 4, 2002

REFERENCES

[AB+98] P. Andreae, R. Biddle, G. Dobbie, A. Gale, L. Miller, and E. Tempero. Surprises in teaching CS1 with JAVA. Technical Report CS-TR-98/9, Department of Computer Science, Victoria University, Wellington, New Zealand, 1998.

[AU92] A. V. Aho and J. D. Ullman. *Foundations of Computer Science*. W. H. Freeman, 1992.

[Bac86] R. C. Backhouse. *Program Construction and Verification*. Prentice Hall International, 1986.

[BT97] R. Biddle and E. Tempero. Learning JAVA: Promises and pitfalls. Technical Report CS-TR-97/2, Department of Computer Science, Victoria University, Wellington, New Zealand, 1997.

[Dro89] G. Dromey. *Program Derivation: The Development of Programs from Specifications*. Addison-Wesley, 1989.

[Gor88] M. J. C. Gordon. *Programming Language Theory and Its Implementation*. Prentice Hall International, 1988.

[Gou88] K. J. Gough. *Syntax Analysis and Software Tools*. Addison-Wesley, 1988.

[Gre] R. Green. JAVA gotchas. Available here: http://www.mindprod.com/gotchas.html.

[LG00] B. Liskov and J. Guttag. *Program Development in JAVA: Abstraction, Specification, and Object-Oriented Design*. Addison-Wesley, 2000.

[Rey81] J. C. Reynolds. *The Craft of Programming*. Prentice Hall International, 1981.

Introduction

A detailed statement of what users (or clients or customers) of a program or program fragment expect it to do *and* what the implementers or developers of the code expect of its environment is called a *specification* for that code. Sometimes the user and developer of the code might happen to be the same person wearing different hats; however, it is best to think of them as independent, possibly with conflicting interests.

If the code being specified is sufficiently complex, several programmers might be involved in writing it and several other programmers might be involved in writing a program to use the code fragment. Furthermore, there might be several different implementations of a specification, and several different applications that use the implementations. A specification is essentially a *contract* among all these developers and users, stating exactly what must be agreed about the observable effects of executing the code and the environment in which it will be executing, and no more. The expectations of the users become obligations on the developers, and vice versa.

Normally, details of how the computational task is to be carried out would *not* be in a specification: the users shouldn't care, and implementers might then be prevented from using *other* implementation techniques. Similarly, a specification would normally *not* contain details of how applications are to use the code: the developers shouldn't care, and this might preclude *other* applications of the code being specified. To summarize, the specification for a program fragment should specify *what* it and its environment are expected to do but as little as possible about *how* or *why*.

The use of specifications is standard practice in every manufacturing and engineering field. For example, if you were considering the purchase of a particular model of printer for use with your home computer, you might want to obtain from the manufacturer or dealer its "technical specifications"; this document would include the following kinds of information:

- speed (pages per minute);

1

- resolution (dots per inch);

- memory (MB);

- input language (PCL, Postscript, etc.);

- duty cycle (maximum number of pages per month);

- power requirements (voltage and frequency ranges);

- power consumption (watts);

- operating systems supported;

- operating environment (acceptable temperature and humidity ranges);

- dimensions and weight;

and so on. Notice that some of these items impose obligations on the printer, whereas others impose obligations on the user of the printer.

In software engineering, the term *formal methods* is often used to describe development and validation techniques that are based on the use of logical and mathematical formalisms in specifications. Ideally, it should be possible to *construct* a software component systematically from its specification and to *verify* its compliance with the specification. This is not substantially different from any other branch of engineering, where it would be considered unprofessional *not* to use appropriate applied mathematics, such as circuit theory or statics. But in the relatively new field of software development, it is often claimed that using mathematical formalisms is unnecessary or impractical.

Unfortunately, conventional development methods are failing. Over 30% of enterprise software projects are canceled without being completed; 30% of the projects that are completed end up costing 150% to 200% of their original budget. Fewer than 10% of software projects in large companies are completed on-time and on-budget.

Defect rates in typical commercial software have been estimated at 10 to 17 per 1,000 lines of code. Studies at the University of Wisconsin have shown that over 40% of popular application programs on Windows operating systems may be made to crash or hang indefinitely simply by supplying them with randomly generated input data. Comparable failure rates have been observed for basic system utilities in some commercial UNIX–like operating systems.*

Developers and software vendors claim that eliminating software defects is impossible and that "bugs" are in any case only minor inconveniences; however, no one who has lost hours of work to a crashing word processor or has had to re-install their operating system is likely to agree. In some situations,

---

*The lowest failure rates were achieved by the open-source GNU utilities used on Linux systems.

defective programs are actually dangerous. A computer-controlled radiation-therapy device called the Therac-25 was involved in at least six incidents between 1985 and 1987 in which massive overdoses of radiation caused death or serious injury; the incidents have been attributed to software faults, exacerbated by inadequate system design, testing, and management procedures.

Even when software defects don't have such serious consequences, they are often very costly. Researchers at The Standish Group International estimate that software defects cost American companies about $100 billion annually in lost productivity and repairs. Here are some of the more spectacular failures of recent years.

- In 1990, the entire AT&T telephone network collapsed for nine hours because of a single programming error.

- In 1994, an error in the floating-point division algorithm implemented on Pentium processors cost Intel over $200 million.

- In 1996, the maiden flight of the *Ariane 5* space launcher ended in an explosion about 37 seconds after lift-off because an input conversion function, which had been used successfully with *Ariane 4*, could not cope with the larger values produced by the new version; the resulting unanticipated exception was handled by aborting execution of the inertial guidance code. The cost of this incident has been reported as being in the range of half a *billion* dollars. Ironically, the outputs of the conversion function were only being used for logging purposes and weren't needed for the actual flight.

- In 1999, an operating-system defect corrupted information in a crucial database, which caused the eBay.com web site to be inoperative for 22 hours.

Are *you* able to write code that correctly solves a simple programming problem? Try the following small exercise, using any programming language.

EXERCISE 1 Suppose A is an array of integers (but possibly with duplicated values) and that n is a nonnegative integer; write code to determine the number nDist of distinct values in A in the subscript range from 0 to n-1, inclusive. For example, if n = 6 and the first six components of A are 45, 13, -15, 13, 13, and 45, respectively, nDist should be set to 3.

Your code is not allowed to change n or A. The code should not be obviously inefficient; however, you may assume that n is sufficiently small that it is not worthwhile to sort (a copy of) the array segment initially.

Did you get the logic right *before* testing your code on a computer? Does your solution work correctly if n = 1? If n = 0? If all components of the array segment are the same? If all are different? Would you be willing to fly on an airplane that is to be controlled by a program that uses your code? We will return to this programming problem in Section 3.6.

As consumers, managers, professional bodies, and regulatory agencies become more aware of the costs, dangers, and liabilities of poor-quality software, they will begin to demand that the software that they purchase or are responsible for be as reliable as other artifacts. Programmers will then have to become more professional than most commercial programmers are now. To keep their jobs, maintain their professional standing, and avoid malpractice suits, they will have to take responsibility for the quality of their products. It is increasingly a requirement on software for safety-critical systems such as aircraft, nuclear power-plant control, and medical equipment that it be supplied with detailed specifications, supported by formal or independent assessments of compliance.

Are you ready for a world in which you might have to take responsibility for the quality of a program? Consider the following amusing examples of this.

- In 1999, Ambrosia Software of Rochester, N.Y., announced that if any of their forthcoming software products subsequently required a bug-fix, their marketing manager would eat real insects at a trade show.*

- The government of China ordered the executive officers of the national airline to be on overnight flights on their airplanes on the night of December 31, 1999.

The program used to control the NASA space shuttles is a significant example of software whose development has been based on specifications and formal methods. A single defect in this program might result in the deaths of six astronauts and the loss of a multibillion dollar piece of equipment. It comes as no surprise that the group responsible for producing and maintaining this software have been obsessed with the correctness of their code.

As of March 1997, the program was some 420,000 lines long. The specifications for all parts of the program filled some 40,000 pages. To implement a change in the navigation software involving less than 2% of the code, some 2,500 pages of specifications were produced before a single line of the code was changed.

Their approach has been outstandingly successful. The developers found 85% of all coding errors before formal testing began, and 99.9% before delivery of the program to NASA. Only one defect has been discovered in each of the last three versions. In the last 11 versions of the program, the total defect count is only 17, an average of fewer than 0.004 defects per 1,000 lines of code.

It might be thought that this is an exceptional case whose success could not be approached in the "real world" of commercial software. But there are

---

*The press release did not say what would happen to the programmer responsible for the error.

commercially successful software houses that use the best available practices and regularly achieve defect rates of 0.03 to 0.05 per 1,000 lines of code. There is no technical or financial reason why at least this level of quality should not be demanded of all commercial and mission-critical software.

This book is an introduction to the use of software specifications. It describes basic formalisms suitable for specifying three kinds of code and practical techniques for systematic construction and verification of program components.

A small fragment of the C programming language is used for almost all the examples; some features of the class notation from C++, an object-oriented extension of C, are used to support information hiding in Part B. For the sake of readability and portability, a number of programming idioms that are specific to C (such as pointer arithmetic) will be avoided. If you have written programs in any similar language (JAVA, PASCAL, MODULA, ADA, TURING, etc.), you will have few difficulties reading the programs or constructing comparable programs.

Program 1

```
# include <stdio.h>
int main(void)
{ printf("Hello, world!\n");
  return 0;
}
```

The traditional first example of a C program is shown as Program 1. The effect of the program is to output the following line:

```
Hello, world!
```

The first line of the program has the effect of including the "header" file for the stdio (standard input-output) library, allowing the program to use the printf function defined in that library. The next line contains the "declarator" (heading) for a function (procedure, method) main, which is always called by the operating system to initiate program execution. The formal-parameter list (void) indicates that the function takes an *empty* argument list.

In C, a function-definition body is always a block (compound statement), which is a sequence of declarations and statements enclosed in curly braces {...}. The printf line is a call to a function that is defined in the stdio library and that may be used for formatted output. In this case, the argument consists of the literal string Hello, world!, terminated by the escape sequence \n, which generates suitable end-of-line control characters. The string is enclosed in double quotes, and the function call itself is terminated by a semicolon. The

---

Program 2

```
/* Test code to determine the number of distinct values in A[0:n-1] */

# include "specdef.i"

int main(void)
{
# define max 256      /* maximum number of entries, > 0           */
  typedef int Entry;  /* type of entries, use == for equality     */
  int n;              /* number of entries                        */
  Entry A[max];       /* A[0:n-1] are the entries                 */
  int nDist;          /* number of distinct entries in A[0:n-1]   */

  printf("Enter n: ");
  if (scanf("%i", &n) != 1) error("input failure");
  if (n<0) error("n must be non-negative");
  if (n > max) error("n must be <= max");
  if (n>0)
  { int i;
    printf("Enter components of A[0:n-1], ");
    printf("separated by white space:\n");
    for (i=0; i<n; i++)
      if (scanf("%i", &A[i]) != 1) error("input failure");
  }

  ASSERT( 0 <= n <= max )

# include "mysolution.i"

  ASSERT( nDist == |A[0:n-1]| )

  printf("Number of distinct components in A[0:n-1] is ");
  printf("%i\n", nDist);
  return 0;
}
```

---

last line of the function body returns the value zero to the environment as an indication of successful completion.

Program 2 on page 6 is more useful; it may be used to test C solutions to Exercise 1 on page 3.

The first line is a comment describing what the program is for; in C, comments are bracketed by the character sequences /* and */. The following include line has the effect of including the file specdef.i, which is listed here as Program 3. Note the use of double quotes " ... " rather than angle brackets < ... > to enclose the file name; this is to make the search for file specdef.i start in the current user folder/directory (rather than in system libraries).

The code in specdef.i includes headers for all the libraries likely to be used for ordinary programs and defines various types, macros, and functions assumed in the program examples in this book. *Our programs will always assume these headers and definitions, even if they are not shown explicitly.* The type defini-

---

Program 3

```
/* specdef.i:  headers and definitions for "Specifying Software" */

# include <stdlib.h>
# include <stdio.h>
# include <math.h>
# include <ctype.h>
# include <limits.h>
# include <string.h>

# ifndef __cplusplus
typedef enum {false, true} bool;   /* not needed for C++ */
# endif

/* null macros:  */
# define ASSERT(P)
# define FACT(P)
# define INVAR(P)

void error(char msg[]) /* abort with stderr message msg */
{ fprintf(stderr, "Error: %s.\n", msg);
  exit(EXIT_FAILURE);
}
```

---

tion introduces an "enumerated" type bool of the two truth values, false and true; the compiler preprocessor is instructed to exclude this definition if the code is being processed by a C++ processor because the extended language predefines a bool type. The "null" macros ASSERT(P), FACT(P), and INVAR(P) allow for the use of special comment forms in programs; this usage will be explained in detail in subsequent chapters. The error function uses function fprintf to print out its error-message argument msg to the error stream and then aborts program execution by calling the exit function, using the constant EXIT_FAILURE as an indication of unsuccessful termination.

The body of the main function

- defines various constants and variables and the type name Entry;

- reads and verifies values for n and array components A[0] to A[n-1] using the scanf function from stdio (note the use of the ampersand "address" operator & on the input variables);

- executes the code found in a separate file mysolution.i, which has been included into the program by the preprocessor; and

- outputs the result.

The ASSERT lines are macro calls; these are essentially comments because the corresponding macro-definition body is empty. The significance of such "assertions" will be explained later.

Note the use of == in one of the assertions. Value equality tests are written this way in C programs; the = operator is used for the assignment operation. But when programs are discussed in the text, the usual = symbol for mathematical equality will often be used, and similarly for other relational operators, such as ≠ and ≤.

Appendix A gives a compact reference manual for the programming language used in this book.

Additional Reading

The Therac-25 incidents are discussed in [LT93, Lev95, Neu95]. The *Ariane* incident is discussed in [JM97, Nus97]. The University of Wisconsin studies referred to are described in [MK⁺95, FM00]. The NASA space-shuttle control program is discussed in [Fis96]. The Usenet news group comp.risks carries discussions of errors and security loopholes in computer software.

Traditional attitudes to formal methods are criticized in [Hal90, BH95, LG97]. Real-world use of formal methods is described in [JS90, Hay92, Lin94, GCR94, CGR95, Har95, HB95, CW96, HB99, KH⁺00]. An overview of formal methods and introductions to a variety of formal specification languages may be found in [Win90]. Many additional bibliographical references on formal methods may be found here:

> http://www.comlab.ox.ac.uk/archive/formal-methods/pubs.html

References

[BH95]   J. P. Bowen and M. G. Hinchey. Seven more myths of formal methods. *IEEE Software*, 12(4):34–41, 1995.

[CGR95]   D. Craigen, S. Gerhart, and T. Ralston. Formal methods reality check: Industrial usage. *IEEE Transactions Software Engineering*, 21(2):90–8, 1995.

[CW96]   E. M. Clarke and J. M. Wing. Formal methods: State of the art and future directions. *ACM Computing Surveys*, 28(4):626–43, 1996.

[Fis96]   C. Fishman. They write the right stuff. *Fast Company*, 6:95–9 and 104–6, December 1996. Available here:
          http://www.fastcompany.com/online/06/writestuff.html.

[FM00]   J. E. Forrester and B. P. Miller. An empirical study of the robustness of Windows NT applications using random testing. In *Proc. 4th USENIX Windows Systems Symposium*, Seattle, August 2000. Available here:
          ftp://grilled.cs.wisc.edu/technical_papers.

[GCR94]   S. Gerhart, D. Craigen, and T. Ralston. Experience with formal methods in critical systems. *IEEE Software*, 11(1):21–8, 1994.

[Hal90]   J. A. Hall. Seven myths of formal methods. *IEEE Software*, 7(5):11–19, 1990.

[Har95]   J. M. Hart. Experience with logical code analysis in software maintenance. *Software Practice and Experience*, 25(11):1243–62, November 1995.

[Hay92] I. Hayes. *Specification Case Studies*. Prentice Hall International, 1992.

[HB95] M. G. Hinchey and J. P. Bowen, editors. *Applications of Formal Methods*. Prentice Hall International, 1995.

[HB99] M. G. Hinchey and J. P. Bowen, editors. *Industrial-Strength Formal Methods in Practice*. Springer Verlag, 1999.

[JM97] J.-M. Jézéquel and B. Meyer. Design by contract: The lessons of Ariane. *IEEE Computer*, 30(2):129–30, 1997.

[JS90] C. B. Jones and R. Shaw. *Case Studies in Systematic Software Development*. Prentice Hall International, 1990. Available here: `ftp://ftp.ncl.ac.uk/pub/users/ncbj/cases.ps.gz`.

[KH⁺00] S. King, J. Hammond, R. Chapman, and A. Pryor. Is proof more cost-effective than testing? *IEEE Trans. Software Engineering*, 26(8):675–86, 2000.

[Lev95] N. G. Leveson. *Safeware: System Safety and Computers; A Guide to Preventing Accidents and Losses Caused by Technology*. Addison-Wesley, 1995.

[LG97] Luqi and J. A. Goguen. Formal methods: Promises and problems. *IEEE Software*, 14:73–85, Jan. 1997.

[Lin94] R. C. Linger. Cleanroom process model. *IEEE Software*, 11(2):50–8, March 1994.

[LT93] N. G. Leveson and C. S. Turner. An investigation of the Therac-25 accidents. *IEEE Computer*, 26(7):18–41, 1993.

[MK⁺95] B. P. Miller, D. Koski, C. P Lee, V. Maganty, R. Murthy, A. Natarajan, and J. Steidl. Fuzz revisited: A re-examination of the reliability of UNIX utilities and services. Technical Report 1268, University of Wisconsin-Madison, Computer Sciences, April 1995. Available here: `ftp://grilled.cs.wisc.edu/technical_papers`.

[Neu95] P. G. Neumann. *Computer Related Risks*. ACM Press, 1995.

[Nus97] B. Nuseibeh. Ariane 5: Who dunnit? *IEEE Software*, 14(3):15–16, 1997.

[Win90] J. Wing. A specifier's introduction to formal methods. *IEEE Computer*, 23(9):8–24, 1990.

Part A

Algorithms

Introduction to Part A

We first consider techniques for *algorithms* (i.e., relatively small program components whose functional behavior may be specified in terms of "before" and "after" properties). Chapter 1 discusses how to specify what a simple algorithmic code fragment should do. Chapter 2 describes basic techniques for *verifying* code (i.e., proving mathematically that it does what its specification says it should do). Chapter 3 discusses a variety of small examples of these methods, demonstrating also how they may be used to *construct* (i.e., systematically code) correct programs. Chapter 4 describes some additional verification techniques and further examples.

Additional Reading

[Wir73, AA78, Rey81, Bac86, Gor88, Dro89, Dah92, BE$^+$94, Cas94, Sta99, MS01] are recommended for further explanation and additional examples. A more formal approach to algorithm development is described in [Gri81, DF88, Kal90, Coh90, Mor94].

REFERENCES

[AA78]   S. Alagić and M. A. Arbib. *The Design of Well-Structured and Correct Programs.* Springer-Verlag, 1978.

[Bac86]   R. C. Backhouse. *Program Construction and Verification.* Prentice Hall International, 1986.

[BE$^+$94]   K. Broda, S. Eisenbach, H. Khoshnevisan, and S. Vickers. *Reasoned Programming.* Prentice Hall International, 1994.

[Cas94]   C. Casey. *A Programming Approach to Formal Methods.* McGraw-Hill International, 1994.

[Coh90]   E. Cohen. *Programming in the 1990s: An Introduction to the Calculation of Programs.* Springer Verlag, 1990.

[Dah92]   O.-J. Dahl. *Verifiable Programming.* Prentice Hall International, 1992.

[DF88]   E. W. Dijkstra and W. H. J. Feijen. *A Method of Programming*. Addison-Wesley, 1988.

[Dro89]   G. Dromey. *Program Derivation: The Development of Programs from Specifications*. Addison-Wesley, 1989.

[Gor88]   M. J. C. Gordon. *Programming Language Theory and Its Implementation*. Prentice Hall International, 1988.

[Gri81]   D. Gries. *The Science of Programming*. Springer-Verlag, 1981.

[Kal90]   A. Kaldewaij. *Programming: The Derivation of Algorithms*. Prentice Hall International, 1990.

[Mor94]   C. C. Morgan. *Programming from Specifications*, 2nd edition. Prentice Hall International, 1994.

[MS01]   J. J. Mead and A. M. Shende. *Persuasive Programming*. ABF Content, Franklin, Beedle, and Associates, 2001.

[Rey81]   J. C. Reynolds. *The Craft of Programming*. Prentice Hall International, 1981.

[Sta99]   A. M. Stavely. *Toward Zero-Defect Programming*. Addison-Wesley Longman, 1999.

[Wir73]   N. Wirth. *Systematic Programming, An Introduction*. Prentice Hall, 1973.

Chapter 1

Specifying Algorithms

1.1 Case Study: Searching an Array

Professor Higgins wants his programmer, Eliza Doolittle, to write a code fragment that is to test for the presence or absence of a value x in an array A. Here is the intended application: A is to contain the student numbers of all the students currently enrolled in his course on computational metaphysics, and x might be the student number of a student who is trying to verify that he or she is properly registered.

EXERCISE 1.1 Before reading on, pretend that you are Eliza Doolittle and try to write the desired code. Also, try to write an application program that uses the code.

As you will quickly discover if you try to write the desired code, or to write a program to use it, the preceding paragraph is an inadequate specification. Here are some of the questions that must be answered before (or during) the development of the desired code or any associated applications.

1. What is the range of allowed subscript values for A, and what segment of the array should be searched?

2. What is the type of variable x (also, presumably, the component type of the array), and how should values of this type be compared?

3. How should the result be recorded?

4. Is the array segment sorted in, say, ascending order, to allow use of a more efficient search method?

5. Is it possible for the value x to occur *more* than once in (the relevant part of) A, and if so, is it required that this be determined as well?

6. Is it possible that "the relevant part of A" is *empty* (i.e., *no* entries), and if so, how should the program fragment react? Is this an error or a "normal" state of the search table?

7. Which variables must not be changed, and which may be changed? For example, the programmer might wish to re-arrange the array or to re-move duplicated entries. If only part of the array is to be searched, the other components might be used during the search.

Notice that all these issues are concerned with the *interface* between the code fragment and applications that will use it and the search table A; none of them are solely concerned with *implementation* of the array-searching code.

Let us be optimistic and assume that all the relevant issues have actually been raised. Who now answers such questions? Who answers depends on the environment: possibly a senior programmer or supervisor; possibly the user(s) of the code; possibly the developer(s); or possibly the user(s) and developer(s) must negotiate an agreement. For our case study, we will simply assume that Professor Higgins gives the following answers to the questions and take these to be the (informal) specification for the array-searching code.

1. What is the range of allowed subscript values for A, and what segment of the array should be searched?

   The array will be physically large enough to be indexable by integers in the range from 0 to max-1, where max is an upper limit for the class size. The value of an int variable n will determine the segment A[0:n-1] that is to be searched, that is, the current *logical* size of the search table. Between searches, the value of n may change as entries are added to or removed from the search table.

2. What is the type of variable x, and how should values of this type be compared?

   The type of both x and A will be some defined data type Entry; it may be assumed that equality of Entry values may be tested using the usual operator ==.

   For many applications, a search-table entry would contain information in addition to the "key" or "unique identifier" that distinguishes it from other entries; it would then be necessary to specify a suitable function to use for comparisons. In some programming languages, the operation == is used for *reference* equality, rather than *value* equality; this would not be appropriate for some applications.

3. How should the result be recorded?

   The result of the search is to be recorded in a bool variable present; if x occurs in A[0:n-1], the final value of present should be true, and false otherwise.

For some applications, it would be necessary to know also *where* x occurs in the array, if it does, or where x should be added if it *doesn't* occur in the array. This feature would be easily added to any particular implementation, but the details will often depend on the search method being used. To simplify the exposition, this feature has been omitted from the specification.

4. Is the array segment sorted in, say, ascending order, to allow use of a more efficient search method?

   The entries need not be in any particular order. Ordering the entries would allow faster searches but would complicate adding or removing entries.

5. Is it possible for the value x to occur *more* than once in (the relevant part of) A, and if so, is it required that this be determined as well?

   The target value x might occur more than once in A[0:n-1], but this need not be tested for.

6. Is it possible that "the relevant part of A" is *empty* (i.e., *no* entries) and if so, how should the program fragment react? Is this an error or a "normal" state of the search table?

   The search table may be logically empty (i.e., n = 0) when the search code is invoked, but this should *not* be treated as an error; rather, the variable present should be assigned false when n = 0 because x clearly will *not* be found in an empty array segment. On the other hand, the value of n should never be negative, nor greater than max (which might be the allocated size of the array).

7. Which variables must not be changed, and which may be changed?

   The values of variables x and n and the entries of array segment A[0:n-1] are not to be changed by the search; however, the rest of the array may be considered to be "garbage," and the components may be used in the search.

EXERCISE 1.2 Explain why it would be undesirable or incorrect to add either of the following statements to the specification.

(a) The array segment A[0:n-1] is not ordered.

(b) A linear search is to be used.

EXERCISE 1.3 Discuss the advantages and disadvantages of weakening the requirements to allow A[0:n-1] to be re-arranged or to allow duplicated entries to be removed.

We now have a specification that seems reasonably complete, but it is verbose and imprecise. To express the specification in a more compact and precise form, we will *formalize* the requirements and assumptions as much as possible.

1.2 Declarative Interface for Array Search

Most modern programming languages require that the kind and type of all identifiers be specified by declarations, definitions, or parameter specifications. We will adopt the same approach for specifications because many of the requirements involve *static* properties of identifiers that allow access to data or operations to be shared between the search code and associated operations. We will, therefore, specify a *declarative interface* (or "signature" or "context") giving the assumed kind and type (and other static properties) of all such identifiers, as in the following:

```
const int max;        /* maximum number of entries */
typename Entry;       /* type of entries, use == for equality */
const int n;          /* number of entries */
const Entry x;        /* search target */
Entry A[max];         /* A[0:n-1] are the entries to search */
bool present;         /* search result */
```

The qualifier const is used to indicate that the identifier so qualified is a constant or a variable whose value must *not* be changed by the search code. Here, max (the maximum number of entries), n (the number of array components currently in use), and x (the search target) are all specified with const. Variables like x and n might have their values changed in *other* program components, but not in the search code. We assume that the compiler in use will enforce the const qualification in the implementing code.

The typename line indicates that Entry is a type name, but the actual type it names is not relevant. This notation has been borrowed from C++.

The identifier A is specified as naming an array of Entry values that allows subscripts in the range from 0 to max−1 (at least), and present is specified as being a bool variable; these are *not* qualified with const.

The comments help to explain the requirements and add other relevant information, such as that the usual operator == is to be used to test equality of values of type Entry.

Although it is convenient to use notation from the programming language as much as possible, the declarative interface should not be thought of as being part of the program. It is part of the *specification* for the desired program. The program, including the declarations, definitions, and parameter declarations, must be compatible with the specification, but no part of the program need necessarily be identical to anything in the specification.

EXERCISE 1.4 Ms Doolittle has asked that a declaration of an index variable i used in her code be added to the declarative interface part of the specification. Should Professor Higgins grant the request?

EXERCISE 1.5 Develop a declarative interface for a code fragment that is to determine the number of distinct values in an array segment.

EXERCISE 1.6 Develop a declarative interface for a code fragment that, given an array segment that may contain duplicated values, constructs a new array with the same entries but without any duplicates.

The following aspects of the informal specification have not yet been adequately formalized:

- the requirements on the value of present after the search;
- the assumptions on the value of n before the search; and
- the requirement that the array segment A[0:n-1] not be changed.

These are concerned with the initial and final values of some of the variables, and relations between them, rather than with fixed or static properties of identifiers. Before studying how these *dynamic* requirements might be expressed formally, we first review some concepts and associated notation from logic.

1.3   Assertions

We will use *logical formulas* to express properties of the values of program variables (normally, at particular execution states); the formulas will be termed *assertions*. For example, $x < y$ is a simple assertion about the values of two program variables, x and y. If an assertion P is true at some computational state, we say that the state *satisfies P* or that *P holds at* that state.

Assertions are essentially like bool expressions (conditions) in a programming language. In fact, we allow any bool expression to be used as an assertion (provided that it does not involve any assignment operations and its evaluation terminates normally), but we will also use notation (such as quantifiers) that cannot be used in bool expressions in programs. In the following, we discuss the forms of assertion that are *not* conventional bool expressions.

1.3.1   CONNECTIVES

In logic, the operators used to form complex formulas from simpler ones are termed *connectives*. In addition to the familiar ! (negation, not), && (conjunction, and), and || (disjunction, or) in C, we use the following in assertions:

- the binary infix operator `implies` (which is also written →, ⊃, ⇒, or if ... then ...) for *conditional*, yielding `false` if the value of the first operand (the *precedent*) is not `false` and the value of the second operand (the *consequent*) is `false`, and `true` in *all* other cases, even if both operands yield `false`.

- the binary infix operator `iff` (i.e., if and only if, also written ↔, ≡, or ⇔) for *(logical) equivalence*, yielding `true` if both operands yield `false` or neither operand does, and `false` otherwise.

If P `implies` Q is `true`, P is said to be *stronger* than Q, and Q is said to be *weaker* than P (even if Q `implies` P is *also* `true`); this technical usage of "stronger" and "weaker" is, therefore, different from colloquial usage. If P is stronger than Q and Q does *not* imply P, we say that P is *strictly* stronger than Q. Note that P `iff` Q is equivalent to (P `implies` Q)`&&`(Q `implies` P); this equivalence explains where the "if and only if" terminology comes from. These connectives will be assumed to have lower precedence than any of the standard C connectives.

EXERCISE 1.7 Are the following always valid? If not, suggest a counterexample.

(a) P `&&` Q implies P `||` Q

(b) P `||` Q implies P `&&` Q

EXERCISE 1.8 How might P `implies` Q and P `iff` Q be expressed in C? Note that, in C, a condition with any *nonzero* integer value is regarded as being (equivalent to) `true`.

1.3.2 QUANTIFICATION

If I is an identifier and P is an assertion (possibly with occurrences of I), the assertions

- `ForAll` (I) P (also written ∀I. P) and
- `Exists` (I) P (also written ∃I. P)

denote *universal* and *existential quantification*, respectively. The first is `true` only if P is `true` for I taking on every possible value, and the second is `false` only if P is `false` for every possible value of I. Thus, the quantifiers represent iterated conjunction (`&&`) and disjunction (`||`), respectively, of the assertion P over all possible values for I.

The quantified identifier I is said to be *bound* in `ForAll` (I) P and in `Exists` (I) P, and the assertion is termed the *scope* of the binding. If it is not obvious from context, a type specification for the bound identifier of a quantification may be added, as in `ForAll` (`int` I) P; see also the range abbreviations in Section 1.3.3. Normally, a bound identifier would be chosen so as not to conflict with any of the program variables in use.

Syntactically, the usual convention is that the scope of a quantifier extends as far to the right as possible. Parentheses may be used to restrict the scope if necessary:

(ForAll (*I*) *P*) ···

(Exists (*I*) *P*) ···

1.3.3 ABBREVIATIONS

It is often convenient to use abbreviated forms of assertion. For example, a <= i < b will be recognized as an abbreviation for a <= i && i < b. For any assertion *P* possibly containing occurrences of i of type int, we will use ForAll (i=a; i<b) *P* as an abbreviation for the following *bounded* quantification:

ForAll (int i) a <= i < b implies *P*

For example, the following assertion is one way to formalize the property that the entries of an array segment A[0:n-1] are distinct:

ForAll (i=0; i<n) ForAll (j=0; j<n) i != j implies A[i] != A[j]

EXERCISE 1.9 Explain why it is necessary to precede A[i] != A[j] with the construct i != j implies ... in the preceding example.

EXERCISE 1.10 What does the following assertion say about A[0:n-1]?

ForAll (i=0; i<n) ForAll (j=0; j<i) A[i] != A[j]

If it happens that $b \leq a$, the assertion ForAll (i=a; i<b) *P* is *vacuously* true, no matter what *P* happens to be; this is because, for every int value i, the precedent a <= i < b must be false and so the conditional

a <= i < b implies *P*

must be true.

For convenience, we are using a C-like notation for bounded quantification, but many other notations are in use. Here are some examples:

$\forall (a \leq i < b). P$

$\forall i: a \leq i < b: P$

$\forall (i \mid a \leq i < b). P$

$\forall i \in [a, b). P$

Constructions such as

ForAll (int i) (int j) *P*

and

>   ForAll (i=0; i<n) (j=0; j<n) P

are acceptable as abbreviations for *multiple* quantifications. But, note that it is improper to use connectives such as && between quantifiers, as in

>   ForAll (i=0; i<n) && ForAll (j=0; j<n) P

(even though this reads well as English), or between a quantifier and an assertion, as in

>   ForAll (i=0; i<n) && P

Also, C-like extensions such as

>   ForAll (j=0; j<n && j != i) P

and

>   ForAll (i=0,j=0; i<n && j<n) P

should be avoided; the interpretations of the corresponding constructions in C are *not* what is usually intended with quantifiers.

Similarly, we will use Exists (i=a; i<b) P as an abbreviation for the bounded existential quantification:

>   Exists (int i) a <= i < b && P

This assertion is vacuously false if $b \le a$ because a <= i < b is false for *every* int value i. For example, here are two ways to assert that an entry of A[0:n-1] occurs more than once in that segment:

>   Exists (i=0; i<n) Exists (j=0; j<n) A[i] == A[j] && i != j

>   Exists (i=0; i<n) (j=0; j<n) A[i] == A[j] && i != j

It is also possible to "mix" the two quantifiers; for example, the following assertion states that the largest value in A[0:n-1] occurs just once:

>   Exists (i=0; i<n) ForAll (j=0; j<n) i != j implies A[i] > A[j]

EXERCISE 1.11 Give assertions that formalize each of the following properties, which an array segment A[0:n-1] might have.

  (a) All the entries are equal to the value of variable x.

  (b) All the entries are equal.

  (c) The entries are in increasing order.

  (d) The value of x occurs exactly once in the array segment.

  (e) Every entry occurs more than once.

(f) Exactly one entry occurs more than once.

If A is an array and x has the appropriate type, the following abbreviations may be used:

- `x in A[a:b-1]` is an abbreviation for `Exists (i=a; i<b) x == A[i]`
- `x < A[a:b-1]` is an abbreviation for `ForAll (i=a; i<b) x < A[i]`

and similarly for `x <= A[a:b-1]` and other relational operators. Array diagrams, a pictorial form of assertion, will be discussed in Section 3.5.

EXERCISE 1.12 What do `x in A[a:b-1]` and `x < A[a:b-1]` mean when $b \leq a$?

EXERCISE 1.13 Why would it be redundant to introduce the notation `x !in A[a:b-1]` as an abbreviation for `ForAll (i=a; i<b) x != A[i]` ?

EXERCISE 1.14 Explain why the following pairs of assertions are not equivalent in general:

(a) `x == A[a:b-1]` and `x in A[a:b-1]`

(b) `x != A[a:b-1]` and `!(x == A[a:b-1])`

EXERCISE 1.15 Are any two of the following assertions equivalent?

- `ForAll (i=0, i<n) A[i] == B[i]`
- `ForAll (x) x in A[0:n-1] iff x in B[0:n-1]`
- `ForAll (i=0, i<n) A[i] in B[0:n-1]`

1.3.4 ASSERTIONS AS COMMENTS

Assertions may be used to provide useful documentation in programs. The macro definition

```
# define ASSERT(P)
```

allows assertions to be added to programs as comments, as in the following:

```
ASSERT(x != 0)
if (x<0)
{ ASSERT(x<0)
  x = -x;
}
ASSERT(x>0)
```

Unless it is a loop invariant (to be discussed in Section 2.9) or a representation invariant (to be discussed in Section 5.5), an assertion comment is always interpreted as follows: it is expected that whenever program execution passes through the comment, the assertion would be true *if* it were evaluated;

however, we do *not* expect that the assertions are actually evaluated during program execution.

The `assert` library in C defines a macro or function `assert` that *does* evaluate its argument (and aborts program execution if the assertion fails); but only legal expressions of the programming language are allowed as arguments. This feature is useful for debugging and to prevent damage from "impossible" situations during execution. Our assertions (possibly containing nonexecutable connectives) will be used for documentation, specification, and reasoning about programs.

An assertion comment that appears at the *end* of a code fragment (such as the assertion x>0 in the preceding example) documents a property of the variables expected to be `true` immediately after executing the code fragment; it is termed a *post-condition* or "consequent" or "output assertion" for the code. Post-conditions may be thought of as properties that are to be *achieved* by execution of the code fragment.

Of course, a post-condition would not be applicable if control were to "jump" out of the code, rather than execute to completion. In this introductory exposition, we will normally assume that there are no jumps out of code (except calls to the `exit` library function to abort program execution in error situations). This assumption precludes some uses of `break` and `continue` in loops and the use of `return` in function definitions, except at the very *end* of a function definition, as well as the use of `goto` statements.

An assertion comment that appears at the *beginning* of a code fragment (such as the assertion x != 0 in the preceding example) documents the expectation that the code fragment will be used only when that assertion is (initially) `true`; it is then termed a *pre-condition* or "precedent" or "input assertion" for the code. Pre-conditions are properties that might be *required* for correct execution of the code. Adding or strengthening pre-conditions generally makes it *easier* for developers of the code, but the resulting code may not be as useful.

Note that if the code fragment were executed for an initial state that does *not* satisfy its pre-condition, anything at all might happen: it might fail with an error message, go into an infinite loop, produce an invalid final state, crash the system, or blow up the computer! The code fragment itself is *allowed* to test the pre-condition, but it does not become *obligated* to do so merely by using an assertion as a comment. In practice, it is often appropriate to improve the *robustness* of a program (i.e., its ability to tolerate improper inputs) by inserting checks to ensure that pre-conditions are satisfied, particularly when such checking is easy, the users are untrusted, and failing to do the checks could have serious consequences.

EXERCISE 1.16 What is the significance of using the assertion `true` as a pre-condition? As a post-condition? What about `false`?

1.4 Completing the Specification for Array Search

1.4.1 Post-Conditions

We may now return to our array-searching problem. The primary requirement that must be formalized involves the result variable, present. What Professor Higgins wants is that, after the search, present have value true if and only if A[0] = x or A[1] = x or ... or A[n-1] = x. We may express this more compactly by the following assertion:

```
present iff Exists (k=0; k<n) A[k] == x
```

or, using the abbreviated notation introduced in Section 1.3.3,

```
present iff x in A[0:n-1]
```

This assertion is required to be true immediately *after* execution of the search code, and so it is a *post-condition* for that code. Note that nothing needs to be said in the assertion about *how* the value of present is to be computed.

EXERCISE 1.17 Give counterexamples that show why each of the following would not be satisfactory as the *only* post-condition for the desired searching code:

(a) `present implies x in A[0:n-1]`

(b) `x in A[0:n-1] implies present`

EXERCISE 1.18 What does `present iff x in A[0:n-1]` mean when $n = 0$? Is this the desired property in this case?

EXERCISE 1.19 Professor Higgins also wants a code fragment that assigns to variable m of type int the larger of the integer values x and y. He specifies the following declarative interface:

```
int x,y,m;
```

and gives Ms Doolittle the following assertion as the desired post-condition:

```
m >= x && m >= y
```

(a) Eliza returns with the following code: `x = 0; y = 0; m = 0;`. Does her code achieve the stated post-condition?

(b) Professor Higgins then revises the interface declarations of x and y as follows:

```
const int x,y;
```

Eliza returns with the following code: `m = INT_MAX;` where the constant `INT_MAX` is defined by the standard limits library in C to be the largest representable int value. Does her code achieve the stated post-condition?

(c) State a stronger post-condition that specifies what Professor Higgins intends the code to achieve.

1.4.2   Pre-Conditions

We will assume that it is the responsibility of *users* of the code to ensure *before* executing the search code that the value of n is neither negative nor too large. The tests are not difficult, but it is not evident what should be done by the search code if a test fails, apart from aborting the execution entirely. We therefore adopt the assertion 0 <= n <= max as a *pre-condition* for the code.

EXERCISE 1.20   Why are there no pre-conditions on the values of x and present?

1.4.3   Relating Initial and Final Values

The final requirement that must be imposed on the array-searching code is that the *final* state of array segment A[0:n-1] is to be the same as its *initial* state. One way to express this requirement formally is as follows. We introduce a fresh identifier A0 to name the initial state of the array and add the assertion A == A0 to the pre-condition. This is to be interpreted as stating that A0 has the same *value* as A (rather than the "reference equality" used in some circumstances in, for example, JAVA). Then we add the assertion

```
ForAll (i=0; i<n) A[i] == A0[i]
```

to the post-condition, which allows components with indices greater than or equal to n to be modified by the code. It also allows components in A[0:n-1] to be *temporarily* changed, as long as the initial values are restored.

To give a formal binding of the initial-value identifier, we may use a pseudodefinition in a comment, as in

```
/*   const Entry A0[max];   */
```

Note that A0 should *not* be declared in the declarative interface of the specification; it is only used locally, and not in application programs. Of course, A0 may only be referred to in comments, and not in executable code. Such names for *fixed* values will be termed *ghost identifiers*; other terms that have been used are "specification variables" and "logical variables". The notational convention of using an existing variable name (such as A) with an appended 0 as the ghost identifier that denotes the "initial" value of the variable is just a convenience and is not obligatory.

EXERCISE 1.21   Specify a code fragment that is to exchange the values of two variables.

EXERCISE 1.22   Develop a specification for a code fragment that, given values a and b, should determine whether the equation $ax + b = 0$ has a *unique* solution, it has *no* solution, or *every* number is a solution. If there *is* a unique solution, it should be computed as well. The values a and b and the solution x are to be represented in float variables; you may assume (unrealistically) that float arithmetic is error-free.

EXERCISE 1.23 Without using $\sqrt{\ }$, specify a code fragment that is to compute the square root of a number x.

EXERCISE 1.24 Develop a declarative interface and pre- and post-conditions for a code fragment that is to determine the value of the largest entry in an array segment.

EXERCISE 1.25 By stating appropriate pre- and post-conditions, complete the specification you started in Exercise 1.5 for code to determine the number of distinct values in an array segment. You may want to use the notation $|S|$ to stand for the *cardinality* of (i.e., number of elements in) the set S; that is,

$$|S| = \begin{cases} 0, & \text{if } S = \emptyset \quad \text{(the empty set)} \\ 1 + |S - \{a\}|, & \text{if } a \in S \end{cases}$$

EXERCISE 1.26 Complete the specification for the code described in Exercise 1.6.

EXERCISE 1.27 Develop a specification for a code fragment that, given an array segment that may contain duplicated values, constructs a new array containing (without duplicates) just the entries that *are* duplicated in the original array.

1.5 Correctness of Code

As we have already seen, the specification for a code fragment may often be formalized by giving

- a declarative interface, to declare the static properties of all identifiers that must be available to both the code itself and to its users;

- a pre-condition assertion P, to specify properties that are assumed to hold of the variables before execution of the code; and

- a post-condition assertion Q, to specify properties that are required to hold of the variables after execution of the code, including relations between final and initial values.

Code C satisfying the syntactic constraints of the declarative interface may be said to be *correct* (relative to such a specification), or to (correctly) *satisfy*, *realize*, or *implement* the specification, if every execution of C that starts from a state satisfying P must result in a final state satisfying Q.

This definition should not be interpreted too literally. In the real world, execution of a code fragment may result in a final state at which the post-condition fails for reasons one might not have expected.

- An insecurity in the operating system may allow another process to interfere with "our" variables.

- The compiler in use may be generating incorrect code.

- An operation may fail to return a "correct" result. For example, the C language standard allows an implementation to do *anything* (including returning garbage without any warning) if an overflow (i.e., calculation of a number too large to be represented in the space allocated for it) has occurred in a (signed) int operation. Similarly, if an array subscript is out of range, it is in principle illegal; but few implementations produce an error message.

Furthermore, an execution may fail to reach a "final state" at which a postcondition could be evaluated for any of a number of reasons:

- an infinite loop;

- a run-time error that causes program abortion, such as division by zero;

- execution of a break, return, continue, or goto that transfers control outside the code;

- a call to abort or exit from the code, or from a function called from the code;

- exhaustion of some implementation resource, such as available "stack" space (usually because of an infinite recursion);

- an operating-system interrupt.

Several of these issues (compiler bugs, operating-system insecurities, interrupts) are clearly outside the scope of what may be addressed by using assertions in our programs, and we will simply assume that they do not happen. Also, to simplify reasoning about program correctness, we will generally be avoiding "jumps" in our programs. The function error given on page 7 may be used to abort program execution if a code fragment or function is executed when its pre-condition is false; this makes the program more robust, but it has no effect on its correctness.

Overflows are especially problematical. Unlike division by 0, overflows are not easily precluded by a simple test *before* the operation. An int operation in C will overflow if the result would be greater than INT_MAX or less than INT_MIN (implementation-dependent constants defined in the limits library); so, for example, the following test would be needed to prevent an int operation i+j from overflowing:

```
if ( (i>0 && j > INT_MAX - i) || (i<0 && j < INT_MIN - i) )
  error("addition overflow");
else /* cannot overflow */
  return i+j;
```

This is obviously inefficient and inconvenient. It is much easier to let the hardware detect the overflow *during* the operation, but C does not support a portable way of detecting a signed int or long overflow *after* it has happened. Some compilers may be configured so that overflows signal an exception or result in program abortion, but this is by no means true of every C implementation.

We will not try in this book to address this issue, which is both language dependent and implementation dependent. Except for variables of types bool or char and bit-string representations of sets in Section 6.4, type int will be used for *all* integer-valued variables, even when long or unsigned would be more likely in practice, and we will naively assume that our implementation uses unlimited-precision int arithmetic.

The remaining issues, which we *will* attempt to address, are infinite looping (and, in one example program, infinite recursion) and easily preventable runtime errors, such as division by zero and illegal array subscripts.

So, how may "correctness" (as we have qualified it) be established? It is almost always impossible to establish correctness *computationally* (i.e., to consider *every* possible state, run the code for all states that satisfy the precondition, and check that the corresponding final states satisfy the postcondition). Instead, correctness must be evaluated by careful testing and by informal or formal reasoning about the program; in this book, we will be focusing on reasoning about programs. In Chapter 2, we motivate and describe a *formal system* of axioms and inference rules oriented to verifying program correctness.

1.6 Additional Reading

The use of assertions as comments is usually attributed to [Nau66, Flo67]; for some earlier references, see [Jon92]. More sophisticated implementations of the standard assert library exist [Ros95, Mak99]; they are more efficient and allow failures to be handled by a debugger. The combined use of pre- and post-conditions as algorithm specifications is from [Hoa69].

REFERENCES

[Flo67] R. W. Floyd. Assigning meanings to programs. In J. T. Schwartz, editor, *Mathematical Aspects of Computer Science*, volume 19 of *Proceedings of Symposia in Applied Mathematics*, pages 19–32. American Mathematical Society, 1967.

[Hoa69] C. A. R. Hoare. An axiomatic basis for computer programming. *Comm. ACM*, 12(10):576–80 and 583, 1969.

[Jon92] C. B. Jones. The search for tractable ways of reasoning about programs. Technical Report UMCS-92-4-4, Department of Computer Science, University of Manchester, 1992.

[Mak99] P. J. Maker. GNU Nana, improved support for assertions and logging in C and C++, 1999. Available here: http://www.gnu.org.

[Nau66]   P. Naur. Proof of algorithms by general snapshots. *BIT*, 6:310–16, 1966.

[Ros95]   D. S. Rosenblum. A practical approach to programming with assertions. *IEEE Trans. Software Engineering*, 21:19–31, 1995.

Chapter 2

Verifying Algorithms: Basic Techniques

> Program testing can be used to show the presence of bugs,
> but never to show their absence!
>
> Edsger W. Dijkstra[*]

> One does not need to give a formal proof of an obviously
> correct program; but one needs a thorough understanding of
> formal proof methods to know when correctness is obvious.
>
> John C. Reynolds[†]

2.1 Some Programs for Array Searching

In Chapter 1, we developed a *specification* for the desired array-searching code, consisting of

- a declarative interface:

```
const int max;      /* maximum number of entries */
typename Entry;     /* type of entries, use == for equality */
const int n;        /* number of entries */
const Entry x;      /* search target */
Entry A[max];       /* A[0:n-1] are the entries to search */
bool present;       /* search result */
```

- a pre-condition: 0 <= n <= max && A == A0, and

- a post-condition:

```
(present iff x in A[0:n-1]) && (ForAll (i=0; i<n) A[i] == A0[i])
```

It is now time to consider some programs for array-searching and evaluate their correctness relative to this specification.

---

[*]In [Dij72].
[†]In [Rey81].

Program 2.1

```
{ int i;
  present = false;
  for (i=0; i<n; i++)
    if (A[i] == x) present = true;
}
```

Consider Program 2.1.

EXERCISE 2.1 Before reading on, decide whether Program 2.1 is correct.

This simple code seems correct: initially, present is set to false and its value changed to true only if A[i] = x for some i in the range 0:n-1; every such entry is considered. Notice that if n = 0, the code works correctly without any need for a special-case test: the loop body (i.e., the indented if statement that immediately follows for (...)) is then not executed at all, and the value of present stays at false. But though the code is correct, it is unnecessarily inefficient because, after the first assignment of the value true to present, its value will not change, and the loop could immediately terminate.

Consider the attempt in Program 2.2 to improve on the efficiency of Program 2.1.

Program 2.2

```
{ int i;
  present = false;
  for (i=0; !present && i<n; i++)
    if (A[i] == x) present = true;
}
```

EXERCISE 2.2 Before reading on, decide whether Program 2.2 is correct.

This code is also correct. The loop condition is now more complicated: the iteration will stop if *either* present is true *or* i >= n.

Suppose that we try to simplify the code, as in Program 2.3. Note that the loop body in this case is an "empty" compound statement {}.

EXERCISE 2.3 Before reading on, decide whether Program 2.3 is correct.

This code will always give correct results whenever it terminates normally; however, consider what will happen if x does *not* occur in A[0:n-1]. Then the value of i will increase to n and A[n] will be compared to x; however,

---

Program 2.3

```
{ int i;
  for (i=0; A[i] != x && i<n; i++)
  {}
  present = i<n;
}
```

---

when n = max, there may not *be* an array component A[n]! This would then be a violation of the ISO/ANSI standard for C and, on a *secure* system, would result in a run-time exception.

EXERCISE 2.4 Experiment to see what your implementation of C does when code attempts to access a nonexistent A[i].

Most C implementations do *not* check for illegal array accesses during execution, even as an option, and their effect is *unpredictable*. In some contexts, such "buffer overflows" have serious consequences, and are the most frequent causes of system insecurities and crashes in C code. In practice, a conscientious programmer should *always* ensure that illegal array accesses and updates do not occur.

In the preceding example, the problem may easily be avoided by interchanging the two operands of the && in the loop condition, as follows: i<n && A[i] != x. In logic, P && Q is equivalent to Q && P; however, the && operation is evaluated "sequentially" in C, so that, if i ≥ n, the array comparison is "short-circuited" (i.e., not evaluated). This approach is more efficient than evaluating both operands and avoids the attempted access to a nonexistent array component.

Consider now Program 2.4, which illustrates a programming style used by some programmers. The for(;;) construct sets up a (potentially) *infinite* iteration of the loop body, which is exited using break statements.

Program 2.4

```
{ int i;
  present = false; i = 0;
  for(;;)
  { if (A[i] == x)
    { present = true; break; }
    if (i >= n-1) break;
    i++;
  }
}
```

EXERCISE 2.5 Before reading on, decide whether Program 2.4 is correct.

This code will *almost* always give correct results; but it is *not* correct code.

EXERCISE 2.6 If you haven't already found the bug, try to find it by testing the code before reading on.

Here is the bug: if $n = 0$ *and* the "garbage" component A[0] happens to contain the search target x, Program 2.4 will assign true to present, whereas the correct result is false. It is not easy to find this bug by testing the code, but it may well occur in actual use.

EXERCISE 2.7 In what circumstances would this bug occur in Professor Higgins's application?

Consider now Program 2.5, which uses an additional local variable m to terminate the search loop without using a flag or jumps.

Program 2.5

```
{ int i, m;
  i = 0; m = n;
  while (i < m)
    if (A[i] == x)
      m = i;
    else
      i++;
  present = (i<n);
}
```

EXERCISE 2.8 Before reading on, decide whether Program 2.5 is correct.

This code is correct: the variable m acts as an upper limit for the iteration counter i. It is initialized to the value of n; but if an entry equal to the seach target is found, m is assigned the current value of the iteration counter, and the loop terminates when the loop condition is next evaluated. If no entry equal to x is found, the loop terminates with i equal to the initial value of m.

Finally, consider Program 2.6.

EXERCISE 2.9 Before reading on, decide whether Program 2.6 is correct.

This code will almost always work correctly, but it will fail in some circumstances. The intention is to use the "garbage" component A[n] as a *sentinel* to terminate the loop if x does *not* occur in A[0:n-1]. But the assignment to A[n] may be illegal if $n = \text{max}$! If it is possible to change the specification of

---

Program 2.6

```
{ int i;
  A[n] = x; i = 0;
  while (A[i] != x) i++;
  present = (i<n);
}
```

A in the declarative interface to Entry A[max+1] to ensure the existence of an additional array component A[max], the code would be correct, and with some compilers it may be 40% more efficient (on average) than any of the other solutions we have considered so far because each iteration requires just a single comparison.

EXERCISE 2.10 Find an example showing that the following code is *not* a correct implementation of the specification for array search.

```
{ int i; Entry t;
  t = A[0];  /* save the value of A[0] */
  A[0] = x;  /* use A[0] as a sentinel */
  i = n-1;
  if (i>0)
     while (A[i] != x) i--;
  A[0] = t; /* restore the value of A[0] */
  present = i>0 || t == x;
}
```

These examples, though small, have shown that it is very difficult to be *sure* whether code is correct, particularly when the programmer has used an unfamiliar coding style or has tried to write very efficient code. And we have seen that both testing and ad hoc informal reasoning may not be sufficiently trustworthy. In Section 2.2, we begin discussing a method that supports sound reasoning about program behavior.

2.2 Correctness Statements

Let us assume that we have an idealized implementation that uses unlimited-precision arithmetic, aborts on run-time errors such as illegal array subscripts, doesn't have bugs or insecurities, and so on. Suppose that C is a statement (without exiting jumps) and that P and Q are, respectively, the pre-condition and the post-condition appropriate to C; in the following sections, we will discuss techniques for mathematically *proving* that it is valid to use assertion comments as follows:

ASSERT(P) C ASSERT(Q)

In other words, if code C is executed with an initial state satisfying pre-condition P, any resulting final state will satisfy post-condition Q. We will frequently abbreviate this to $P\{C\}Q$, using curly braces $\{\dots\}$ to enclose the code; the notation $\{P\}C\{Q\}$ is also widely used, particularly with languages that use curly braces to enclose comments, such as PASCAL.

We may consider this combination of a statement with pre- and post-conditions to be a *logical* formula (i.e., either true or false), which we term a *correctness statement*. Of course, it will still be necessary in general to show that execution of C from a state satisfying P terminates and doesn't have run-time errors before we may declare it *correct*, but validity of $P\{C\}Q$ ensures that executing C on an idealized implementation is "safe" in the following sense:

> Executing C will not produce a normal (i.e., nonaborted) final state at which the desired post-condition Q fails, provided that the corresponding initial state satisfied the assumed pre-condition P.

This property is sometimes termed *partial* or "conditional" correctness: the code is correct *provided* that it is also verified that nontermination and, when necessary, run-time errors will not occur.

Note that a correctness statement $P\{C\}Q$ involves two assertions, P and Q, but is not itself an assertion, as we use this term. A correctness statement is either true (valid) or false (invalid), independent of any particular state of a computation; however, an assertion may be true for some states and false for others. An assertion asserts a property of computational *states*; a correctness statement is essentially a statement about *code* satisfying a pre- and post-condition specification.

2.3   Simple Assignment Statements

In this section, we discuss correctness statements for code of the form $V = E$;, where V is a variable identifier and E is a suitable expression (i.e., simple assignment statements). For example, it is evident that the correctness statement

```
n == n0 { n = n-1; } n == n0-1
```

is valid. Suppose that we try to generalize this reasoning pattern by stating the following *axiom scheme*:

$$V == I \{V = E;\} V == [E](V \mapsto I)$$

with the *side condition* that identifier I be distinct from V, and $[E](V \mapsto I)$ is (roughly) the expression E with occurrences of V substituted by I. This substitution concept will be discussed in more detail in Section 2.4.

Symbols such as V, E, and I that occur in such an axiom scheme (or in an inference rule or proof-tableau scheme, to be discussed later) are known as (syntactic) *metavariables*; here V stands for a variable identifier, E stands for an expression (of appropriate type), and I stands for an identifier. The correctness statement discussed earlier may be obtained as an *instance* of the axiom scheme by instantiating metavariable V to the program variable n, I to the ghost identifier n0, and E to the expression n-1.

If a metavariable (such as V) occurs more than once in a rule or axiom scheme, all the occurrences must be instantiated to the *same* variable or expression or identifier; however, *distinct* metavariables (such as E_0 and E_1, or V and V') may, in general, be instantiated to the *same* expression or variable identifier (unless this is specifically disallowed by a side condition). If *every* (allowed) instance of an axiom scheme is a valid correctness statement, the axiom scheme is said to be *sound*.

EXERCISE 2.11 Give a counterexample showing that the proposed axiom scheme would *not* be sound if the side condition were omitted.

EXERCISE 2.12 Explain why the following is a sound axiom scheme:

Empty Statement:

   $P \{\} P$

The axiom scheme proposed for assignments, though sound, is not very useful: the pre-condition must be of the form $V == I$ where V is the left-hand side of the assignment. For example, is the following correctness statement valid?

   n>0 { n = n-1; } n >= 0

The axiom scheme stated earlier does not help us answer this question because the pre-condition is not of the form $V == I$. It turns out that validity of the correctness statement in question depends on the type of n; the code satisfies the specification if n is of type int, but not if n is of type float.

EXERCISE 2.13 Devise a counterexample to illustrate that the preceding correctness statement is invalid when n is of type float.

It is possible to generalize the proposed axiom scheme to allow for arbitrary pre-conditions [Flo67]; however, the resulting scheme is somewhat inconvenient to use. C. A. R. Hoare described a simpler approach [Hoa69]. Here is Hoare's axiom scheme for assignments:

Assignment:

   $[Q](V \mapsto E) \{V = E;\} Q$

where $[Q](V \mapsto E)$ is, roughly, assertion Q with E substituted for occurrences of V; a detailed treatment will be given in Section 2.4.

Note that this axiom scheme is used in the "backwards" direction; that is, starting from any *post*-condition Q, it determines a *pre*-condition $[Q](V \mapsto E)$ with respect to which the code is correct. Informally, the axiom scheme may be justified as follows: if Q is to be true of V *after* the assignment, it must be that Q is true of the value of expression E *before* the assignment of E to V. For example, the following is an instance of the assignment scheme:

```
n-1 >= 0 { n = n-1; } n >= 0
```

This is not quite the correctness statement that we asked about earlier, but it *is* valid, whether n is of type int or type float. In Section 2.5, we will see how to verify n>0 { n = n-1; } n >= 0 if n is of type int.

EXERCISE 2.14 What should pre-condition P be in each of the following correctness statements for the statement to be an instance of Hoare's axiom scheme? All variables are of type int.

  (i) P { x = 0; } x==0

  (ii) P { x = 0; } x >= 0

  (iii) P { x = 0; } x>0

  (iv) P { x = 0; } y>0

  (v) P { x = x+1; } x==1

  (vi) P { x = x+1; } x>0

  (vii) P { x = x+1; } x==y

  (viii) P { x = x-1; } x == y-1

EXERCISE 2.15 Derive axiom schemes for the C statements V++; and V--;, where V is a simple variable; assume that these are equivalent to $V=V+1$; and $V=V-1$;, respectively.

2.4   Substitution into Assertions

In general, if Q is an assertion, I is an identifier, and E is an expression, we use the notation* $[Q](I \mapsto E)$ to denote the assertion that is like Q except that E has been substituted for occurrences of I; for example, $[A[j] > 0](j \mapsto j-1)$ is A[j-1] > 0. Substitution is much like the effect of a macro substitution or a "replace" operation in a text editor; however, there are some subtle aspects of *mathematical* substitution.

When substituting an expression E for identifier I, the substitution should not otherwise change the syntactic structure of the assertion; therefore, it may

---

    *Many other notations are in use, including $Q[E/I]$, $Q|_I^E$, and $Q[I := E]$.

be necessary to use additional parentheses around E. For example, the substitution [2 * i == j](i ↦ i-1) should yield 2 * (i - 1) == j, rather than just 2 * i - 1 == j; the latter is equivalent to (2 * i) - 1 == j, because * takes precedence over -.

To discuss two other issues, we remind the reader of some important terminology from logic. If an identifier occurs in an assertion or expression but that occurrence is not bound *within* that assertion or expression, the identifier is said to have a *free* occurrence in the assertion or expression. Programmers use the term "nonlocal" identifier for essentially the same concept. For example, in the assertion

```
n>0 implies Exists (i=0; i<n) A[i] == x
```

the identifers n, A, and x all occur freely; however, every occurrence of i in the assertion is a bound occurrence.

EXERCISE 2.16 Give an example of an assertion in which identifier i has both free *and* bound occurrences.

In general, when substituting E for I in Q, it is only the *free* occurrences of I that are to be replaced by E. Substituting for an identifer from "outside" an assertion should not have any effect on bound occurrences that, because of an unfortunate choice of bound identifier, look the same. For example, the result of the substitution

```
[ForAll (i=0; i<n) A[i] > 0](i ↦ i-1)
```

is the given assertion without any change, because i only occurs in it bound. On the other hand,

```
[ForAll (i=0; i<n) A[i] > 0](n ↦ n-1)
```

produces

```
ForAll (i=0; i<n-1) A[i] > 0
```

because the occurrence of n is free. This issue may be avoided by always choosing a "fresh" identifier as the bound identifier of a quantification (i.e., an identifier that is not already in use).

EXERCISE 2.17 Substitute i-1 for i in your answer to Exercise 2.16.

Finally, another kind of identifier clash occurs if substituting expression E for occurrences of identifier I in assertion Q would result in free identifiers of E becoming bound within the assertion; all occurrences of the *bound* identifier in the assertion must first be systematically changed to prevent this. For example, the substitution

$$[\text{ForAll } (i=0; \ i<n) \ A[i] \ > \ j](j \mapsto i-1)$$

should *not* produce

```
ForAll (i=0; i<n) A[i] > i-1
```

in which the last occurrence of i has been "captured" by the quantifier. A correct result of the substitution is

```
ForAll (k=0; k<n) A[k] > i-1
```

in which the quantified identifier has first been changed to a "fresh" identifier k. Again, the justification for this is that a free identifier in the substituted expression should be regarded as distinct from a bound identifier of the assertion, even if they happen to look the same.

EXERCISE 2.18 Carry out the following substitutions:

(a) $[\text{ForAll } (x) \text{ Exists } (y) \ y>x](y \mapsto x)$

(b) $[\text{ForAll } (x) \text{ Exists } (y) \ x<z \text{ implies } x<y<z](z \mapsto x)$

2.5   Using Mathematical Facts

We saw in Section 2.3 that we may validate the correctness statement

```
n-1 >= 0 { n = n-1; } n >= 0
```

by using Hoare's axiom scheme. To verify

```
n>0 { n = n-1; } n >= 0
```

we note that the assertion

```
n>0 implies n-1 >= 0
```

is true in *every* state; that is, it is a *mathematical* fact, independent of computational state, provided that n is of type int. This justifies the validity of

```
ASSERT(n>0)
ASSERT(n-1 >= 0)
n = n-1;
ASSERT(n >= 0)
```

because the mathematical fact ensures that if n>0 is true in any execution state, so is n-1 >= 0. (Note that n>0 implies n-1 >= 0 is *not* generally valid when n has type float.) In this example, n-1 >= 0 also implies n>0 and so they are logically *equivalent*; however, we will also see examples where a *strictly* stronger pre-condition is used.

In general, if P implies P' is a mathematical fact, an instance of P as a comment may validly appear immediately before an instance of P' as a comment:

⋮

```
ASSERT(P)
ASSERT(P')
```

⋮

Note that P and P' themselves need not be mathematical facts.

Use of a mathematical fact to strengthen a pre-condition is formalized by the following *inference rule*:

Pre-Condition Strengthening:

$$\frac{P' \ \{C\} \ Q \qquad P \ \text{implies} \ P'}{P \ \{C\} \ Q}$$

An inference rule allows the derivation of the statement *below* the horizontal line if the premises *above* the horizontal line may be proved (after the metavariables have been properly instantiated). In the preceding rule, there are two premises; the first premise is a correctness statement, and the second is a mathematical fact. Note that P implies P', but $P \ \{C\} \ Q$ is derived *from* $P' \ \{C\} \ Q$; the reversal arises because pre-conditions are precedents rather than consequents of code execution.

EXERCISE 2.19 Where possible, express the pre-conditions in Exercise 2.14 more neatly using mathematical facts and pre-condition strengthening.

Similarly, mathematical facts may be used to *weaken* post-conditions. For example,

```
n > 0 implies  n >= 1
```

is a mathematical fact when n has type int, which allows the derivation of

```
ASSERT(n-1 > 0)
n = n-1;
ASSERT(n > 0)
ASSERT(n >= 1)
```

in which the new post-condition is implied by the post-condition of an instance of the assignment axiom scheme.

In general, we have the following inference rule:

Post-Condition Weakening:

$$\frac{P \ \{C\} \ Q \qquad Q \ \text{implies} \ Q'}{P \ \{C\} \ Q'}$$

Mathematical facts used to justify instances of either of these inference rules are often termed *verification conditions*.

2.6   Formal Proofs and Proof Tableaux

A *formal proof* (with respect to a formal system of axioms and inference rules) consists of a sequence of logical statements. Each statement must be an axiom or the conclusion of an instance of one of the inference rules, all of whose premises occur earlier in the sequence (i.e., have already been proved). Axiom schemes may be regarded as inference rules with *no* premises and so their instances may be used anywhere in a proof; in particular, the *first* statement in a formal proof will normally be an axiom or an instance of an axiom scheme. A formal proof is said to be a *proof of* the last statement in the sequence.

For example, if we allow the mathematical facts `n>1 implies n-1 > 1` and `n>0 implies n >= 0` to be used as axioms, the following is a formal proof (with annotations justifying each step) involving the axiom scheme of assignment (ASGN) and the inference rules of pre-condition strengthening (PRE) and post-condition weakening (POST):

1.   `n-1 > 0 { n = n-1; } n > 0`   ... ASGN
2.   `n>1 implies n-1 > 1`   ... MATH. FACT
3.   `n>1 { n = n-1; } n>0`   ... PRE, from lines 1 and 2
4.   `n>0 implies n >= 1`   ... MATH. FACT
5.   `n>0 { n = n-1; } n >= 1`   ... POST, from lines 3 and 4

However, such formal proofs are difficult to read, particularly when any of the "statements" may consist of several lines of code plus pre- and post-conditions!

We will find it much easier to present correctness verifications as *proof tableaux*, consisting of program code, pre- and post-conditions, *and* all intermediate assertions, as in

```
ASSERT(n>1)
ASSERT(n-1 > 0)
n = n-1;
ASSERT(n > 0)
ASSERT(n >= 1)
```

It is, of course, implicit that the assignment axiom scheme justifies the use of the "inner" assertions before and after the assignment statement, and that the pre- and post-condition rules (and appropriate mathematical facts) justify the use of the "outer" assertions before and after these, respectively. In general, it should be possible to reconstruct a detailed formal proof from such a proof tableau and, possibly, some additional justifications for mathematical facts.

When the implication justifying a use of the pre-condition or post-condition rules depends on a mathematical fact P that may not be obvious to a reader, it may be made explicit in a program with a comment of the form FACT(P) if the "null" macro definition

```
# define FACT(P)
```

is provided. A fact differs from an assertion in that it is true for mathematical or logical reasons, rather than because program variables have appropriate values. Hence, any FACT(...) comment could, in principle, be used *anywhere* in a program; of course, it is appropriate to place it as close as possible to where it is relevant. It may also be useful on occasion to add explanatory comments to the program text, as in the following:

```
ASSERT(x>0)
ASSERT(x-1 >= 0) /* x has type int */
x = x-1;
ASSERT(x >= 0)
```

Here the comment explains what might otherwise be a mysterious inference if the reader has forgotten the type of variable x.

EXERCISE 2.20 Are the following correctness statements valid?

(a) n<0 { n = n*n; } n>0

(b) n != 0 { n = n*n; } n>0

(c) true { n = n*n; } n >= 0

(d) false { n = n*n; } n<0

Give a proof tableau and a formal proof for each valid statement, indicating the relevant mathematical facts. For each invalid statement, give a counterexample (i.e., an initial state that satisfies the pre-condition but for which the corresponding final state fails to satisfy the post-condition). Assume that variable n has type int.

2.7 Sequencing

Consider the following correctness statement for code that is supposed to exchange the values of two variables, x and y, using an auxiliary variable z:

```
ASSERT(x==x0 && y==y0)
z = x;
x = y;
y = z;
ASSERT(y==x0 && x==y0)
```

The ghost identifiers x0 and y0 are used to name the initial values of variables x and y, respectively.

To validate the correctness statement, we may use the assignment axiom scheme to work backwards from the given post-condition to get a pre-condition for the third assignment, as follows:

```
ASSERT(z==x0 && x==y0)
y = z;
ASSERT(y==x0 && x==y0)
```

Then consider the resulting pre-condition for the third assignment as a post-condition for the second assignment and again use the assignment axiom as follows:

```
ASSERT(z==x0 && y==y0)
x = y;
ASSERT(z==x0 && x==y0)
```

Finally, consider the resulting pre-condition for the second assignment as the post-condition for the first assignment; the assignment axiom then gives us

```
ASSERT(x==x0 && y==y0)
z = x;
ASSERT(z==x0 && y==y0)
```

Putting these together, we have demonstrated the validity of the following correctness statement:

```
ASSERT(x==x0 && y==y0)
z = x;
x = y;
y = z;
ASSERT(y==x0 && x==y0)
```

Here is the code annotated to show the intermediate assertions:

```
ASSERT(x==x0 && y==y0)
z = x;
ASSERT(z==x0 && y==y0)
x = y;
ASSERT(z==x0 && x==y0)
y = z;
ASSERT(y==x0 && x==y0)
```

Each intermediate assertion between assignment statements is *both* a post-condition for the preceding statement *and* a pre-condition for the succeeding statement.

The following inference rule formalizes this approach to reasoning about statement sequences:

Sequencing:

$$\frac{P\{C_0\}Q \qquad Q\{C_1\}R}{P\{C_0\ C_1\}R}$$

This rule has two premises, which are correctness statements for the two sub-statements C_0 and C_1, and a conclusion, which is a correctness statement for the composite statement $C_0\ C_1$. Informally, this rule is justified as follows: assume that the initial state satisfies P; according to the first premise, the state after execution of C_0 must satisfy Q and so, according to the second premise, the state after executing C_1 must satisfy R.

EXERCISE 2.21 Write out a complete formal proof of the correctness statement for the exchange code.

The following is a proof-tableau scheme that implicitly uses the sequencing rule:

```
ASSERT(P)
C₀
ASSERT(Q)
C₁
ASSERT(R)
```

and makes explicit the intermediate assertion Q. Of course, it will not always be as easy as in the example to determine the intermediate assertions; often it will be necessary to use mathematical facts to strengthen pre-conditions or weaken post-conditions appropriately.

EXERCISE 2.22 Verify the validity of

```
ASSERT(i >= 0 && y == power(x,i))
y = y * x;
i++;
ASSERT(i >= 0 && y == power(x,i))
```

where * denotes multiplication and power(x,i) denotes x^i (for nonnegative integers i only); that is, for any x, power(x,0) = 1 and power(x,n+1) = x * power(x,n).

EXERCISE 2.23 Verify the validity of

```
ASSERT(k>0 && f == Fib(k) && g == Fib(k-1))
t = f+g;
g = f;
f = t;
ASSERT(k >= 0 && f == Fib(k+1) && g == Fib(k))
```

where Fib(n) denotes the n'th Fibonacci number; that is, Fib(0) = 0, Fib(1) = 1, and, for all n > 1, Fib(n) = Fib(n-1) + Fib(n-2).

EXERCISE 2.24 What pre-condition P would allow the following code to achieve its post-condition:

```
ASSERT(P)
t = f+g;
g = f;
f = t;
k++;
ASSERT(k>0 && f == Fib(k) && g == Fib(k-1))
```

Use the results of Exercise 2.23.

EXERCISE 2.25 Are the following alternative implementations of the specification in Exercise 2.23 valid?

(a)
```
ASSERT(k>0 && f == Fib(k) && g == Fib(k-1))
t = f;
f = f + g;
g = t;
ASSERT(k >= 0 && f == Fib(k+1) && g == Fib(k))
```

(b)
```
ASSERT(k>0 && f == Fib(k) && g == Fib(k-1))
f = f + g;
g = f - g;
ASSERT(k >= 0 && f == Fib(k+1) && g == Fib(k))
```

EXERCISE 2.26 Is the following correctness statement valid? If so, give a proof; if not, obtain a pre-condition that is just strong enough to make the correctness statement valid.

```
ASSERT(x==x0 && y==y0)
x = x - y;
y = x + y;
x = y - x;
ASSERT(x==y0 && y==x0)
```

2.8 If *Statements*

To validate a correctness statement of the form

$$P \ \{ \ \text{if} \ (B) \ C_0 \ \text{else} \ C_1 \ \} \ Q$$

we must validate correctness statements for the constituent code fragments C_0 and C_1; but what pre- and post-conditions should be used? To ensure that Q is true after executing C_0 *or* C_1, assertion Q should be the post-condition for *both* of them. If the evaluation of B is assumed not to change the state, pre-condition P may be assumed to be true initially by both; furthermore, if C_0 is executed, we may assume B as a pre-condition, and if C_1 is executed, we may assume that $!B$ holds. This informal argument suggests the intermediate assertions in the following proof-tableau scheme:

```
ASSERT(P)
if (B)
   ASSERT(P && B)
   C0
   ASSERT(Q)
else
   ASSERT(P && !B)
   C1
   ASSERT(Q)
ASSERT(Q)
```

Here is the corresponding inference rule:

If:

$$\frac{P \text{ \&\& } B \{C_0\} \, Q \qquad P \text{ \&\& } !B \{C_1\} \, Q}{P \{\text{if } (B) \, C_0 \text{ else } C_1\} \, Q}$$

Note that the `bool` condition B from the code is used in the pre-condition assertions in the premises.

As a simple example, suppose that Ms Doolittle has finally submitted the following code as her solution to the problem posed by Professor Higgins (Exercise 1.19):

```
if (x>y)
    m = x;
else
    m = y;
```

We want to verify the code with respect to the following specification:

- Declarative interface:

```
const int x, y;
int m;
```

- Pre-condition: `true`

- Post-condition: `m >= x && m >= y && ( m == x || m == y )`

We first match the metavariables in the preceding tableau scheme or inference rule to our problem: P is the pre-condition, Q is the post-condition, B is the condition x>y, C_0 is the statement `m = x;`, and C_1 is the statement `m = y;`.

According to the inference rule or tableau scheme, we must verify two substatements, but these verifications may be done separately and independently. We choose (arbitrarily) to verify the first substatement first. Because `true && x > y` is equivalent to `x > y`, we simplify the pre-condition and then prove the following correctness statement:

```
ASSERT( x > y )
m = x;
ASSERT( m >= x && m >= y && ( m == x || m == y ) )
```

Use of the assignment axiom scheme gives us the intermediate assertion in

```
ASSERT( x > y )
ASSERT( x >= x && x >= y && ( x == x || x == y ) )
m = x;
ASSERT( m >= x && m >= y && ( m == x || m == y ) )
```

which is valid by pre-condition strengthening, using the logical properties of `||` and `&&`, and the mathematical facts that `x == x` and `x >= x`, and that `x > y` implies `x >= y`.

EXERCISE 2.27 Complete the verification of the conditional in the preceding example by verifying the correctness statement for the else part suggested by the proof tableau or inference rule.

EXERCISE 2.28 Professor Higgins has just realized that what he *really* wants is that m be assigned the largest of the values of *three* variables x, y, and z. Give a formal specification of the problem, write code to solve it, and verify the code.

EXERCISE 2.29 Professor Higgins has just changed his mind again: what he *now* wants is that m be assigned the *median* (middle value) of x, y, and z. Give a formal specification of the problem, write code to solve it, and verify the code.

EXERCISE 2.30 Explain informally why the following inference rule for a "one-branch" if statement is valid:

One-Branch If:

$$\frac{P \text{ \&\& } B \{C\} Q \qquad (P \text{ \&\& } !B) \text{ implies } Q}{P \{\text{if } (B) C\} Q}$$

The corresponding proof-tableau scheme is best written using a dummy else part for the two assertions of the second premise, as follows:

```
ASSERT(P)
if (B)
  ASSERT(P && B)
  C₀
  ASSERT(Q)
else
  ASSERT(P && !B)
  {}
  ASSERT(Q)
ASSERT(Q)
```

EXERCISE 2.31 Suppose that we try to "work backwards" from a given post-condition Q to a suitable pre-condition P, assuming that we may derive from Q suitable pre-conditions P_0 and P_1 to C_0 and C_1, respectively:

```
ASSERT(P)
if (B)
  ASSERT(P₀)
  C₀
  ASSERT(Q)
else
  ASSERT(P₁)
  C₁
  ASSERT(Q)
ASSERT(Q)
```

Explain why $(B \text{ implies } P_0)$ && $(!B \text{ implies } P_1)$ is valid as a pre-condition P.

EXERCISE 2.32 Consider the following specification for a program fragment that, given values *a* and *b*, is to determine whether the equation $a \cdot x + b = 0$ has a *unique* solution, it has *no* solution, or *all* numbers *x* are solutions. If there *is* a unique solution, the program should also compute it.

- Declarative interface:

```
const float a, b;        /* equation parameters */
enum {none, one, all} NumSol;  /* number of solutions */
float x;                 /* the solution (if NumSol == one) */
```

- Pre-condition: true

- Post-condition:

```
( NumSol == all  iff  ForAll (float y) a * y + b == 0 ) &&
( NumSol == none iff  ForAll (float y) a * y + b != 0 ) &&
( NumSol == one  iff  ForAll (float y) a * y + b == 0 => y==x )
```

Implement the specification and verify the code. You may assume (unrealistically) that `float` arithmetic is error-free.

EXERCISE 2.33 Give an inference rule or proof-tableau scheme for `switch` statements:

```
switch (N)
{ case K₀: C₀ break;
  case K₁: C₁ break;
     ⋮
  case K_{n-1}: C_{n-1} break;
  default: Cₙ break;
}
```

where *N* is an `int` expression, the K_i are `int` constants with distinct values, and the C_i are statement sequences. The `break;` statements are used to terminate each of the `case` sections; otherwise, control would just continue on to the next `case`. You should assume that the effect of the `switch` statement form is equivalent to (but more efficient than)

```
if (N==K₀) { C₀ }
else if (N==K₁) { C₁ }
   ⋮
else if (N==K_{n-1}) { C_{n-1} }
else { Cₙ }
```

2.9 While *Statements*

At first, it might seem quite difficult to treat *loops*; will it be necessary to consider each iteration separately, using a whole sequence of intermediate assertions? In practice, a single well-chosen assertion called a *loop invariant* is normally sufficient. The following inference rule shows what is needed for a `while` loop:

While:

$$\frac{I\ \&\&\ B\ \{C\}\ I}{I\ \{\texttt{while }(B)\ C\}\ I\ \&\&\ !\,B}$$

The assertion I in this rule is the loop invariant. Here is the corresponding proof-tableau scheme:

```
ASSERT(I)
while (B)
  ASSERT(I && B)
  C
  ASSERT(I)
ASSERT(I && !B)
```

Note that assertion I occurs four times, as explained in the following.

- Assertion I must be *preserved* by any execution of C, the loop body, whenever B, the loop condition, is also `true` initially. Assertion I is both a precondition *and* the post-condition for the loop body. Note that I may be *temporarily* `false` during execution of C; however, at the end of any such execution, I must again hold.

- Assertion I is the pre-condition of the loop, and so it is required to be `true` *before* execution of the loop. The invariant may follow directly from a given pre-condition; or some additional code such as initializing assignments may be needed immediately before the loop.

- Assertion I, and the negation of B, are then `true` *after* execution of the loop, no matter how many times the loop body is executed (including *zero* times, if the loop condition B happens to be `false` initially). This claim may be justified by a mathematical induction on the number of iterations.

  In many examples, $I\ \&\&\ !\,B$ will logically imply the desired post-condition; but if not, it is necessary to bridge the gap between $I\ \&\&\ !\,B$ and the desired post-condition by some appropriate "finalization" code immediately after the loop.

As a simple example, consider the following loop:

```
while (i != n)
{ y = y * x;
  i++;
}
```

We may prove the following about the body of the loop using the assignment axiom scheme and the sequencing rule:

```
ASSERT(i+1 >= 0 && y * x == power(x,i+1))
y = y * x;
i++;
ASSERT(i >= 0 && y == power(x,i))
```

Then, the following mathematical facts:

- `y == power(x,i)` implies `y * x == power(x,i+1)`
- `i >= 0` implies `i+1 >= 0`

allow us to use the rule of pre-condition strengthening to derive

```
ASSERT(i >= 0 && y == power(x,i) && i != n)
y = y * x;
i++;
ASSERT(i >= 0 && y == power(x,i))
```

This annotated code has the form of the premise of the while rule if we take *I* to be the assertion `i >= 0 && y == power(x,i)`. We may then use the while rule to derive

```
ASSERT(i >= 0 && y == power(x,i))
while (i != n)
{ y = y * x;
  i++;
}
ASSERT( i >= 0 && y == power(x,i) && !(i != n))
```

To achieve `i >= 0 && y == power(x,i)` initially, we may use the two assignments

```
i = 0; y = 1;
```

because $power(x,0) = 1$ for all x. Finally, the post-condition of the loop

```
i >= 0 && y == power(x,i) && !(i != n)
```

is easily seen to imply that $y = power(x,n)$. Hence, we have derived

```
ASSERT(true)
i = 0; y = 1;
while (i != n)
{ y = y * x;
  i++;
}
ASSERT(y == power(x,n))
```

showing that, on termination, the code will have assigned $power(x,n)$ to y.[*]

It is clear from this example that an appropriate invariant assertion is the key to reasoning about a program with a while loop. So, where does such

---

[*]Recall that we are ignoring the possibility of int overflows.

an "appropriate" invariant assertion come from? Often, the invariant may be obtained by generalizing the post-condition of the specification. A simple technique that frequently works is to replace a "size" constant by a variable that is used as a counter. For example, the assertion y == power(x,i) used in the invariant for the preceding loop is obtained from the post-condition y == power(x,n) by replacing n by i. For various reasons, such as to prove termination or legality of array subscripts, it will usually be necessary to add range conditions on such a counter; for example, we added the assertion i >= 0 to the invariant to ensure that power(x,i) was meaningful.

In general, for an assertion to be "appropriate" to prove the correctness of a loop, it must have at least the following properties.

- It is preserved by the loop body.

- It may be established initially by suitable assignments, taking into consideration the assumed pre-conditions.

- Together with the negation of the loop condition, it implies the desired post-condition, perhaps after some finalizing code is executed.

In addition, it might be necessary that an invariant be strong enough to ensure termination of a loop or legality of array subscripts; these issues will be discussed in the examples in the following chapters. Experience with many examples is the best way to develop expertise with loop invariants. After you understand the concept well, you will use invariants not just to verify code already written but also to help *develop* correct code.

Because of its importance in understanding and verifying a loop, a suitable invariant assertion is often provided as a comment, with an indication that it is not merely a conventional assertion, but an invariant for a loop, as in the following:

```
while (B) INVAR(I)
   C
```

in the scope of the macro definition

```
# define INVAR(I)
```

The use of INVAR(I) may be thought of as an abbreviation for the proof-tableau scheme we discussed earlier:

```
ASSERT(I)
while (B)
   ASSERT(I && B)
   C
   ASSERT(I)
ASSERT(I && !B)
```

It is usually convenient to place the INVAR comment for a while loop immediately after the loop condition, where the assertion happens to be true; but this is not essential: an INVAR comment is associated with a loop *as a whole*, not with a particular program point.

EXERCISE 2.34 Use the suggested invariant (and the results of Exercise 2.24) to prove that, after executing the following code, variable f has the value Fib(n):

```
f = 1; g = 0; k = 1;
while (k != n)
INVAR(k>0 && f == Fib(k) && g == Fib(k-1))
{ t = f+g; g = f; f = t; k++;
}
```

In Sections 4.1 and 4.3, inference rules for for and do ... while loops will be *derived* from the while rule presented here.

2.10 Termination of Loops

In Section 2.9, we discussed the validity of correctness statements of the form $P\{C\}Q$ when C is a while loop. However, this is not quite all that must be done to ensure correctness of the code. What has been shown is that immediately after any execution of C that starts in a state satisfying P, the postcondition Q is satisfied. But in the case of a while loop, there is the possibility that execution *never* terminates because of an infinite loop, and so the code would then *not* be correct according to the definition in Section 1.5 (if the initial state satisfied the pre-condition).

For example, execution of

```
i = 0; y = 1;
while (i != n)
INVAR( i >= 0 && y == power(x,i) )
{ y = y * x;
  i++;
}
```

will not terminate if $n < 0$. If we now adopt the pre-condition $n \geq 0$, it is straightforward to verify termination of the loop in the example. The variable i is initialized to 0, and its value is incremented each iteration. However, n is nonnegative, and its value is not changed; consequently, the loop condition i != n eventually will fail, and the loop will then terminate. Finally, we note that there is nothing in the loop body that could go into an infinite loop or fail to terminate normally.* We may conclude that the code *is* correct whenever n is greater than or equal to 0.

---

*As discussed in Section 1.5, we assume that interrupts and so on do not occur.

EXERCISE 2.35 What pre-condition is sufficient to ensure termination of the program in Exercise 2.34?

EXERCISE 2.36 Modify the program in Exercise 2.34 so that it is correct if the pre-condition is n ≥ 0.

In some examples, it may be more difficult to verify termination of a loop. A convenient and elegant technique is to show the existence of a suitable *variant* or "bound," an int expression N such that, for every execution of the loop body (i.e., whenever the invariant and the loop condition are both true), $N > 0$ initially and the value of N is strictly *decreased* by the loop body. The loop must then terminate because it is impossible for the value of an int expression such as N to be *indefinitely* decreased and remain greater than zero. Note that the only role of the loop condition in this argument is as an additional pre-condition to the loop body.

For example, we may verify that, if the assertion i <= n is added to the invariant, the expression n-i is a variant for the loop in the example. When the (new) invariant and the loop condition are both true, n-i is greater than 0; and every execution of the loop body increases the value of i and so decreases the value of n-i. This may not be repeated indefinitely, and so the loop must terminate.

EXERCISE 2.37 Consider the following attempt to compute powers:

```
ASSERT( n >= 0 )
i = 0; y = 1;
while (i != n)
INVAR(i >= 0 && y == power(x,i))
{ y = y * x * x;
  i = i + 2;
}
ASSERT( y == power(x,n) )
```

(a) Verify the *partial* correctness of this algorithm.

(b) What is the flaw in the following reasoning: the value of expression n-i is greater than 0 initially, and its value is strictly decreased because i is increased; hence, the loop must eventually terminate.

(c) Now add i <= n to the invariant assertion and reconsider the preceding partial correctness and termination arguments.

(d) Now add n % 2 == 0 (i.e., n is even) to the pre-condition and to the invariant, add i % 2 == 0 to the invariant, and reconsider the correctness arguments.

Unfortunately, a suitable loop variant is not always so obvious. Consider the simple loop in Program 2.7; x is an int variable and the expression x % 2 == 1 is true if x is an odd number.

Program 2.7

```
ASSERT(x >= 1)
while (x != 1)
{ if (x % 2 == 1)
    x = 3 * x + 1;
  else x = x/2;
}
ASSERT(x==1)
```

EXERCISE 2.38 Execute the code in Program 2.7 to termination if x is initially 7.

It is immediately evident from the loop condition that the only possible final value for x is 1; so, the loop is *partially* correct relative to the pre-condition $x \geq 1$ and post-condition $x = 1$. And for every value of x that has been tried (up to several billion), the loop did eventually terminate. But nobody currently knows whether this simple loop terminates for *all* positive values of x; consequently, its correctness has not been proved (yet)!

EXERCISE 2.39 Suggest a correct and efficient way to achieve the post-condition $x = 1$.

Fortunately, proving program termination is usually rather more straightforward than for this notorious example from number theory. However, our inability to be more definite about this example suggests that there is no *general* way to verify termination properties of arbitrary code (other than by using a programming language that does not have features such as the while loop). This is indeed the case; furthermore, it will be explained in Chapter 12 why this fact is an inevitable part of computational life.

2.11 Local Variables

The following example illustrates the use of a variable that should be defined locally:

```
ASSERT(n >= 0)
i = 0; y = 1;
while (i != n)
{ y = y * x;
  i++;
}
ASSERT(y == power(x,n))
```

Although the code uses the variable i, the pre- and post-conditions do not mention i. In other words, variable i is *local* to the code; it should *not* be mentioned in the interface, but it should be defined in the implementing code, as locally as possible.

The variable i may be defined locally using a block statement as follows:

```
{ int i;
  i = 0; y = 1;
  while (i != n)
  { y = y * x;
    i++;
  }
}
```

Here is an inference rule for local-definition blocks:

Local-Variable Block:
$$\frac{P\{C\}Q}{P\{T\,I;\,C\,\}Q}$$

where T is a type, with the "side condition" that identifier I not be free in P or Q. The rule essentially says that defining a local variable doesn't affect reasoning about a program, provided that the relevant pre- and post-conditions may be expressed without referring to the variable.

For example, the annotated code in Program 2.8 illustrates an application of this rule. In practice, one of the pairs of duplicate assertions would be omitted.

Program 2.8

```
ASSERT(n >= 0)
{ int i;
  ASSERT(n >= 0)
  i = 0; y = 1;
  while (i != n)
  { y = y * x;
    i++;
  }
  ASSERT(y == power(x,n))
}
ASSERT(y == power(x,n))
```

EXERCISE 2.40 Improve the program in Exercise 2.34 by using local-variable definitions.

EXERCISE 2.41 Give a proof-tableau scheme corresponding to the inference rule for local-variable blocks.

Some programming-language implementations ensure that a local variable is "automatically" initialized to a default value; others detect attempts to use a variable before it has been initialized. But to avoid unpleasant surprises when moving to another implementation or to another programming language, it is best to get into the habit of *explicitly* initializing *every* (simple) variable.

2.12   Discussion

2.12.1   FORMAL AND INFORMAL REASONING

The use of formal axioms and inference rules as discussed in this chapter will undoubtedly seem too fussy to be feasible with practical code. But with practice, the techniques may be used "semiformally"; that is, invariants and key assertions are stated explicitly, but most intermediate assertions and the detailed derivations justifying them may be omitted when they are intuitively clear. This is the method mathematicians normally use. Proofs are, in principle, *formalizable* but, in practice, are hardly ever completely formal (except when one is studying logic). Furthermore, verification concepts such as invariants may be used *constructively*, while the code is being written, and not merely to verify correctness a posteriori, after code has been written. This technique will be illustrated by examples in Chapters 3 and 4.

We will treat program termination and run-time errors *informally*, demonstrating techniques by giving examples rather than by presenting formal rules; even so, the assertions and interface qualifiers of our specifications and the intermediate assertions such as loop invariants of our partial-correctness reasoning will provide essential information for this.

2.12.2   SOUNDNESS

Although we have tried to give intuitive justifications for the axioms and rules we have stated, a proper demonstration of their soundness requires a detailed semantic analysis. This type of analysis is outside the scope of this presentation, but it is important to be aware of the assumptions about the programming language that underlie the formal rules we are using.

It has already been mentioned that, apart from error aborts, we do not allow jumps such as goto, break, or return (except at the end of a function definition) out of statements. To use bool expressions as assertions, we must assume that expression evaluations in assertions do not *change* the state, for example, by executing assignment operations; such state changes are termed *side effects*. This restriction is also needed for soundness of the assignment axiom scheme and of the rules for the if and while statements: the conditions in these statements should not have side effects.

Another assumption needed to ensure soundness of the assignment axiom scheme is that all variables are *disjoint*, that is, assignment to one variable does not affect any other variable. In most programming languages, it is possible by using reference parameters or other techniques to create *aliases* that circumvent this assumption. Other difficulties arise from possible "interference" between functions. Finally, object assignments in object-oriented languages such as JAVA may not in general be soundly reasoned about using Hoare's axiom scheme because they are assignments "by reference" rather than "by value."

2.13   Additional Reading

The axioms and rules discussed were introduced in [Flo67, Hoa69]. Soundness was first discussed in [Lau71, HL74]; see, for example, [Ten91, Rey98] for modern treatments. See [DLP79, Fle89] for dissenting opinions on the practicality of program verification.

The problem of proving termination of the loop in Program 2.7 is discussed in [Cra78, Guy94]. Two examples of "buffer overflows" with serious consequences are discussed here:

    http://www.cs.berkeley.edu/~srhea/morris-internet-worm.html

    http://www.microsoft.com/technet/security/bulletin/MS01-023.asp

A free multiplatform implementation of C that checks array indices may be found here:

    http://www.kd-dev.com/~eic/

Efficient implementation of array-bound checking for C programs is described here:

    http://gcc.gnu.org/projects/bp/main.html

Verification techniques that allow for jumps are described in [CH72, dB80, Rey81, Ten91]. See [Rey81, Rey78] for two approaches to the problems caused by interference.

REFERENCES

[CH72]   M. Clint and C. A. R. Hoare. Program proving: Jumps and functions. *Acta Informatica*, 1:214–24, 1972.

[Cra78] R. E. Crandall. On the '$3x + 1$' problem. *Mathematics of Computation*, 32:1281–92, 1978.

[dB80]   A. de Bruin. Goto statements. In *Mathematical Theory of Program Correctness*, pages 401–43. Prentice Hall International, 1980.

[Dij72] E. W. Dijkstra. Notes on structured programming. In O.-J. Dahl, E. W. Dijkstra, and C. A. R. Hoare, *Structured Programming*, pages 1–82. Academic Press, 1972.

[DLP79] R. DeMillo, R. J. Lipton, and A. J. Perlis. Social processes and proof of theorems and programs. *Comm. ACM*, 22(5):271–80, 1979.

[Fle89] J. H. Fletzer. Program verification: The very idea. *Comm. ACM*, 31(9):1048–63, 1989.

[Flo67] R. W. Floyd. Assigning meanings to programs. In J. T. Schwartz, editor, *Mathematical Aspects of Computer Science*, volume 19 of *Proceedings of Symposia in Applied Mathematics*, pages 19–32. American Mathematical Society, 1967.

[Guy94]   R. K. Guy. *Unsolved Problems in Number Theory*. Springer-Verlag, 1994.

[HL74]   C. A. R. Hoare and P. E. Lauer. Consistent and complementary formal theories of the semantics of programming languages. *Acta Informatica*, 3(2):135–53, 1974.

[Hoa69]   C. A. R. Hoare. An axiomatic basis for computer programming. *Comm. ACM*, 12(10):576–80 and 583, 1969.

[Lau71]   P. Lauer. Consistent formal theories of the semantics of programming languages. Technical Report TR 25.121, IBM Laboratory, Vienna, Austria, 1971.

[Rey78]   J. C. Reynolds. Syntactic control of interference. In *Conference Record of the Fifth Annual ACM Symposium on Principles of Programming Languages*, pages 39–46, Tucson, Arizona, January 1978. ACM.

[Rey81]   J. C. Reynolds. *The Craft of Programming*. Prentice Hall International, 1981.

[Rey98]   J. C. Reynolds. *Theories of Programming Languages*. Cambridge University Press, 1998.

[Ten91]   R. D. Tennent. *Semantics of Programming Languages*. Prentice Hall International, 1991.

Chapter 3

Verifying Algorithms: Some Examples

In this chapter, we apply the techniques discussed in Chapter 2 to some small but realistic examples. Our main aim is to verify program *correctness*; however, good programmers normally try to write code that is *efficient*, as well as correct. Unfortunately, achieving the best performance may make it more difficult to ensure correctness; the simplest and most "obviously" correct codings may not be the most efficient ones. But this only makes using techniques that help achieve correctness more important. We will discuss the correctness of efficient as well as straightforward solutions to the programming problems we consider; however, the techniques of efficiency analysis and execution profiling are outside the scope of this presentation.

3.1 Searching an Array

In Chapter 1, we discussed the problem of searching for x in an array segment A[0:n-1]. Initially, we simplify the verification problem by considering a slightly more demanding specification with the following declarative interface:

```
const int max;        /* maximum number of entries */
typename Entry;       /* type of entries, use == for equality */
const int n;          /* number of entries */
const Entry x;        /* search target */
const Entry A[max];   /* A[0:n-1] are the entries to search */
bool present;         /* search result */
```

The new const qualifier on the declaration for array A precludes *any* changes to the array, even to the "garbage" components, so that we may simplify the pre- and post-conditions to 0 <= n <= max and present iff x in A[0:n-1], respectively.

Consider initially the following simple (albeit inefficient) solution to the problem; it is just a re-formulation of Program 2.1 using a while loop rather than a for loop:

```
{ int i;
  present = false; i = 0;
  while (i != n)
  { if (A[i] == x) present = true;
    i++;
  }
}
```

To show that the post-condition present iff x in A[0:n-1] is achieved by the while loop, we need to use a loop invariant.

Clearly, the value of variable i is changing throughout, and the value of present might also change from false to true. But what remains *invariant* is that the value of i stays within an appropriate range and that the value of present records whether or not an entry equal to x has been found in the array segment so far examined.

More precisely, consider the following assertion, which we call *I*:

```
0 <= i <= n && (present iff x in A[0:i-1])
```

The first part of *I* specifies the *range* of values for index i, and the second part is simply the desired post-condition with n replaced by i. We will now argue informally that *I* is in fact an appropriate invariant assertion for the loop in this code.

Initially, we have $i = 0$ and present $=$ false. Clearly, i is in the allowed range, and present has the right value because the condition

```
x in A[0:i-1]
```

is false when $i = 0$. (Recall that x in A[0:i-1] is an abbreviation for an assertion of the form Exists(k=0, k<i)..., and this is vacuously false when $i = 0$, no matter what assertion ... might be.)

The truth of *I* is preserved by any execution of the loop body, for the following reasons:

- i is increased by one, but the loop condition i != n ensures that this does not take i outside the allowed range;

- present will be assigned true if A[i] $= x$, and so will have the correct value when i is incremented;

- the value of present remains unchanged if A[i] $\neq x$, and so will have the correct value when i is incremented.

We have therefore verified (informally) that assertion *I* is in fact an invariant for the while loop.

Because assertion *I* is true initially and preserved by any execution of the loop body, *I* will be true both before and after the loop body, no matter how many times the body of the loop is executed (including 0 times). In particular, assertion *I* will be true when execution leaves the loop. Furthermore, the *negation* of the loop condition is true when execution leaves the while loop. The negation of our loop condition i !=n is i = n, and so we have verified that present iff x in A[0:n-1] is achieved by any terminating execution of the code fragment.

This informal argument may be formalized using the axioms and rules of Chapter 2, together with some simple mathematical facts. Program 3.1 gives a complete proof tableau; however, in practice, only the pre- and post-conditions and the loop invariant would appear explicitly in the code, as in Program 3.2 on page 64.

EXERCISE 3.1 Justify each use of pre-condition strengthening or post-condition weakening implicit in the tableau of Program 3.1.

Program 3.1

```
ASSERT(0 <= n <= max)
{ int i;
  ASSERT(0 <= n <= max)
  ASSERT(0 <= 0 <= n && (false iff x in A[0:-1]))
  present = false;
  ASSERT(0 <= 0 <= n && (present iff x in A[0:i-1]))
  i = 0;
  ASSERT(0 <= i <= n && (present iff x in A[0:i-1]))
  while (i != n)
  { ASSERT(0 <= i <= n && (present iff x in A[0:i-1]) && i != n)
    ASSERT(0 <= i < n && (present iff x in A[0:i-1]))
    if (A[i] == x)
    { ASSERT(0 <= i < n && (present iff x in A[0:i-1]) && A[i] == x)
      ASSERT(0 <= i < n && (true iff x in A[0:i]))
      present = true;
      ASSERT(0 <= i < n && (present iff x in A[0:i]))
    }
    else
    { ASSERT(0 <= i < n && (present iff x in A[0:i-1]) && A[i] != x)
      ASSERT(0 <= i < n && (present iff x in A[0:i]))
    }
    ASSERT(0 <= i < n && (present iff x in A[0:i]))
    ASSERT(0 <= i+1 <= n && (present iff x in A[0:i+1-1]))
    i++;
    ASSERT(0 <= i <= n && (present iff x in A[0:i-1]))
  }
  ASSERT(0 <= i <= n && (present iff x in A[0:i-1]) && !(i != n))
  ASSERT(present iff x in A[0:n-1])
}
ASSERT(present iff x in A[0:n-1])
```

Program 3.2

```
ASSERT(0 <= n <= max)
{ int i;
  present = false; i = 0;
  while (i != n)
  INVAR( 0 <= i <= n && (present iff x in A[0:i-1]) )
  { if (A[i] == x) present = true;
    i++;
  }
}
ASSERT(present iff x in A[0:n-1])
```

To complete the verification, we must check that there are no run-time errors and that the loop will always terminate (when the pre-condition is initially true). The only subscript expression is i, and we have shown that 0 <= i < n at that point. Furthermore, we have that n ≤ max, and so the subscript is in the allowed range 0:max-1 specified for A in the interface. Finally, it is evident that the loop will terminate for any n ≥ 0 because n-i is a variant: the invariant and the loop condition imply that n-i is positive, and the loop body increments i. It may finally be concluded that the program is indeed correct.

EXERCISE 3.2 Assume the following interface:

```
const int max;      /* maximum number of entries */
typename Entry;     /* type of entries, use == for equality */
const int n;        /* number of entries */
const Entry A[max], B[max];
                    /* A[0:n-1] and B[0:n-1] are the entries in use */
bool equal;         /* result */
```

Verify the correctness of the following code using a suitable loop invariant.

```
ASSERT(0 <= n <= max)
{ int i;
  equal = true; i = 0;
  while (i != n)
  { if (A[i] != B[i]) equal = false;
    i++;
  }
}
ASSERT(equal iff ForAll (k=0, k<n) A[k] == B[k])
```

EXERCISE 3.3 Using the *same* invariant as in Program 3.2, verify informally the correctness of the following more efficient program, which is a re-formulation of Program 2.2:

```
{ int i;
  present = false; i = 0;
  while (i != n && !present)
  { if (A[i] == x) present = true;
    i++;
  }
}
```

EXERCISE 3.4 Design and verify a more efficient implementation of the specification in Exercise 3.2.

EXERCISE 3.5 Use the following loop invariant to verify the correctness of Program 2.5:

```
0 <= i <= m <= n && x != A[0:i-1] && (m<n implies x == A[m])
```

3.2 Minimal Entry of an Array

The problem considered in this section is to set variable m to the index of a minimal entry of a nonempty segment of array A. An appropriate interface would be

```
const int max;      /* maximum number of entries */
typename Entry;     /* type of entries;
                       use == and < for equality and ordering */
const int n;        /* number of entries */
const Entry A[max]; /* A[0:n-1] are the entries in use */
int m;              /* index of minimal entry in A[0:n-1] */
```

The pre-condition is 0 < n <= max, and the post-condition is

```
0 <= m < n && A[m] <= A[0:n-1]
```

Notice that, for this problem, we require that n be strictly positive ($n > 0$). If the minimal value occurs more than once in the array, m may be set to any of the corresponding indices.

EXERCISE 3.6 Strengthen the specification to require m to be set to the index of the *first* occurrence of the minimal value, if this value occurs more than once in the array.

Program 3.3 is a straightforward solution to the problem. The stated invariant is derived from the post-condition by substituting the iteration index i for n and imposing appropriate range constraints; essentially, it asserts that A[m] is a minimal entry of the array segment A[0:i-1] examined so far.

Program 3.3

```
{ int i;
  m = 0; i = 1;
  while (i != n)
  INVAR(0 <= m < i <= n && A[m] <= A[0:i-1])
  { if (A[i] < A[m]) m = i;
    i++;
  }
}
```

In outline, the verification is as follows.

1. Initially, the proposed invariant is achieved by setting m to 0; in effect, A[0] is taken to be a minimal entry of the one-component segment A[0:0].

2. The body of the loop increases i but preserves the invariant because m is updated if A[i] is found to be less than A[m], the current minimal value. More formally, the body of the loop satisfies the following specification:

```
ASSERT(0 <= m < i < n && A[m] <= A[0:i-1])
if (A[i] < A[m])
  m = i;
i++;
ASSERT(0 <= m < i <= n && A[m] <= A[0:i-1])
```

The following tableau gives the outline of a formal proof:

```
ASSERT(0 <= m < i < n && A[m] <= A[0:i-1])
if (A[i] < A[m])
{ ASSERT(0 <= m < i < n && A[i] < A[m] <= A[0:i-1])
  ASSERT(0 <= i < i+1 <= n && A[i] <= A[0:i])
  m = i;
  ASSERT(0 <= m < i+1 <= n && A[m] <= A[0:i])
}
else
{ ASSERT(0 <= m < i < n && A[m] <= A[0:i])
  ASSERT(0 <= m < i+1 <= n && A[m] <= A[0:i])
}
ASSERT(0 <= m < i+1 <= n && A[m] <= A[0:i])
i++;
ASSERT(0 <= m < i <= n && A[m] <= A[0:i-1])
```

3. The invariant, together with the negation of the loop condition, implies the desired post-condition; that is,

```
0 <= m < i <= n && A[m] <= A[0:i-1] && i == n
```

implies

```
0 <= m < n && A[m] <= A[0:n-1]
```

Finally, the subscript expressions are easily seen to be in range, and termination of the loop is obvious when n > 0.

Can you do better than Program 3.3? A more efficient solution to (a slightly revised version of) this problem is described in Section 4.3.

EXERCISE 3.7 Verify that Program 3.3 satisfies the stronger specification of Exercise 3.6.

3.3 Powers

In this section, our aim is to compute power$(x,n) = x^n$ when n is a non-negative int value; that is, for any x, power$(x,0) = 1$ and power$(x,n+1) = x * $ power(x,n). Assuming the interface

```
const int x, n;
int y;
```

we want a program fragment to achieve the post-condition y = power(x,n), with pre-condition $n \geq 0$.

A program that solves this problem by *increasing* an iteration index was discussed in Section 2.9. Program 3.4 is a "counting-down" version; variable i records the number of multiplications by x still required. This solution also requires n multiplications and so is no more efficient; however, as we will soon see, this code may be improved easily. The stated invariant is initially true because $i = n \geq 0$ and $y = 1$. The body of the loop preserves the stated invariant because y * power$(x,i) = $ y * x * power$(x,i-1)$ when $i > 0$, so that multiplying y by x and reducing i by one preserves the equivalence of y * power(x,i) to the fixed value of power(x,n). If the loop terminates, $i = 0$, and so y * power$(x,0) = $ y * 1 = y = power(x,n). The loop must terminate because i is a variant.

Program 3.4

```
{ int i;
  i = n; y = 1;
  while (i > 0)
  INVAR(i >= 0 && y * power(x,i) == power(x,n))
  { y = y * x;
    i--;
  }
}
```

EXERCISE 3.8 What will happen if this algorithm is executed with n negative?

Program 3.5

```
{ int i, z;
  i = n; y = 1; z = x;
  while (i > 0)
  INVAR(i >= 0 && y * power(z,i) == power(x,n))
  { while (i%2 == 0)
    INVAR(i > 0 && y * power(z,i) == power(x,n))
    { FACT( i%2 == 0 implies power(z * z, i/2) == power(z,i) )
      z = z * z; i = i/2;
    }
    y = y * z; i--;
  }
}
```

A much more efficient program may be obtained by taking advantage of the following fact about powers; when i is an *even* positive integer,

```
power(x,i) = power(power(x,2), i/2) = power(x * x, i/2)
```

that is, the value of power(x,i) is preserved by squaring x and halving i. This fact is used in Program 3.5 to reduce significantly the number of multiplications needed to compute power(x,n). Because we are not allowed to change x itself, we introduce a new local variable z initialized to the value of x. The only change, apart from the use of z rather than x, is the new inner loop, which repeatedly uses the squaring-and-halving method while i is an even number. For example, if x = 5 and n = 13, the successive values of variables i, z, and y are as follows:

i	z	y
13	5	1
12	5	5
6	$25 = 5 \times 5$	5
3	$625 = 25 \times 25 = 5^4$	5
2	625	$3{,}125 = 5 \times 625 = 5^5$
1	$390{,}625 = 625 \times 625 = 5^8$	3,125
0	390,625	$1{,}220{,}703{,}125 = 3{,}125 \times 390{,}625 = 5^{13}$

EXERCISE 3.9 Verify the partial correctness of Program 3.5, both *without* and *with* the inner loop.

We also need to consider *termination*. The inner loop terminates because i is a variant, for when i is even and *strictly* greater than zero, division by 2 decreases its value. The outer loop of Program 3.5 terminates because i is also a variant for this loop: the loop condition states that i > 0, and i is strictly *decreased* (by being decremented and possibly repeatedly halved) by *each* execution of the loop body. Therefore, the code is correct; it is also more efficient for sufficiently large n than the other power-computing code we have seen, despite the presence of *nested* loops.

EXERCISE 3.10 What is the order-of-magnitude execution time for Program 3.5 if you assume that n is a power of 2?

EXERCISE 3.11 Assume the same interface as we have been using for computing powers (page 67) and show how to compute y = n * x efficiently for n ≥ 0, using addition, and multiplication and division by 2 *only*. Use the following fact: i * x = (i/2) * (2*x) when i is an even positive integer. State suitable invariants for any loops in your solution.

3.4 Division

In this section, we consider the problem of writing code to compute the quotient quot and remainder rem when numerator num is divided by divisor den. This problem may be specified more formally by requiring the post-condition

```
num == quot * den + rem && 0 <= rem < den
```

where the pre-condition is num >= 0 && den > 0 and the interface is

```
const int num, den;   /* numerator and denominator */
int quot, rem;        /* quotient and remainder */
```

For example, if num = 17 and den = 5, the code should assign 3 to quot and 2 to rem. The first post-condition is satisfied because 17 = 3 * 5 + 2, and the second is satisfied because the remainder rem = 2 is less than the denominator den = 5.

The following is a simple approach using repeated subtraction.

```
quot = 0; rem = num;
while (rem >= den)
INVAR( num == quot * den + rem && 0 <= rem && 0 < den )
{ rem = rem - den;
  quot++;
}
```

Note that the invariant is obtained from the post-condition by removing the condition rem < den. Termination is assured because, for each execution of the loop body, rem initially has a value greater than 0, and its value is decreased by the assignment rem = rem - den because den is assumed positive.

EXERCISE 3.12 Verify the code using the suggested invariant.

Program 3.6

```
{ int mult, k;
  mult = den; k = 0;
  while (mult <= num)
  INVAR( k>=0 && mult == power(10,k) * den )
  { mult = mult * 10;
    k++;
  }
  quot = 0; rem = num;
  while (k > 0)
  INVAR
  ( k>=0 && mult == power(10,k) * den &&
    num == quot * mult + rem && 0 <= rem < mult
  )
  { quot = quot * 10;
    mult = mult / 10;
    k--;
    while (rem >= mult)
    INVAR
    ( k>=0 && mult == power(10,k) * den &&
      num == quot * mult + rem && 0 <= rem
    )
    { rem = rem - mult;
      quot++;
    }
  }
}
```

A faster algorithm uses a process analogous to "long division," as in Program 3.6. A preliminary computation calculates the sequence of values den, $10 \times$ den, $100 \times$ den, $10^3 \times$ den, and so on until one of them is greater than the numerator num; this value is saved as the value of mult. To see the correspondence with long division, compare the intermediate results in the following example of dividing 1,713 by 5, with the successive values of variables quot and rem after the initial assignments:

$$
\left. \begin{array}{r} 2 \\ 40 \\ 300 \end{array} \right\} = 342
$$

$$
\begin{array}{r}
5\overline{)1713} \\
\underline{1500} = 5 \times 300 \\
213 \\
\underline{200} = 5 \times 40 \\
13 \\
\underline{10} = 5 \times 2 \\
3
\end{array}
$$

EXERCISE 3.13 Verify the stated invariants and other assertions in Program 3.6, and use them to verify the code.

EXERCISE 3.14 Give variants for each of the loops in Program 3.6.

EXERCISE 3.15 In practice, one would most likely use a *binary* (base 2) rather than *decimal* (base 10) computer. What changes would be needed to make the code use multiplication and division by 2?

3.5 Binary Search in a Sorted Array

> I don't like debuggers. Without a debugger, you tend to think about
> problems another way; you want to understand things on a different *level*.
> It's partly "source versus binary," but it's more than that. You have to look
> at the level *above* sources, at the meaning of things. Without a debugger,
> you basically have to go the next step: understand what the program does.
>
> Linus Torvalds*

An array segment A[0:n-1] is said to be *sorted (in ascending order)* if

```
ForAll (i=0, i<n)(j=0, j<n) i < j implies A[i] <= A[j]
```

for an ordering <= on the type of the components. This definition allows for duplicated entries; that is, "ascending" really means nondescending, rather than *strictly* ascending.

EXERCISE 3.16 Prove that A[0:n-1] is sorted (as just defined) if and only if

```
ForAll (i=1, i<n) A[i-1] <= A[i]
```

EXERCISE 3.17 Develop and verify code to test whether A[0:n-1] is sorted.

If it is feasible to keep the entries of an array segment sorted, a very efficient search algorithm known as *binary search* may be used. Consider again the specification of Section 3.1, but now suppose that the relational operator <= may be used to compare values of type Entry, and that we add to the pre-condition the assumption that A[0:n-1] is sorted. Because A cannot be modified, this additional property of A[0:n-1] may be assumed throughout.

The basic idea is very straightforward: the middle component A[mid] of the array may be compared to the target x and if A[mid] > x or A[mid] < x, approximately one half of the array may be eliminated from contention. This process continues until the outcome of the search is known. Correct implementation of this idea is not as easy as most programmers think, however.[†]

EXERCISE 3.18 Try to write a correct version of binary search (without looking ahead or referring to another textbook).

---

[*]Posted to the Linux-kernel mail list on September 6, 2000.
[†]Experiments have shown that, without access to reference material or computers, 90% of professional programmers are unable to code a correct binary search.

Program 3.7 is a typical *incorrect* solution.

Program 3.7

```
/* an INCORRECT version of binary search */
{ int left, right;
  left = 0; right = n; present = false;
  while (left != right && !present)
  { int mid;
    mid = (left + right)/2;
    ASSERT( left <= mid < right )
    if (x < A[mid])
      right = mid;
    else if (x > A[mid])
      left = mid;
    else ASSERT( x == A[mid] )
      present = true;
  }
}
```

EXERCISE 3.19 Before reading on and without using a computer, try to find the error in Program 3.7.

Did you try to find the problem by hand-executing a few test cases? If you hadn't been told initially that there *is* a problem, might you have decided after one or two successful tests that the code is correct? Even if you did the computations correctly *and* were lucky enough to hit on a problematic case (or used systematic testing), did you then have any idea of how to fix the problem? Is it the initialization, the termination condition, the updates to left and right, or something else that needs to be fixed? Would you, after an attempt to fix the problem, know whether the attempted correction was successful or whether there might still be other problems to be corrected?

A much better approach is to try to *verify* the code. This attempt will presumably fail, but out of that failure will come some high-level understanding of exactly what is going on: why the code *sometimes* works and how to correct it so that it *always* works.

Because an invariant has not been provided with the code, we must devise one. The most important idea behind this approach to binary search is that the indices left and right determine an array segment A[left:right-1] within which any occurrences of x must lie (if there are any in A[0:n-1]); that is,

0 <= left <= right <= n <= max

x > A[0:left-1]

x < A[right:n-1]

These assertions may be presented in a convenient pictorial form as follows:

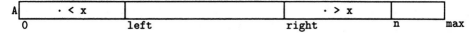

This is termed an *array diagram*. The long box represents array A. The array is partitioned into several segments. The expressions below the box (0, left, right, n, max) are various indices, which are placed to the immediate right (or left) of a segment boundary, never immediately *below* the boundary. The indices are usually for components of the array, and the partitions come *between* components. Note, however, that max does not index an A[max] component but only indicates the assumed physical size of the array.

Segments are allowed to be *empty*; for example, if left = 0, the leftmost segment is empty, and if right = n, the segment A[right:n-1] is empty. But a segment boundary cannot be moved *past* a neighboring boundary; for example, the conditions $0 \leq$ left $\leq$ right $\leq$ n $\leq$ max are implicit in this diagram.

The expression $\cdot$ < x in the leftmost segment simply means that (all) the entries in this segment of the array have the property of being less than x, and similarly for $\cdot$ > x in A[right:n-1]. If left = 0, the first segment in the diagram would be empty, but such a state would satisfy the constraint vacuously because the assertion implicitly has the form ForAll (k=0, k < left) P. Note, however, that, if the constraint were instead A[left-1] < x, it would be meaningless when left = 0 because there would not be an array component A[left-1]. There are no conditions on the entries in the "middle" segment A[left:right-1] or on the entries in A[n:max-1].

If this is in fact an invariant of the loop and the loop terminates because left and right are equal, then it is evident that x does not occur in A[0:n-1]: the central segment A[left:right-1] in which entries equal to x (if any) must occur is then empty. To handle the case that an occurrence of x *is* found, we add (using &&) the following assertion to our tentative invariant:

```
present implies x in A[0:n-1]
```

This part of the invariant can't be shown on the array diagram.

EXERCISE 3.20 Verify that the conjunction of all the assertions in the preceding discussion *is* an invariant of the while loop in Program 3.7. You must use the fact that $0 \leq$ left < right implies that left $\leq$ (left+right)/2 < right (because int division by 2 in C truncates *down* when the operands are nonnegative and the numerator is odd). Then verify that the invariant and the negation of the loop condition imply the desired post-condition. *Hint:* consider separately the cases present = true and present = false. Also, verify that all array subscripts are in range.

So have we in fact verified the correctness of Program 3.7? Not quite. We haven't considered termination! In fact, when `right = left+1` and `x > A[mid]`, the assignment to `left` leaves its value unchanged, and so, in these circumstances, the `while` loop will not terminate.

How can this problem be fixed? During the attempted verification in Exercise 3.20, you should have noticed that, if `x > A[mid]`, the assignment of `mid+1` rather than `mid` to `left` would still maintain the invariant; furthermore, infinite looping would be avoided because the difference `right - left` decreases. We can easily verify that `right - left` also decreases if `x < A[mid]`. Hence the following `int` expression is a variant for the loop:

```
present ? 0 : (right - left)
```

This is a "conditional expression" in C, equivalent to

$$\begin{cases} 0, & \text{if present} \\ \text{right - left,} & \text{if !present} \end{cases}$$

Nothing else in the code or the verification needs to be changed.

There are other approaches to binary search. Program 3.7 may require up to *two* array comparisons per iteration. A good compiler should be able to combine these into a single hardware comparison, but let us try to implement a binary search that uses only *one* array comparison per iteration: `x ≤ A[mid]`. This undertaking leads to the following assertion as a potential invariant:

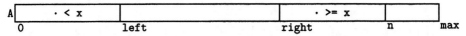

To achieve it initially (before testing array values), the segments to the left of `left` and to the right of `right` must be empty so the initializing assignments are

```
left = 0; right = n;
```

The loop is to terminate when the central segment becomes empty (i.e., when `left = right`). The central segment is made smaller and the invariant is preserved if, after selecting any value `mid` in the index range `left:right-1`, the following choice is made:

```
if (x <= A[mid])
   right = mid;
else
   left = mid+1;
```

On average, the best performance is obtained by doing

```
mid = (left + right)/2;
```

that is, by selecting the middle component of the central segment. After the loop, the invariant and the negation of the loop condition tell us that x is present if and only if right < n and A[right] = x. This analysis gives us Program 3.8, which is very similar to (the corrected form of) Program 3.7, except that variable present is not assigned until after the loop.

Program 3.8

```
{ int left, right;
  left = 0; right = n;
  while (left != right)
  { int mid;
    mid = (left + right)/2;
    ASSERT( left <= mid < right )
    if (x <= A[mid])
      right = mid;
    else
      left = mid+1;
  }
  present = right < n && A[right] == x;
}
```

EXERCISE 3.21 Describe an example that would give incorrect results if the assignment after the loop in Program 3.8 were replaced by present = (A[right] == x).

EXERCISE 3.22 Verify that the loop in Program 3.8 will always terminate properly.

When programmers see this code, many think that it is *less* efficient than Program 3.7 because the test for equivalence to x doesn't occur until after the loop has terminated. But unless such a test is essentially "free" (because it may be combined with the other array comparison in the loop), it is in fact better placed *outside* the loop. A test inside the loop to determine whether A[mid] = x saves further testing only if it succeeds. However, success is a rather unlikely outcome until the segment A[left:right-1] becomes very short and there will be few array comparisons left to do by then!

EXERCISE 3.23 Develop and verify a version of binary search from the following invariant:

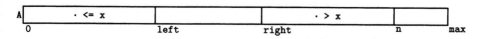

EXERCISE 3.24 Is the following implementation of binary search correct?

```
{ int left, right;
  left = 0; right = n;
  while (left < right-1)
  INVAR( 0 <= left < right <= n &&
         x in A[0:n-1] implies x in A[left:right-1] )
  { int mid;
    mid = (left + right)/2;
    if (x <= A[mid]) right = mid;
    else left = mid;
  }
  present = (A[left] == x);
}
```

EXERCISE 3.25 The library function bsearch in C implements a binary search assuming a comparison function that returns, respectively, a negative int value, zero, or a positive int value according to whether its first argument is less than, equal to, or greater than its second argument. Implement and verify a binary search that uses this kind of comparison function instead of < or ==.

EXERCISE 3.26 Specify, code, and verify a program fragment that, given any array segment A[m:n] with A[m]<=0 and A[n]>0, finds an index i such that A[i]<=0 and A[i+1]>0. Do *not* assume that the array is sorted. Each iteration should roughly halve the size of the segment being searched.

3.6   The Number of Distinct Values in an Array

The problem we address in this section (cf. Exercise 1 in the Introduction) is to determine the number of distinct values in an array segment. An appropriate interface specification would be

```
const int max;        /* maximum number of entries */
typename Entry;       /* type of entries, use == for equality */
const int n;          /* number of entries */
const Entry A[max];   /* A[0:n-1] are the entries in use */
int nDist;            /* number of distinct entries in A[0:n-1] */
```

with a pre-condition of 0 <= n <= max. The post-condition would require that nDist = |A[0:n-1]|, where |A[0:n-1]| is an abbreviation for the cardinality of (number of elements in) the set {A[k] | $0 \leq k < n$} (i.e., the number of distinct values in the array segment A[0:n-1]). The const qualifications in the interface specify that max, n, and A are not to be modified.

For this problem, we may use the familiar technique of changing the occurrence of n in the post-condition nDist = |A[0:n-1]| to an iteration index i, and adopt 0 <= i <= n && nDist == |A[0:i-1]| as a loop invariant; this leads to the following program outline:

```
{ int i;
  nDist = 0; i = 0;
  while (i != n)
  INVAR( 0 <= i <= n && nDist == |A[0:i-1]| )
  { if ("A[i] does not occur in A[0:i-1]")
      nDist++;
    i++;
  }
}
```

Implementing the "A[i] does not occur in A[0:i-1]" test obviously requires a search. Here, entry A[i] is the search target and may be used as a sentinel (as in Program 2.6), leading to Program 3.9.

Program 3.9

```
{ int i;
  nDist = 0; i = 0;
  while (i != n)
  INVAR( 0 <= i <= n && nDist == |A[0:i-1]| )
  { int j;
    j = 0;
    while (A[j] != A[i]) /* A[i] is a sentinel */
    INVAR( 0 <= j <= i && A[i] != A[0:j-1] )
      j++;
    if (j == i)
      ASSERT( A[i] != A[0:i-1] )
      nDist++;
    i++;
  }
}
```

EXERCISE 3.27 Use an array diagram to express the invariant for the inner loop.

EXERCISE 3.28 Explain why this code works correctly when n = 0 or n = 1.

EXERCISE 3.29 Verify that i - j is suitable as a variant expression for the inner loop.

EXERCISE 3.30 Develop a solution to this problem using the following as a loop invariant: 0 <= i <= n && nDupl == i - |A[0:i-1]|. The quantity i - |A[0:i-1]| is the number of duplicates (repeated values) in the array segment A[0:i-1]. For example, if the array segment consists of the values 45, 13, -15, 13, 13, and 45, the number of duplicates is 3 (two 13s and one 45). The code should work correctly when n = 0 or n = 1.

EXERCISE 3.31 Specify and code a program fragment that tests whether all the entries of an array segment are distinct.

A more efficient solution to this problem is possible if there is an ordering <= for values of type Entry. Suppose that array segment A[0:n-1] has previously been sorted; then, if there exist one or more values that duplicate A[i], one such duplicate must occur at A[i-1]. Consequently, a full search isn't necessary.

EXERCISE 3.32 Try to write code that solves this problem, using the following invariant:

```
0 <= i <= n && nDist == |A[0:i-1]|
```

Does your solution for the preceding exercise treat the cases n = 0 and n = 1 correctly? Consider the following code:

```
ASSERT(A[0:n-1] sorted)
{ int i;
  nDist = 0; i = 0;
  while (i != n)
  INVAR( 0 <= i <= n && nDist == |A[0:i-1]| )
  { if (i==0 || A[i] != A[i-1])
      nDist++;
    i++;
  }
}
```

Unfortunately, the if condition is rather awkward and inefficient; the i==0 test and the "short-circuit" evaluation of || prevent an illegal access to A[-1] the first time through the loop body.

One alternative is to partially "unroll" the loop, so that the cases when n ≤ 1 are treated separately, as in Program 3.10. We will discuss another approach (based on the suggestion in Exercise 3.30) in Section 4.5.

Program 3.10

```
ASSERT(A[0:n-1] sorted)
if (n <= 1) nDist = n;
else
{ ASSERT(n>1)
  int i;
  nDist = 1; i = 1;
  while (i != n)
  INVAR( 1 <= i <= n && nDist == |A[0:i-1]| )
  { if (A[i] != A[i-1])
      nDist++;
    i++;
  }
}
```

Of course, it will usually be necessary to *sort* A[0:n-1] (or a copy) to establish the additional pre-condition. But if an O(n log n) sorting algorithm such

as quicksort (Section 4.4.3) or heapsort is used, this approach will be, for sufficiently large values of n, much more efficient on average than the $O(n^2)$ search-
based algorithm we initially described.

EXERCISE 3.33 Do experiments to determine approximately how large n must be for this
approach to be more efficient on average.

3.7 Additional Reading

Most of the algorithms discussed are standard examples that may be found in
such textbooks as [Wir73, AA78, Rey81, Bac86, Gor88, Dro89, Dah92, BE$^+$94,
Cas94, Sta99].

REFERENCES

[AA78]   S. Alagić and M. A. Arbib. *The Design of Well-Structured and Correct Programs.*
          Springer-Verlag, 1978.

[Bac86]   R. C. Backhouse. *Program Construction and Verification.* Prentice Hall
          International, 1986.

[BE$^+$94] K. Broda, S. Eisenbach, H. Khoshnevisan, and S. Vickers. *Reasoned
          Programming.* Prentice Hall International, 1994.

[Cas94]   C. Casey. *A Programming Approach to Formal Methods.* McGraw-Hill
          International, 1994.

[Dah92]   O.-J. Dahl. *Verifiable Programming.* Prentice Hall International, 1992.

[Dro89]   G. Dromey. *Program Derivation: The Development of Programs from
          Specifications.* Addison-Wesley, 1989.

[Gor88]   M. J. C. Gordon. *Programming Language Theory and Its Implementation.*
          Prentice Hall International, 1988.

[Rey81]   J. C. Reynolds. *The Craft of Programming.* Prentice Hall International, 1981.

[Sta99]   A. M. Stavely. *Toward Zero-Defect Programming.* Addison-Wesley Longman,
          1999.

[Wir73]   N. Wirth. *Systematic Programming, An Introduction.* Prentice Hall, 1973.

Chapter 4

Additional Verification Techniques

In this chapter, we discuss a number of additional techniques for verifying correctness statements: how to reason about `for` and `do...while` loops, how to deal with assignments to array components, and how to combine two or more correctness statements for the same code. We also discuss an important class of examples: array sorting algorithms.

4.1 For *Loops*

So far, our verification examples have used only `while` loops. In this section, we consider verification rules for `for` loops of the form

$$\text{for } (A_0; B; A_1) C$$

where A_0 and A_1 are assignments (i.e., assignment statements without the terminating semicolon), B is a `bool` condition, and C is a statement. This is defined to be equivalent to

$$A_0; \text{ while } (B)\{C\ A_1;\}$$

The following proof-tableau scheme shows how code of this form would be verified:

```
ASSERT(P)
A₀;
ASSERT(I)
while (B)
{ ASSERT(I && B)
    C
    A₁;
    ASSERT(I)
}
ASSERT(I && !B)
ASSERT(Q)
```

where I is the loop invariant, P is the pre-condition, and Q is the post-condition. This tableau makes it clear that the program verifier has the following obligations when reasoning about a for loop.

1. The pre-condition P must be sufficient to ensure that invariant assertion I holds immediately after executing the initialization A_0:

   ```
   ASSERT(P)
   A_0
   ASSERT(I)
   ```

2. The assertion I must be an invariant of the sequence C A_1; , where it may also be assumed that the loop condition B holds initially:

   ```
   ASSERT(I && B)
   C
   A_1;
   ASSERT(I)
   ```

3. The invariant assertion I and the negation of the loop condition B must together imply the desired post-condition Q:

   ```
   ASSERT(I && !B)
   ASSERT(Q)
   ```

For example, consider Program 2.1, one of the array-searching algorithms discussed in Section 2.1:

```
ASSERT(0 <= n <= max)
{ int i;
  present = false;
  for (i=0; i<n; i++)
    if (A[i] == x) present = true;
}
ASSERT( present iff x in A[0:n-1] )
```

We may verify this using the following as an invariant assertion:

```
0 <= i <= n && (present iff x in A[0:i-1])
```

The assertion is "initially" true because i is set to 0 by the initialization assignment, present has been assigned false, and the pre-condition states that $n \geq 0$. The assertion is preserved by the loop body (followed by the "update" assignment) because of the validity of

```
ASSERT( 0 <= i <= n && (present iff x in A[0:i-1]) && i < n )
if (A[i] == x) present = true;
i++;
ASSERT( 0 <= i <= n && (present iff x in A[0:i-1]) )
```

Finally, the invariant and the negation of the loop condition (i.e., i >= n) imply the desired post-condition present iff x in A[0:n-1]. Termination and validity of the array subscript are easily verified.

EXERCISE 4.1 Establish the (partial) correctness of Program 2.3 using the following assertion as the loop invariant: `0 <= i <= n && x != A[0:i-1]` .

EXERCISE 4.2 Re-formulate Programs 3.2, 3.9 and 3.10 to use `for` loops wherever possible and verify their correctness using suitable invariants.

EXERCISE 4.3 State an inference rule that formalizes the reasoning pattern implicit in the preceding tableau scheme. The rule should have a separate premise for each of A_0, A_1, and C.

4.2 Array-Component Assignment Statements

The axiom scheme for assignment statements discussed in Section 2.3 is not directly applicable to assignments of the form $A[I] = E$; . The effect of an array-component assignment is easily understood. If we assume that $0 \leq I < n$, where n is the length of the array, then the effect on the array A is as follows, where the "after" state of A is drawn beneath the "before" state:

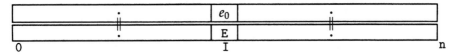

All the components of A are left unchanged *except* for the component indexed by I, which is set to E, overwriting the value e_0 that was there previously.

But how are we to formalize reasoning about array-component assignments? The following example illustrates that this will not be as straightforward as one might expect. Suppose A is an `int` array and consider the following correctness statement, which claims that the code swaps the contents of A[i] and A[j]:

```
ASSERT(A[i]==x0 && A[j]==y0)
A[i] = A[i] - A[j];
A[j] = A[i] + A[j];
A[i] = A[j] - A[i];
ASSERT(A[i]==y0 && A[j]==x0)
```

It might be thought that this is completely analogous to the following, from Exercise 2.26:

```
ASSERT(x==x0 && y==y0)
x = x - y;
y = x + y;
x = y - x;
ASSERT(x==y0 && y==x0)
```

But the latter is *valid* and the former is *not*!

EXERCISE 4.4 What effect will the first code have if $i = j$?

To formalize correctness arguments for array-component assignments, we adopt the following idea: an assignment of E to $A[I]$ is equivalent in effect to an assignment to A of an entire array of values that is like A except that the component indexed by I is E. Unfortunately, C does not provide notation to express the concept of "an array that is like A except that the component indexed by I is E." So, we simply introduce a suitable notation for use in our assertions.

For any array A, appropriate index expression I, and component expression E, let $(A \mid I \mapsto E)$ denote the array such that

- $(A \mid I \mapsto E)[I'] = E$ when $I' = I$, and
- $(A \mid I \mapsto E)[I'] = A[I']$ when $I' \neq I$.

For example, suppose that A is the following array:

3	5	2	1	3	4	7	8
0	1	2	3	4	5	6	7

Then we may regard the array-component assignment

    A[3] = 6;

as being an abbreviation for a pseudo-assignment

    A = (A | 3 +-> 6);

where +-> is an ASCII representation of $\mapsto$, so that A becomes the array such that the value of the component indexed by 3 is 6, and all the other components are exactly the same as before:

3	5	2	6	3	4	7	8
0	1	2	3	4	5	6	7

The notation $(A \mid I \mapsto E)$ should not be confused with the substitution notation $[Q](V \mapsto E)$ which is *about* assertions, rather than notation that is used *in* assertions.

We may now state the following axiom scheme, which is essentially a special case of Hoare's assignment axiom (Section 2.3).

Array-Component Assignment:

$$[Q](A \mapsto A')\,\{A[I] = E;\}\,Q$$

where $[Q](A \mapsto A')$ is, as before, the result of substituting A' for A in Q, and A' is $(A \mid I \mapsto E)$. Like Hoare's axiom, this axiom allows a sufficient pre-condition to be mechanically generated from an arbitrary post-condition.

Of course, it is essential to verify separately that the value of the subscript expression I is within the range of subscripts allowed for array A. Adding a suitable constraint to the pre-condition would certainly be conceivable, but doing this would only address assignments *to* array components, and not accesses *from* array components in expressions. We prefer to deal with subscript checks separately and less formally.

Here is an example of this axiom in action:

```
ASSERT( (A | i +-> 2)[j] == (A | i +-> 2)[i] )
A[i] = 2;
ASSERT(A[j] == A[i])
```

The assignment is regarded as an abbreviation for A = (A | i +-> 2). The pre-condition is therefore derived from the post-condition by substituting (A | i +-> 2) for each of the two occurrences of A in the post-condition. The resulting pre-condition looks intimidating, but it may easily be simplified.

- The right-hand side of the equation, (A | i +-> 2)[i], simplifies immediately to 2.

- The left-hand side, (A | i +-> 2)[j], also simplifies to 2 when $i = j$.

- When $i \neq j$, the left-hand side simplifies to A[j].

The pre-condition may therefore be equivalently expressed as follows:

```
i != j implies A[j] == 2
```

Note that the pre-condition does not constrain the value of A[j] if $i = j$.

EXERCISE 4.5 Using the indicated invariant assertion, verify the following correctness statement. The code implements a search for x in A[0:n-1] using A[n] as a sentinel (compare with Program 2.6).

```
ASSERT(0 <= n <= max)
{ int i;
  A[n] = x; i = 0;
  while (A[i] != x)
  INVAR( 0 <= i <= n && x != A[0:i-1] && A[n] == x )
    i++;
  present = (i<n);
}
ASSERT(present iff x in A[0:n-1])
```

You will need to use the array-component assignment axiom to treat the assignment to A[n]. You may assume that an array component A[max] exists.

As a second example, the following tableau validates the usual method of swapping the values of two components of int array A using a temporary variable:

```
ASSERT(A[j] == y && A[i] == x)
ASSERT(((A | i +-> A[j]) | j +-> A[i])[i] == y && A[i] == x)
{ int z;
  z = A[i];
  ASSERT(((A | i +-> A[j]) | j +-> z)[i] == y && z == x)
  A[i] = A[j];
  ASSERT((A | j +-> z)[i] == y && z == x)
  ASSERT((A | j +-> z)[i] == y && (A | j +-> z)[j] == x)
  A[j] = z;
}
ASSERT(A[i] == y && A[j] == x)
```

To verify that $A[j] = y$ implies

$$((A \mid i \mathrel{+\!\!-\!\!>} A[j]) \mid j \mathrel{+\!\!-\!\!>} A[i])[i] = y$$

we consider separately the cases $i = j$ and $i \neq j$. If $i = j$, the second assertion simplifies to $A[i] = y$ and so $A[j] = y$; on the other hand, if $i \neq j$, the assertion simplifies directly to $A[j] = y$. So, in both cases, the assertion is logically equivalent to $A[j] = y$.

Finally, consider Program 4.1, which is intended to "left-shift" array segment $A[m:n-1]$ one position. The invariant essentially says that the concatena-

---

Program 4.1

```
ASSERT(0 < m <= n <= max && A == A0)
{ int i;
  i = m;
  while (i != n)
  INVAR
  ( m <= i <= n &&
    (ForAll (k=m; k<i) A[k-1] == A0[k]) &&
    (ForAll (k=i; k<n) A[k]   == A0[k])
  )
  { A[i-1] = A[i];
    i++;
  }
}
ASSERT(ForAll (k=m; k<n) A[k-1] == A0[k])
```

---

tion of the array segments $A[m-1:i-2]$ and $A[i:n-1]$ matches $A0[m:n-1]$. The component $A[i-1]$ may be considered to be a "hole" between the segments; as the iteration proceeds, the hole moves from component $m-1$ up to $n-1$ as more and more of the array is shifted left:

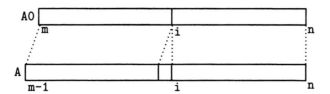

The array-component assignment axiom gives the following correctness statement for the array-component assignment in the loop body:

```
ASSERT
( m <= i < n &&
    (ForAll (k=m; k<i+1) (A | i-1 +-> A[i])[k-1] == AO[k]) &&
    (ForAll (k=i+1; k<n) (A | i-1 +-> A[i])[k] == AO[k])
)
A[i-1] = A[i];
ASSERT
( m <= i < n &&
    (ForAll (k=m; k<i+1) A[k-1] == AO[k]) &&
    (ForAll (k=i+1; k<n) A[k] == AO[k])
)
```

The second `ForAll` conjunct in the pre-condition immediately simplifies to

```
ForAll (k=i+1; k<n) A[k] = AO[k]
```

because $k > i-1$. For the first `ForAll`, we use case analysis.

- When $k = i$, the assertion is that `A[i]` = `AO[k]`, which may be combined with the preceding simplified assertion to get

  ```
  ForAll (k=i; k<n) A[k] = AO[k]
  ```

- For $m \le k < i$, the assertion simplifies to

  ```
  ForAll (k=m; k<i) A[k-1] = AO[k]
  ```

The invariant assertion implies the simplified assertions in both cases. The rest of the verification is routine.

EXERCISE 4.6 Specify, implement, and verify code to "right-shift" array segment `A[m:n-1]` one position.

EXERCISE 4.7 Is the following correctness statement valid? If so, give a proof; if not, state a (simplified) pre-condition that is just strong enough to make the correctness statement valid.

```
ASSERT(true)
A[A[0]] = 1;
ASSERT( A[A[0]] == 1 )
```

We have seen that it is important to simplify assertions involving the $(\cdot \mid \cdot \mapsto \cdot)$ notation as much as possible, to keep the complexity manageable. The following proposition is an example of a mathematical fact about arrays involving this notation.

PROPOSITION 4.1 $(A \mid I \mapsto A[I]) = A$.

Proof. Consider any suitable index expression I';

- if $I' = I$: $(A \mid I \mapsto A[I])[I'] = A[I] = A[I']$
- if $I' \neq I$: $(A \mid I \mapsto A[I])[I'] = A[I']$

In either case, $(A \mid I \mapsto A[I])[I'] = A[I']$. Because this has been shown for *any* (in-range) index I', the array of values described by $(A \mid I \mapsto A[I])$ is the same as A. $\square$

EXERCISE 4.8 Verify the following properties for any appropriate A, I, I', E, and E':

(i) $((A \mid I \mapsto E) \mid I' \mapsto E') = ((A \mid I' \mapsto E') \mid I \mapsto E)$, provided $I \neq I'$

(ii) $((A \mid I \mapsto E) \mid I \mapsto E') = (A \mid I \mapsto E')$

4.3 Do-While *Loops*

In this section, we consider the do . . . while form of loop in C. Provided that code C has no labels or break, continue, or return statements, the loop

```
do C while (B);
```

is equivalent to the compound statement

```
{ C
  while (B) C
}
```

The loop body C is always executed once *before* evaluating the loop condition B for the first time. Because of this equivalence, it should be evident that the do . . . while construct is primarily useful when the loop body C is sufficiently large that it is undesirable to write it more than once.

An invariant assertion I for the while loop in the equivalent construct would mean the following:

```
C
ASSERT(I)
while (B)
  ASSERT(I && B)
  C
  ASSERT(I)
ASSERT(I && !B)
```

So this is what we take as the meaning of an invariant associated with a do...while loop. Notice that the invariant assertion is not necessarily true (or even well-defined) immediately *before* execution of the do...while loop, but it is required to be true *after* every execution of the loop body. Consequently, it is often convenient to place an INVAR comment immediately *before* the while (...) phrase, as in

```
do
  C
INVAR(I)
while (B);
```

Here is the formal inference rule derived from this analysis:

Do-While:

$$\frac{P\{C\}I \qquad I \text{ \&\& } B\{C\}I}{P\{\text{do } C \text{ while } (B);\} I \text{ \&\& } !B}$$

Notice that there are *two* premises involving C; one of them treats the *first* execution of C, and the other treats any further executions.

As an example, consider again the problem of determining the index m of a minimal component of an array segment, as discussed in Section 3.2. Program 3.3 might seem to be an efficient program, but notice that there are *two* tests per iteration: one is the array comparison A[i] < A[m], and the second is the i != n test controlling the loop. This property raises the possibility that the sentinel technique might be applicable to this problem. If it is allowable to use A[n] as a sentinel (even if n = max), Program 4.2 is correct and usually more efficient than Program 3.3; i is compared to n only when a new minimal element (or the sentinel) is encountered.

Program 4.2

```
ASSERT( 0 < n <= max )
{ int i;
  i = 0;
  do {
    m = i;
    A[n] = A[m]; /* sentinel */
    do i++; while (A[i] > A[m]);
  }
  while i != n;
}
ASSERT( 0 <= m < n && A[m] <= A[0:n-1] )
```

The outer do...while loop may be verified using the conjunction of the following assertions as an invariant:

- 0 <= m < i <= n <= max

- $A[m]$ <= $A[0:i-1]$ ($A[m]$ is the current minimal component)

- $A[i]$ <= $A[m]$ ($A[i]$ might be a smaller component)

- $A[n]$ == $A[m]$ ($A[n]$ is a sentinel to stop the inner loop)

Notice that variable m is initialized only when the body of the (outer) loop is executed for the first time, and so this assertion might not be well-defined if it were to be evaluated before the first execution of the loop body.

The inner loop in the code is also (perhaps unnecessarily in this case) a do ... while loop; the invariant for this loop is simply the invariant for the outer loop *without* the condition $A[i] \le A[m]$.

EXERCISE 4.9 Verify the code using the suggested invariants and the do-while rule.

EXERCISE 4.10 Will Program 4.2 satisfy the stronger requirements of Exercise 3.6?

EXERCISE 4.11 The following C loop, which copies the standard input stream stdin to the standard output stdout, illustrates a pattern sometimes called the "n-and-a-half" loop.

```
for (;;)
{ c = getc(stdin);
  if (c == EOF) break;
  putc(c, stdout);
}
```

Note the use of break to terminate the loop. Give a proof-tableau scheme or inference rule for reasoning about any loop of the form

```
for (;;)
{ C₀
INVAR(I)
  if (B) break;
  C₁
}
```

by treating it as being equivalent to

```
C₀
while (!B)
INVAR(I)
{ C₁
  C₀
}
```

4.4   Sorting an Array

We will assume the following declarative interface for the problem of sorting (re-arranging into ascending order) an array segment.

```
const int max;      /* maximum number of entries */
typename Entry;     /* type of entries;
                       use == and < for equality and ordering */
const int n;        /* number of entries */
Entry A[max];       /* A[0:n-1] are the entries to sort */
```

The pre-condition assumed for sorting is $0 \leq n < max$. The desired post-condition is, first, that A[0:n-1] be in ascending order; that is,

```
ForAll (i=0, i<n)(j=0, j<n) i <= j implies A[i] <= A[j]
```

second, that A[0:n-1] be a permutation (re-arrangement) of the initial value; and, third, that A be otherwise unchanged. We will be focusing on the first requirement. The other requirements are normally treated informally; for example, they are always achieved if the only changes to the array are "swaps" within the appropriate range.

There are many array-sorting methods. The following sections discuss some of the more important of these.

4.4.1   SELECTION SORT

One of the simplest array-sorting algorithms is called *selection sort*, or sorting by successive minima. Here is the relevant invariant:

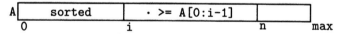

Segment A[0:i-1] is sorted, and every entry of segment A[i:n-1] is greater than or equal to every entry of the sorted segment. This property is sometimes described by saying that the entries of A[0:i-1] are in their *final positions*. The basic algorithm is then

```
ASSERT( 0 <= n <= max )
{ int i;
  for (i=0; i<n; i++)
  INVAR(I)
  { int m;
    "determine m so that A[m] <= A[i:n-1]";
    ASSERT( I && i <= m < n && A[m] <= A[i:n-1] )
    swap(A, i, m);
  }
}
ASSERT( A[0:n-1] sorted )
```

where *I* is the following invariant assertion:

```
0 <= i < n && A[0:i-1] sorted && ForAll (k=i, k<n) A[k] >= A[0:i-1]
```

and `swap(A,i,j)` exchanges the values of `A[i]` and `A[j]`. Putting a minimal entry of `A[i:n-1]` in `A[i]` ensures that the invariant holds again after `i` is increased by one.

EXERCISE 4.12 Code the "`determine m ...`" step and complete the verification of the algorithm using the indicated assertions.

EXERCISE 4.13 Verify that the termination condition for the `for` loop may be changed to `i < n-1`.

EXERCISE 4.14 The algorithm known as *bubble sort* is, in its simplest form, similar to selection sort except that the body of the (outer) loop is replaced by the following:

```
{ int m;
  for (m = n-1; m>i; m--)
  INVAR( i <= m < n && A[m] <= A[m:n-1] )
    if ( A[m-1] > A[m] )
      swap(A, m-1, m);
}
```

Verify the correctness of this inner loop using the specified invariant and the correctness of the outer loop using the invariant for the outer loop of selection sort.

EXERCISE 4.15 The inner loop of the bubble sort of Exercise 4.14 may be modified as follows to determine the index `ls` of the entry *last* switched (or, if there are no swaps, to set `ls` to `n-1`):

```
{ int m;
  ls = n-1;
  for (m = n-1; m>i; m--)
  INVAR
  ( i <= m <= ls < n &&
    A[m:ls-1] sorted &&
    ForAll (k=m; k<ls) A[k] <= A[ls:n-1]
  )
    if ( A[m-1] > A[m] )
    { swap(A, m-1, m); ls = m;}
}
```

Verify this code using the invariant and show how to redesign the *outer* loop of bubble sort to take advantage of `ls`.

4.4.2   INSERTION SORT

The basic idea of insertion sort is successively to insert a new entry into a sorted segment of the array, preserving the ordering:

```
{ int i;
  for (i=0; i<n; i++)
  { Entry x;
    int j;
    x = A[i];
    "search for an insertion position j, shift A[j:i-1] right";
    A[j] = x;
  }
}
```

The invariant for the outer loop is

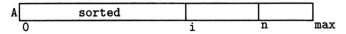

EXERCISE 4.16 Would it be correct to initialize i to 1 rather than 0?

We now consider the code necessary to find an insertion position j and to shift larger values right to make room for x; the assumed pre-condition is $0 <= i < n$ && $A[0:i-1]$ sorted. The "search" is to determine a position j at which the sorted array segment $A[0:i-1]$ is such that

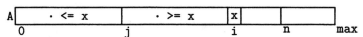

Here are three ways this could be implemented:

- a linear search for the rightmost entry that is $\leq$ x, starting at the right-hand end of the array segment $A[0:i-1]$;

- a linear search for the leftmost entry that is $\geq$ x, starting at the left-hand end of the array and using $A[i] = x$ as a sentinel;

- a binary search for the leftmost entry that is $>$ x in the sorted array segment $A[0:i-1]$.

EXERCISE 4.17 Implement and verify each of these search methods using an appropriate invariant. For example, an invariant suitable for the suggested *binary* search would be

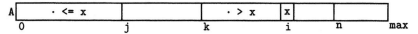

EXERCISE 4.18 Before reading on, evaluate the advantages and disadvantages of these possibilities.

It turns out that binary search is *not* the approach usually used in insertion sort. One reason is that insertion sort is most often used to complete the sorting of partially sorted arrays; in these circumstances, the insertion position is on average very close to position i. Another reason is that if a linear search is started at the right-hand end of the array segment (index i), it is possible to combine the search and the necessary shifting of entries into a single loop, as in the following code:

```
j=i;
while (j>0 && A[j-1] > x)
{ A[j] = A[j-1];
  j--;
}
```

EXERCISE 4.19 State a suitable invariant for this loop and verify its correctness.

EXERCISE 4.20 In the circumstances described, running off the left-hand end of the array would be a very rare occurrence and so the repeated j>0 tests almost always succeed. The sentinel technique may be used to simplify the loop condition. The first iteration of selection sort may be used to put a minimal entry of the entire array segment A[0:n-1] into A[0]; then this value will act as a sentinel for insertion of the remaining entries. Implement these ideas and verify the code.

EXERCISE 4.21 Yet another way to implement a search for the insertion position is called *exponential search*. Initialize a new variable k to 1 and j to i-1; then, while j ≥ 0 and A[j] > x, do

```
k = 2 * k;
j = j - k;
```

Then do a binary search in the segment A[j:j+k]. Implement and verify this approach.

4.4.3 QUICKSORT

Quicksort (also known as *partition sort*) is one of the most important array-sorting methods. The basic algorithm uses recursion, and so we express it using the following recursive function:

```
void Sort(Entry A[], int m, int n)
/* Sorts A[m:n-1] */
{ if (m < n-1)
    { int i, j;
      "partition A[m:n-1]";
      Sort(A, m, i);
      Sort(A, j, n);
    }
}
```

Note that the lower subscript bound for the array segment to be sorted is the value of parameter m, rather than 0. The crucial partitioning step is expected to re-arrange A[m:n-1] and determine i and j so that

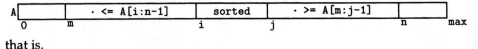

that is,

- segment A[m:i-1] consists of "small" values (less than or equal to any of the values to the right);

- segment A[j:n-1] consists of "large" values (greater than or equal to any of the values to the left);

- the entries of segment A[i:j-1] are in their final positions (i.e., in order, larger than or equal to entries to the left, and smaller than or equal to entries to the right).

There is no predefined concept of what "large" or "small" values are. Ideally, the recursive calls act on subsegments of close to equal length, but any of the three subsegments may be empty after the partitioning step. However, to prevent infinite recursion, we add the following to the post-condition: i<n and j>m.

We will not discuss verification of recursive functions formally, and so we simply assume that the two recursive calls to Sort correctly complete the sort of A[m:n-1] if the partitioning step achieves this post-condition.

Many partitioning approaches have been suggested. Program 4.3 is one of the simplest. Entry A[n-1] is used as the partitioning value x: entries are deemed "small" if they are <x and "large" if they are ≥x. Here is assertion *I*, the invariant for the loop:

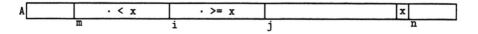

Program 4.3

```
{ Entry x;
  x = A[n-1]; i = m;
  for (j = m; j < n-1; j++)
  INVAR(I)
    if (A[j] < x)
    { swap(A, i, j); i++; }
  A[n-1] = A[i]; A[i] = x;
  j = i+1;
}
```

EXERCISE 4.22 What would be appropriate intermediate assertions immediately after the loop and immediately before and immediately after the swap operation in Program 4.3?

EXERCISE 4.23 Verify that all the desired post-conditions (including i<n and j>m) are achieved by Program 4.3, that the loops terminate, and that all array subscripts are in the range m:n-1.

An approach to partitioning proposed by C. A. R. Hoare, the inventor of quicksort, is to choose any entry in A[m:n-1] (such as A[(m+n)/2], or a randomly selected entry) as the partitioning value, and then to proceed as follows: search rightward starting from position m for a large value, and search leftward from position n-1 for a small value. If the two searches "collide," the partitioning is finished; otherwise, the large and small values are exchanged, and this process continues until the array is partitioned. The basic invariant assertion is then:

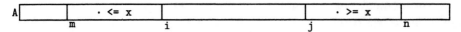

At the end of the partitioning process, the state of the array may be

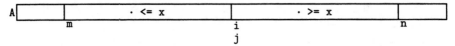

or, if the two searches stop on the same entry (which must be equal to x),

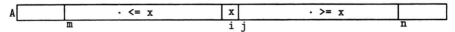

In either case, the pre-condition for the remainder of the sorting algorithm is satisfied, so long as i<n and j>m. To verify these additional properties (and to allow very efficient inner loops), we add the following conditions to the basic invariant assertion:

```
((Exists(k=i, k<n) A[k] >= x) && (Exists(k=m, m<j) A[k] <= x))
```

The entries whose existence is asserted ensure, on termination of the partitioning process, that i<n and j>m. They are initially true (when i = m and j = n) because x is chosen to be one of the entries in A[m:n-1]. The reason these additional invariant conditions allow efficient inner loops is that the large and small entries whose existence is asserted act as *sentinels* for the rightward and leftward searches, respectively. The resulting partitioning code is given as Program 4.4; P is the assertion discussed earlier (i.e., the conjunction of the array diagram and the sentinel-existence assertions).

EXERCISE 4.24 Verify that all parts of the stated invariant (including the existence of sentinels) are preserved by the body of the outer loop.

EXERCISE 4.25 What is a suitable variant expression for the outer loop of Program 4.4?

EXERCISE 4.26 Why can't the inner loops of Program 4.4 be written as follows?
```
while (A[i] <= x) i++;
while (A[j-1] >= x) j--;
```

Program 4.4

```
{ Entry x;
  x = any entry in A[m:n-1];
  i = m; j = n;
  while (A[i] < x) INVAR(P) i++;
  while (A[j-1] > x) INVAR(P && A[i] >= x) j--;
  while (i<j-1)
  INVAR(P && A[i] >= x && A[j-1] <= x)
  { swap(A, i, j-1);
    i++; j--;
    while (A[i] < x) INVAR(P) i++;
    while (A[j-1] > x) INVAR(P && A[i] >= x) j--;
  }
}
ASSERT(P &&  x == A[i:j-1])
```

EXERCISE 4.27 Why is A[(m+n)/2] often chosen to be the value of x in the partitioning code?

EXERCISE 4.28 Express the partitioning algorithm in Program 4.4 more compactly using the loop structure analyzed in Exercise 4.11.

EXERCISE 4.29 The following partitioning code is slightly better than Program 4.4 because it ensures that, after partitioning, the "middle" segment A[i:j-1] cannot be empty; consequently, the recursive calls have less to do.

```
{ Entry x;
  x = A[n-1];
  i = m; j = n-1;
  for (;;)
  { while (A[i] < x) INVAR(P) i++;
    while (j>m && A[j-1] > x) INVAR(P && A[i] >= x) j--;
  INVAR(P && A[i] >= x && A[j-1] <= x)
    if (i >= j-1) break;
    swap(A, i, j-1);
    i++; j--;
  }
  ASSERT(P &&  x == A[i:j-1])
  swap(A, j, n-1);
  j++;
}
```

The invariant for the outer (for) loop has been placed immediately before the if (...) break statement.

(a) What is a suitable assertion P?

(b) Why is the j>m test needed?

EXERCISE 4.30 In practice, arrays that are being sorted may contain "duplicates," records that have the same "key" (but possibly differing additional fields). For efficiency, it is desirable that, after partitioning, the middle segment A[i:j-1] contain *all* records equivalent to the partitioning value, as in the following:

Design a partitioning algorithm that achieves this post-condition, maintaining the following as the loop invariant:

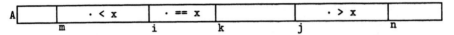

Many other improvements may be made. Severely unbalanced partitioning may usually be avoided by choosing partitioning value x to be the *median* (middle value) of a small sample of the entries in the array segment, such as A[m], A[n], and A[(m+n)/2]. For large array segments, it is worthwhile to calculate medians of three triples of entries, and then to use the median of the three medians.

Improvements may also be made to the basic form of quicksort. One is to replace the *second* recursive call by a single assignment and a loop as follows:

```
void Sort(Entry A[], int m, int n)
/* Sorts A[m:n-1] */
{ while (m < n-1)
    { int i, j;
      "partition A[m:n-1]";
      Sort(A, m, i); m = j;
    }
}
```

This approach is usually more efficient than a function call.

A second improvement is to always use the recursive call for the *shorter* of the two segments; this approach ensures that, in the worst case, the maximal depth of recursion (and hence local storage requirements) is bounded by $\log_2 N$, where $N = n-m$. This is achieved by changing

```
Sort(A, m, i); m = j;
```

to

```
if (i-m < n-j)
  Sort(A, m, i); m = j;
else
  Sort(A, j, n); n = i;
```

Finally, insertion sort is more efficient than quicksort on *small* arrays; consequently, it is desirable to combine the methods. If comparisons are expensive, it is best to incorporate the insertion sort directly into the sorting function:

```
void Sort(Entry A[], int m, int n)
{ if (n-m < K)
    "insertion sort of A[m:n-1]"
  else
  { int i, j;
    "partition A[m:n-1]";
    Sort(A, m, i);
    Sort(A, j, n);
  }
}
```

(and similarly for any of the variants discussed). But if comparisons are cheap, it may be better to modify the recursive sorting function to leave small array segments unsorted, as in the following:

```
void PartialSort(Entry A[], int m, int n)
/* Partially sorts A[m:n-1] */
{ if (n-m >= K)
  { int i, j;
    "partition A[m:n-1]";
    PartialSort(A, m, i);
    PartialSort(A, j, n);
  }
/* No entry more than K positions out of place */
}
```

Then the sort may be completed by doing a single insertion sort of the *entire* array. The optimal value of K is implementation-dependent and usually must be determined experimentally; a typical value is 8.

4.5   Combining Correctness Statements

It is sometimes convenient to decompose the pre- and post-condition specification for a code fragment, to allow independent aspects of a specification to be treated separately. For example, consider again the specification for array-search discussed in Chapter 1. We have so far side-stepped the requirement that the array segment A[0:n-1] must not be changed; we have simply been assuming that, if we qualify the declaration of A by const, the compiler will verify for us that *no* changes will be made to A. But we have seen that there may be legitimate reasons to allow assignments to "garbage" components such as A[n] (when n < max). So let us discuss how to verify a correctness statement such as

```
/* const int x0; */
ASSERT(x == x0)
C
ASSERT(x == x0)
```

which asserts that code fragment C does not change the value of variable x. We will then study how to combine this correctness statement with a more conventional correctness statement for C.

If *P* is any assertion, and code *C* has no assignments to variables used in *P* (and no function calls that may affect such variables), assertion *P* must be an *invariant* of *C*; that is, the following tableau will be valid:

```
ASSERT(P)
C
ASSERT(P)
```

We will refer to this as the *non-interference* principle, and say that code *C* does not *interfere with* (the variables used in) assertion *P*.

For example, consider again Program 2.6, which implements a search for x in A[0:n-1] using A[n] as a sentinel:

```
{ int i;
  A[n] = x;
  i = 0;
  while (A[i] != x) i++;
  present = (i<n);
}
```

The non-interference principle justifies

```
ASSERT( ForAll (k=0, k<n) A[k] == A0[k] )
i = 0;
while (A[i] != x) i++;
present = (i<n);
ASSERT( ForAll (k=0, k<n) A[k] == A0[k] )
```

because there are no assignments to A in this code fragment. By using the pre-condition strengthening and local-variable rules and the array-assignment axiom, we may then obtain the following proof tableau:

```
/* const Entry A0[max+1] */
ASSERT( A == A0 )
{ int i;
  ASSERT( ForAll (k=0, k<n) A[k] == A0[k] )
  ASSERT( ForAll (k=0, k<n) (A | n +-> x)[k] == A0[k] )
  A[n] = x;
  ASSERT( ForAll (k=0, k<n) A[k] == A0[k] )
  i = 0;
  while (A[i] != x) i++;
  present = (i<n);
  ASSERT( ForAll (k=0, k<n) A[k] == A0[k] )
}
ASSERT( ForAll (k=0, k<n) A[k] == A0[k] )
```

Now, let us assume that we have *also* verified (Exercise 4.5) the following correctness statement for the array-searching code:

```
ASSERT(0 <= n <= max)
{ int i;
  A[n] = x; i = 0;
  while (A[i] != x)
  INVAR(0 <= i <= n && x != A[0:i-1] && A[n] == x)
    i++;
  present = (i<n);
}
ASSERT( present iff x in A[0:n-1] )
```

What we want to do now is to *combine* these correctness statements, as follows:

```
/* const Entry A0[max+1]; */
ASSERT(0 <= n <= max && A == A0)
C
ASSERT
( (present iff x in A[0:n-1])  &&
  ForAll (k=0, k<n) A[k] == A0[k] )
)
```

where C is the code fragment. How is this justified?

Pre-condition strengthening may be used to justify the following two tableaux, in which the two *pre*-conditions have been combined using &&:

```
/* const Entry A0[max+1]; */
ASSERT(0 <= n <= max && A == A0)
ASSERT(0 <= n <= max)
C
ASSERT( present iff x in A[0:n-1] )
```

and

```
/* const Entry A0[max+1]; */
ASSERT(0 <= n <= max && A == A0)
ASSERT(A == A0)
C
ASSERT( ForAll (k=0, k<n) A[k] == A0[k] )
```

But, to justify taking the conjunction of the two *post*-conditions, we need the following *new* inference rule:

Post-Condition Conjunction:

$$\frac{P\,\{C\}\,Q_1 \quad P\,\{C\}\,Q_2}{P\,\{C\}\,Q_1\,\&\&\,Q_2}$$

The new rule states that if pre-condition P is sufficient to ensure that executions of C result in states satisfying *both* Q_1 *and* Q_2 separately, then P is also sufficient to ensure that executions of C lead to states satisfying their *conjunction*. Of course, this justifies the desired "combined" correctness statement for our array-searching code.

Another rule allows taking the *disjunction* of two *pre*-conditions:

Pre-Condition Disjunction:

$$\frac{P_1\,\{C\}\,Q \quad P_2\,\{C\}\,Q}{P_1\ ||\ P_2\,\{C\}\,Q}$$

This rule is useful when it is necessary to combine correctness statements that deal separately with cases, such as $n = 0$ and $n > 0$.

For example, consider again the problem (discussed in Section 3.6) of determining the number nDist of distinct elements in a *sorted* array segment A[0:n-1]. Program 4.5 determines nDupl, the number of duplicates in A[0:n-1], and then computes the value of nDist as n - nDupl.

The technique described in Section 4.1 may be used to verify this code using the assertion

```
1 <= i <= n && nDupl == i - |A[0:i-1]|
```

as an invariant, provided that $n \geq 1$; but what if $n = 0$? Note that it is not permissible to weaken the invariant to allow $i = 0$ because of the reference to A[i-1] in the loop.

If $n = 0$, the only effect of the for loop is the initial (and irrelevant) assignment to i. So it is possible to verify that Program 4.5 is correct also when $n = 0$. The rules of pre-condition disjunction (Section 4.5) and pre-condition strengthening (Section 2.5) may then be used to combine these correctness statements for the same code and justify the correctness for *all* $n \geq 0$.

EXERCISE 4.31 Generalize the new rules to allow for k premises, for any $k \geq 0$. What do the rules reduce to when $k = 0$?

Program 4.5

```
ASSERT(A[0:n-1] sorted)
{ int nDupl, i;
  nDupl = 0;
  for (i=1; i<n; i++)
    if (A[i] == A[i-1]) nDupl++;
  nDist = n - nDupl;
}
```

4.6   Additional Exercises

EXERCISE 4.32 Specify, develop, and verify a code fragment that searches in a given two-dimensional bool array B[0:m-1][0:n-1] for a row consisting entirely of true values.

EXERCISE 4.33 Specify, develop, and verify a program that determines the positions of *both* a minimal entry *and* a maximal entry in A[0:n-1].

EXERCISE 4.34 Specify, develop, and verify a code fragment to merge two sorted arrays into a new (sorted) array of all the entries.

EXERCISE 4.35 [BM93] Show how to achieve the "strict" partitioning

using

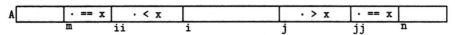

as a loop invariant until i = j, and then swapping all the entries with keys equal to x into a suitable middle segment. Compare with Exercise 4.30.

EXERCISE 4.36 [Rey81] Specify, code, and verify a program fragment that, given a two-dimensional array A[0:m-1][0:n-1], finds a "minimax," which is an entry A[i][j] in the array such that

- A[i][j] is a maximal entry of row A[i]; and

- the maximal entry of each row is at least as large as A[i][j].

EXERCISE 4.37 [Hoa71] Suppose that f satisfies m <= f < n, and that it is desired to re-arrange A[m:n-1] to the following state:

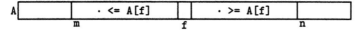

For example, if f = (m+n)/2, the final value of A[f] will be the *median* of A[m:n-1]. Any program that *sorts* A[m:n-1] would be a correct, but often unnecessarily inefficient, solution to this problem. Write a program that uses partitioning to achieve the desired post-condition more efficiently (without changing f).

EXERCISE 4.38 Develop and verify code to search for occurrences of the "pattern" P[0:m-1] as a subarray segment of A[0:n-1]:

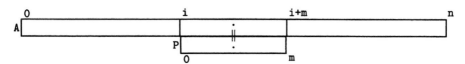

Use the following as the loop invariant:

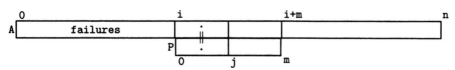

See [KMP77, BM77, Ste94, CR94, CGR99] for more efficient approaches to this problem.

EXERCISE 4.39 [Wir73] It is desired to "mark" certain positions below a line of text with asterisks. The positions to be marked, in the range $0:m-1$, are recorded in a sorted array $A[0:n-1]$ for $n \geq 0$, so that 0 <= $A[i]$ < m for all i in $0:n-1$, and $A[i]$ <= $A[j]$ when i < j. For example, if A is the array $(2,5,8,8,11)$, a line of text and the markings to be output beneath it are as follows:

```
This is a line of text.
  *   *   *   *
```

Which of the following proposed codings are correct? Indicate under what conditions the incorrect ones will fail, and give suitable invariants for the loops in the correct ones.

(a)
```
k = 0;
for (i=0; i<m; i++)
{ if (i == A[k])
  { putchar('*'); k++;
  }
  else putchar(' ');
}
```

(b)
```
k = 0; A[n] = m;
for (i=0; i<m; i++)
{ if (i == A[k])
  { putchar('*');
    do k++; while (A[k] <= i);
  }
  else putchar(' ');
}
```

(c)
```
i = 0;
for (k=0; k<n; k++)
{ do
  { putchar(' ');
    i++;
  } while (i != A[k]);
  putchar('*');
  k++;
}
```

(d)
```
i = 0; k = 0;
do
{ while (i < A[k])
  { putchar(' ');
    i++;
  }
  if (i = A[k])
  { putchar('*');
    i++;
  }
  k++;
} while (k <= n);
```

```
(e) i = 0; k = 0;
    while (k <= n)
    { while (i < A[k])
      { putchar(' ');
        i++;
      }
      putchar('*');
      do k++; while (A[k] > i);
    }
```

4.7 Additional Reading

A good survey of techniques for achieving the best possible performance in algorithm implementations may be found in [Ben82]. Detailed treatments of quicksort-like algorithms are given in [Sed78, BM93].

REFERENCES

[Ben82]   J. L. Bentley. *Writing Efficient Programs.* Prentice Hall, 1982.

[BM77]   R. S. Boyer and J. S. Moore. A fast string-searching algorithm. *Comm. ACM,* 20(10):762–72, 1977.

[BM93]   J. Bentley and D. McIlroy. Engineering a sort function. *Software Practice and Experience,* 23(1):1249–65, 1993.

[CGR99]   M. Crochemore, L. Gacsieniec, and W. Rytter. Constant-space string-matching in sublinear average time. *Theoretical Computer Science,* 218(1):177–95, 1999.

[CR94]   M. Crochemore and W. Rytter. *Text Algorithms.* Oxford University Press, 1994.

[Hoa71]   C. A. R. Hoare. Proof of a program: FIND. *Comm. ACM,* 14(1):39–45, 1971.

[KMP77]   D. E. Knuth, J. H. Morris, Jr., and V. Pratt. Fast pattern matching in strings. *SIAM J. Computing,* 6(2):323–50, 1977.

[Rey81]   J. C. Reynolds. *The Craft of Programming.* Prentice Hall International, 1981.

[Sed78]   R. Sedgewick. Implementing quicksort programs. *Comm. ACM.,* 21:847–57, 1978.

[Ste94]   G. A. Stephen. *String Searching Algorithms,* volume 3 of *Lecture Notes Series on Computing.* World Scientific, 1994.

[Wir73]   N. Wirth. *Systematic Programming, An Introduction.* Prentice Hall, 1973.

Part B

Data Representations

Introduction to Part B

We now turn our attention to the specification, verification, and construction of *data representations*. These combine "private" definitions of data-representation variables (and possibly functions) with definitions of "public" functions (or "methods") that provide a suitably abstract "view" of the data to application programs. Chapter 5 introduces the basic concepts in the context of a simple case study, and Chapter 6 discusses a variety of other examples.

Additional Reading

The following are recommended for further discussion and additional examples: [Hoa72a, Hoa72b, Jon80, Rey81, Jon86, LG86, LG00].

REFERENCES

[Gri78]   D. Gries, editor. *Programming Methodology, A Collection of Articles by IFIP WG 2.3*. Springer-Verlag, 1978.

[HJ89]   C. A. R. Hoare and C. B. Jones, editors. *Essays in Computing Science*. Prentice Hall International, 1989.

[Hoa72a]   C. A. R. Hoare. Notes on data structuring. In O.-J. Dahl, E. W. Dijkstra, and C. A. R. Hoare, *Structured Programming*, pages 83-174. Academic Press, 1972.

[Hoa72b]   C. A. R. Hoare. Proof of correctness of data representations. *Acta Informatica*, 1:271–81, 1972. Reprinted in [Gri78], pages 269–81, and [HJ89], pages 103–15.

[Jon80]   C. B. Jones. *Software Development: A Rigorous Approach*. Prentice Hall International, 1980.

[Jon86]   C. B. Jones. *Systematic Software Development Using VDM*. Prentice Hall International, 1986. Available here: ftp://ftp.ncl.ac.uk/pub/users/ncbj/ssdvdm.ps.gz.

[LG86]   B. Liskov and J. Guttag. *Abstraction and Specification in Program Development*. The MIT Press, 1986.

[LG00]   B. Liskov and J. Guttag. *Program Development in* JAVA: *Abstraction,*
           Specification, and Object-Oriented Design. Addison-Wesley, 2000.
[Rey81]   J. C. Reynolds. *The Craft of Programming.* Prentice Hall International, 1981.

Chapter 5

Data Representation: A Case Study

5.1 Informal Specification

Professor Higgins wants to set up a small database to keep track of which students are enrolled in his course on computational metaphysics. He asks his programmer, Eliza Doolittle, to write a program that will allow him or his secretary to

- add a student record to the database;

- determine whether a particular student is currently enrolled; and

- remove a student record from the database.

Students are to be identified by their student numbers.

Eliza considers the problem and points out that the specification is incomplete: what should happen if a student is "added" when he or she is already enrolled? Or if a student is "removed" when that student has not yet enrolled? Professor Higgins replies that *he* would never make such mistakes; however, because the system will also be used by his secretary, he agrees that such operations should produce appropriate warning messages to the user.

Eliza intends to structure the program as two modules: one to manage the data representation and the other to provide the user interface. She decides that it should not be the responsibility of the data-representation module itself to produce error messages to the user; the user-interface module should do this. But where should the errors be *detected*?

If the data-representation module is responsible for detecting errors, it would be necessary for the operations to return error flags or to raise exceptions, which would significantly complicate the interface between the modules. Furthermore, the data-representation module might be used for other applications in which similar sequences of operations would *not* be erroneous. Eliza therefore adopts an alternative approach: the data-representation operations must ensure only that a particular entry is, respectively, included in, or excluded from, the database. It will be the responsibility of application programs to both detect *and* handle appropriately what they consider to be errors.

The data-representation module is to implement the following interface to the application program:

```
typename Entry;  /* type of entries, use == for equality */
bool contains(Entry e);
void include(Entry e);  /* post-condition: contains(e)  */
void exclude(Entry e);  /* post-condition: !contains(e) */
```

where type name Entry is to be defined as the type of student numbers, and it will be assumed that student numbers may be tested for equality using the == operator. Note that if the operation include(e) is called when e is already contained in the database, it is *not* considered an error; include may simply return without making any change to the database, and similarly for exclude(e) if contains(e) is already false. The post-conditions stated in the comments for include and exclude highlight the most important aspects of these interface operations, but they are not complete specifications of their intended behavior. Note that this is intended to be a "general-purpose" (re-usable) interface; that is, it is not specifically tailored to a particular application.

The database application program itself may use a code fragment similar to the following to add StudentNum (of type Entry) to the database, producing a warning message if that student has already been added:

```
if (contains(StudentNum))
  printf("This student has already been enrolled.\n");
else
  include(StudentNum);
```

Similarly, the following removes a StudentNum from the database, producing a warning message if that student is *not* in the database:

```
if (!contains(StudentNum))
  printf("This student is not currently enrolled.\n");
else
  exclude(StudentNum);
```

Whenever possible, it is best to detect and handle error situations at the *same* program level (i.e., exception handling involving jumps between different levels of abstraction should be avoided if possible). This sometimes introduces performance penalties. For example, each of the preceding code fragments seems to require a repeated search for the *same* target; however, we will see later (Section 5.6) that this inefficiency may be avoided by using an appropriate implementation strategy.

EXERCISE 5.1 Design an interface suitable for each of the following familiar structures:

    (a) a stack of entries of type Entry;

    (b) a queue of entries of type Entry.

EXERCISE 5.2 Design an interface suitable for the representation of a bank account. The interface should support inquiries on the current balance, operations of depositing money to and withdrawing money from the account, and production of a statement of all transactions since the preceding statement (or, for the first statement, since the account was started).

5.2 Formal Specification

Specification of a data-representation module is quite different from specification of an algorithm. What is wanted is a way to specify the desired behavior of the interface operations, but without overcommitting to any particular implementation data structure.

We will use what is termed an *abstract model* to specify the desired behavior of the database. In mathematical logic, a *model* (of a set of axioms) is a mathematical structure, together with interpretations of the function and predicate symbols used in the axioms, such that all the axioms are satisfied. This terminology has been borrowed to describe data-representation specifications based on specifying an appropriate mathematical structure, together with interpretations of the operations, having the desired behavioral properties. The models are described as being *abstract* models because they are *mathematical* structures, rather than *computational* (data) structures.

An appropriate mathematical model for the database we have been considering in this chapter is that it is a (finite) *set* of values of type Entry, recording which students are currently enrolled in the course. If S is considered to be an abstract set-valued variable modeling the database, the interface operations may be interpreted in terms of S using simple assignments and familiar set-theoretic operations as follows:

contains(e)	is interpreted as	$e \in S$
include(e)	is interpreted as	$S = S \cup \{e\}$;
exclude(e)	is interpreted as	$S = S - \{e\}$;

The use of assignment operations in a specification is somewhat unconventional, but the two examples here seem to be both precise and comprehensible.

EXERCISE 5.3 Give specifications of include(e) and exclude(e) using pre- and post-conditions.

Finally, the *initial* state of the data representation may be specified by requiring S to be initialized to the *empty* set, which is denoted by $\emptyset$ or $\{\}$.

Note that the abstract model is not intended to be a computationally realistic *implementation* of the database; implementations will be discussed later.
Even if the programming language in use supports the mathematical structure,
this may not be satisfactory for the application being considered. For example,
the programming language PASCAL provides set types, but we could not use a
set variable to implement the course database in a PASCAL program unless all
the student numbers were within a very small range, such as 0:127. For this
application, other representations of sets are more appropriate.

EXERCISE 5.4 Attempt to specify the desired behavior of the operations you proposed
for a stack and for a queue in Exercise 5.1 using suitable abstract models. *Hint:* use the
mathematical concept of a *sequence*.

EXERCISE 5.5 Attempt to specify the desired behavior of the bank-account operations
you proposed in Exercise 5.2 using a suitable abstract model.

5.3   A Simple Implementation

A set-valued variable whose sets never contain more than a very small fraction
of the universe of *possible* members may be termed a *sparse* set. The database
we are considering may certainly be regarded as a sparse set: there may be
millions of possible student numbers, but at any time only a very small fraction
of them will be enrolled in one particular course.

A sparse set may be represented by storing the current members.   To
avoid the complexities of linked structures and dynamic storage allocation,
Ms Doolittle gets permission from Professor Higgins to adopt an upper limit
on the number of students who are allowed to be enrolled in the course under consideration. This constraint allows the sparse set to be represented by
a partially filled *array* of (distinct) values, each entry representing one of the
elements of the set.

The following definitions may then be used:

```
/* Set S; */
# define max 255       /* maximum number of entries */
Entry A[max+1];        /* A[0:n-1] are the (distinct) entries */
int n = 0;             /* number of entries, <= max */
int i;                 /* search index */
```

The elements of the set are to be stored in array segment A[0:n-1], and these
entries will be distinct so that n is the *cardinality* (number of elements) of the
set being represented. The array is defined with an "extra" component A[max],
which will allow use of the sentinel technique in searches even when n = max.
The order of the entries will not be significant.

The data structure is initialized to be a representation of the *empty* set by
the initialization n = 0; it is not necessary to initialize the array itself. The
variable i will be used as a search index.

Program 5.1

```
void find(Entry x)
{ ASSERT(0 <= n <= max)
  i = 0;
  A[n] = x; /* sentinel */
  while (A[i] != x) i++;
  ASSERT( 0 <= i <= n && A[i] == x && x != A[0:i-1] )
}
```

The function find(x) defined in Program 5.1 will be used in functions contains, include, and exclude to search for an entry equal to x in A[0:n-1]. Note that find does more than merely determine whether or not x is in A[0:n-1]. It also sets variable i to the index of the array component containing x if the search is successful. Furthermore, the sentinel technique discussed in Section 2.1 is used so that A[n] is set to x and i is set to n if the seach is unsuccessful. These "side effects" of find will be important for the implementations of contains, include, and exclude.

The stated post-condition is essential documentation for the function; it has the following consequences: if i < n, the search was successful and x was found at position i; on the other hand, if i = n, the search was unsuccessful (x is not currently in the set), but A[n] was assigned the value x.

Program 5.2 shows how the three set operations may be implemented. Each function calls find as its first step. For include, nothing further is done if the

Program 5.2

```
bool contains(Entry e) /* e in S? */
{ find(e);
  return i<n;
}

void include(Entry e) /* S = S + {e} */
{ find(e);
  if (i==n)
  { ASSERT(A[n] == e) /* A[n] used as a sentinel in find */
    if (n == max) error("the set is too large");
    n++;
  }
}

void exclude(Entry e) /* S = S - {e} */
{ find(e);
  if (i<n)
  { /* replace A[i] by A[n-1] and decrement n */
    n--;
    A[i] = A[n];
  }
}
```

search is successful. If the search is unsuccessful but the new number of entries would exceed the specified limit max, an error message is printed, and program execution is terminated. Note that it isn't necessary to assign e to A[n] because this has already been done by find. In exclude, entry A[i] is "removed" by simply replacing it by A[n-1], taking advantage of the fact that the order of the entries in A[0:n-1] is irrelevant. This method avoids an inefficient "shift" of an array segment to fill in the gap. Comments give specifications for the functions in terms of the abstract model.

EXERCISE 5.6 What are the advantages and disadvantages of requiring the array entries to be *distinct*? Implement the set operations so that their externally visible behavior is unchanged but without requiring that the array entries be distinct. Would this implementation be practical for Professor Higgins's application?

EXERCISE 5.7 What would be the advantages and disadvantages of implementing the set using a *sorted* array segment (without changing the externally visible behavior of the interface operations)? In what circumstances would this be an appropriate implementation method?

5.4 Program Organization

Suppose that the various components of the database implementation discussed in Section 5.3 were put together as follows:

```
typedef int Entry;
# define max 255
Entry A[max+1];
int n = 0;
int i;
void find(Entry x) { ... }
bool contains(Entry e) { ... }
void include(Entry e) { ... }
void exclude(Entry e) { ... }
```

This organizaton would certainly be workable; however, it would make the representation variables (n, i, and A) and the searching function find, which are *not* in the interface, directly accessible to the application program. This visibility would be a serious violation of the basic principles of modularity. The implementation could then not be verified or modified without going through the entire application program. What is wanted is to keep those entities *local to* the data-representation code, allowing application programs to access *only* the three interface operations contains, include, and exclude.

In standard C, such representation hiding is best achieved by separately compiling a SparseSet module that defines the set representation and the interface functions, as in Program 5.3. The representation variables and function find are specified as being static; this qualification precludes access to the representation from other modules. The following "header" file would then

Program 5.3

```
/*  Set S;  */
# define max 255
typedef int Entry;
static Entry A[max+1];
static int n = 0;
static int i;

static void find(Entry x) { ... }

bool contains(Entry e) { ... }
void include(Entry e) { ... }
void exclude(Entry e) { ... }
```

be included into application programs to allow compilation of calls to the interface functions:

```
typedef int Entry;
bool contains(Entry e);
void include(Entry e);
void exclude(Entry e);
```

In many extensions of C and most modern programming languages, the desired separation between implementation and use of a data representation may be achieved in other ways, using facilities termed units, packages, modules, or classes. For example, Program 5.4 shows how the partially filled array implementation of a *class* (programmer-defined type) of sparse sets may be coded in C++, an object-oriented extension of C.

The SparseSet class body consists of definitions and declarations partitioned into two sections: (i) a *private* part, which defines the entities that should

Program 5.4

```
class SparseSet
{ private:

  # define max 255
  Entry A[max+1];
  int n;
  int i;
  void find(Entry x) { ... }

  public:

  SparseSet(void) { n = 0; }
  bool contains(Entry e) { ... }
  void include(Entry e) { ... }
  void exclude(Entry e) { ... }
};
```

not be accessible from outside the class (i.e., variables n, i, and A and function
find), and (ii) a *public* part, which defines entities that *are* accessible outside
the class. The "constructor" function SparseSet (i.e., a function having the
same name as the class itself) is used by the implementation to initialize new
sparse-set objects, when these are created.

An application program would then create and use a sparse set as follows:

```
{ SparseSet CompMetaphys;
  Entry StudentNum;
       :
  if (CompMetaphys.contains(StudentNum))
    printf("This student has already been enrolled.\n");
  else
    CompMetaphys.include(StudentNum);
       :
  if (!CompMetaphys.contains(StudentNum))
    printf("This student is not currently enrolled.\n");
  else
    CompMetaphys.exclude(StudentNum);
       :
}
```

The SparseSet definition creates and initializes object CompMetaphys. The public entities of the class, such as function include, are accessed by using composite identifiers such as CompMetaphys.include. However, a reference such
as CompMetaphys.A would be syntactically erroneous because variable A is not
defined in the public part of the class and so may not be accessed (directly).
Similarly, local variables that are defined in the application program, such as
StudentNum, are not (directly) accessible in the SparseSet class.

This approach to data-representation modularization has the significant advantage over the approach based on static declarations that it allows a programmer to create *several* objects of a class. For example, if it is necessary to
use an *array* of sparse sets, this may be defined as follows:

```
SparseSet Courses[NC];
```

For uniformity, we will use the notation of C++ classes to present data representations, even when just a single instance of a class is needed.

EXERCISE 5.8 In some applications of sparse sets, the operation of inserting a "new"
entry (i.e., one known *not* to be in the set) is often useful. Specify a suitable new interface
operation

```
void insert(Entry e)
```

and implement it so that insert(e) is more efficient than include(e).

EXERCISE 5.9 A *bag* (or *multiset*) is like a set, except that elements may occur in a bag
more than once. The following is a suitable interface for a "sparse" bag of values of
type Entry:

```
typename Entry;          /* type of entries, use == for equality    */
int count(Entry e);      /* number of occurrences of e in the bag    */
void add(Entry e);       /* adds one occurrence of e to the bag      */
void remove(Entry e);    /* removes one occurrence of e from the bag;
                            pre-condition: count(e) > 0      */
```

(a) Implement a SparseBag class using a partially filled array (with duplicated entries as necessary) to represent the entries of a bag B.

(b) Implement SparseBag in another way using "parallel" arrays as follows:

```
Entry A[max+1]; /* A[0:n-1] are entries with > 0 occurrences in B */
int N[max];     /* N[k] is the number of occurrences of A[k] in B */
```

(c) Discuss the advantages and disadvantages of the two representations.

5.5 Verification of a Data Representation

In this section, we illustrate how to verify that a data representation satisfies its formal specification. The key idea is the concept of a *representation invariant*, an assertion that constrains the representation and relates the abstract and concrete implementations such that

- it is *initially* true (i.e., immediately after initialization of the data representation),

- it is *preserved* by every interface function (provided that the appropriate pre-condition is satisfied), and

- it is sufficient to imply the correctness of any values returned by interface functions (and also any values passed back to the application module via reference parameters of interface functions).

A representation invariant appropriate to the array-based implementation of a sparse set described in Section 5.3 is the conjunction of the following three assertions:

- 0 <= n <= max

which specifies the range of values for n;

- ForAll(Entry e) e in A[0:n-1] iff e in S

which asserts that the components of A[0:n-1] represent the elements of S; and

- |A[0:n-1]| = n

which asserts that the entries in A[0:n-1] are distinct. This third assertion is needed to verify the correctness of the exclude operation, which never deletes more than *one* entry of A[0:n-1].

In outline, the argument to show that this conjunction of assertions (let us call it *I*) *is* an invariant proceeds as follows.

- I is established initially by setting n to 0 and S to $\emptyset$; then e in A[0:n-1] and e $\in$ S are both false for every Entry value e, and this establishes the second assertion. The first and third assertions are trivially or vacuously true.

- Every execution of include(e) preserves I. In the abstract model, include(e) has the effect S = S $\cup$ {e};, whereas the implementation appends e to the array segment A[0:n-1] and increments n when e cannot be found in A[0:n-1] but does nothing if e is found. The constraint n $\leq$ max is preserved by aborting program execution if necessary.

- Every execution of exclude(e) preserves I. In the abstract model, exclude(e) has the effect S = S $-$ {e};, whereas the implementation replaces A[i] by A[n-1] and decrements n just if there is some index i such that 0 <= i < n and A[i] = e. The third assertion ensures that this occurrence of e in A[0:n-1] is unique.

- Finally, the value returned by any call of contains(e) is correct because it follows from the assertion and the post-condition of find(e) that i < n if and only if e $\in$ S.

Hence we conclude that I is an invariant for our data representation.

The importance of a representation invariant for verification of a data representation is as follows: provided that the representation invariant is preserved *between* calls to interface functions, it will follow by induction on the number of interface function calls that the data representation returns only *correct* values.

To ensure that assignable program variables referred to in the invariant are not interfered with by *other* parts of the program, such variables should normally be defined, as recommended in Section 5.4, in the private part of the class. Another constraint that must be considered is that interface functions should not normally be called from *within* the class (unless the representation invariant holds at that point). For example, function include might have been written as follows:

```
void include(Entry e) {
  if (!contains(e)) { ... }
}
```

The "internal" call to contains would actually be harmless because it appears as the *first* step of function include where the invariant has been assumed to be true; however, an internal function call might be inappropriate if the representation invariant happened *not* to hold at the call.

In our SparseSet class, all the variables referred to in the invariant are private, and there are no internal calls to interface functions. It follows that the representation invariant will be preserved between calls to interface functions, and so any values returned by the class implementation will in fact be correct.

It should be evident that a representation invariant, together with the abstract model and the abstract interpretations of all the operations, provide important documentation for a data-representation module. The representation invariant should be included as a comment between the private and public parts of a class definition, as illustrated in Program 5.5. If *I* stands for the representation invariant, this kind of use of INVAR(*I*) (not associated with a loop) may be regarded as being an abbreviation for using ASSERT(*I*) as pre- and post-conditions of every interface operation of the class (and as post-condition of the constructor), as in Program 5.6 on page 122.

Program 5.5

```
class SparseSet
{ private:

    /*  Set S;  */
    # define max 255
    Entry A[max+1];
    int n;
    int i;
    void find(Entry x) { ... }

INVAR
( 0 <= n <= max &&
  (ForAll(Entry e) e in A[0:n-1] iff e in S) &&
  |A[0:n-1]| == n
)
    public:

    SparseSet(void) { ... }
    bool contains(Entry e) { ... }
    void include(Entry e) { ... }
    void exclude(Entry e) { ... }
};
```

EXERCISE 5.10 Verify your implementation of a sparse-set class with an insert operation (Exercise 5.8).

EXERCISE 5.11 Give appropriate representation invariants for your implementations of a SparseBag class (Exercise 5.9).

Program 5.6

```
SparseSet(void)
{ ... ASSERT(I) }

bool contains(Entry e) /* e in S? */
{ ASSERT(I) ... ASSERT(I && i<n iff e in S) return i<n; }

void include(Entry e)   /* S = S + {e} */
{ ASSERT(I) ... ASSERT(I) }

void exclude(Entry e)   /* S = S - {e} */
{ ASSERT(I) ... ASSERT(I) }
```

5.6   A Caching Implementation

Many implementations of sparse sets are possible, as we have seen already in Exercises 5.6 and 5.7. In all three of the sparse-set operations, the key step is a *search* (in our implementation, using function find) for a possible set member. This means that many of the sophisticated data structures and algorithms that have been developed in computer science for implementing efficient searching may be adapted to implementing sparse sets.

EXERCISE 5.12 Implement the sparse-set interface of Section 5.2 using each of the following to represent the set:

(a) a linked list;

(b) a hash table;

(c) a binary search tree.

State informally a representation invariant for each implementation. Discuss the advantages and disadvantages of each.

In this section, we describe an optimization strategy that may often be used to improve the performance of sparse-set implementations, irrespective of the data structure used to represent the sparse set. The key observation is that the following patterns are very common in applications that use sparse sets:

```
if (!contains(e)) include(e);
```

and

```
if (contains(e)) exclude(e);
```

This means that there will often be successive searches for the *same* target. It may therefore be possible to improve the average performance of such applications (without changing the interface) by optimizing the representation for repeated searches for the same target value.

This strategy is easy to implement. All that is required is to maintain a suitable *cache* from one call of the searching routine to the next, recording where the search ends. If every call of the searching function checks this cached position first, a real search may be avoided whenever it would be a repeated search for the same target, for the relatively minor additional cost of a single comparison.

Program 5.7 shows how to modify function find and the initialization function SparseSet from our array-based implementation to incorporate a search cache. The value of search index i is preserved between calls to the interface functions and acts as the search cache. The new version of find initially tests whether $A[i] = x$ (for $i < n$), and does a real search only if this test fails. The correctness of the revised find is established as follows (notice the new pre-condition):

- If $A[i] = x$ for $i < n$, the search loop is skipped, but these facts and the pre-condition imply the post-condition;

- otherwise, the same searching code as before is executed.

No changes are needed to any of the other functions (in Program 5.2).

Program 5.7

```
void find(Entry x)
{ ASSERT(0 <= i <= n <= max && A[i] != A[0:i-1])
  if (i==n || A[i] != x)
  { i = 0;   A[n] = x;
    while (A[i] != x) i++;
  }
  ASSERT(0 <= i <= n &&   A[i] == x && x != A[0:i-1])
}

SparseSet(void) { n = 0; i = 0; }
```

Correctness of caching optimizations is often very delicate; the use of a representation invariant helps to prevent subtle bugs because assumptions about interactions between operations must be made explicit. To verify the rest of our caching implementation, we need to add the following assertions to the representation invariant used in Section 5.5:

```
0 <= i <= n && A[i] != A[0:i-1]
```

to ensure the pre-condition for find. We must now verify the augmented representation invariant for our optimized implementation, as follows:

- The revised initialization establishes the new assertions by setting i to 0.

- The include operation in Program 5.2 may increment n, but this change cannot invalidate the assertion i <= n.

- The `exclude` operation in Program 5.2 may decrement n, but only when i<n. Replacing `A[i]` by `A[n-1]` does not invalidate `A[i] != A[0:i-1]` because the entries of `A[0:n-1]` are, according to the original invariant assertion, distinct.

EXERCISE 5.13 Adapt your sparse-set implementations of Exercises 5.6, 5.7, and 5.12 to use search caching. Verify the optimized implementations using appropriate representation invariants.

5.7 Additional Reading

The use of relations as representation invariants was first described in [Mil71]. Good examples may be found in [Rey81]. Soundness and completeness issues are discussed in [Mit91, Ten94, OT95]. Other approaches to formal specification of data representations are described in [LZ77, GM86, AP98, Red98, dRE99].

REFERENCES

[AP98]   V. S. Alagar and K. Periyasamy. *Specification of Software Systems*. Springer-Verlag, 1998.

[dRE99] W.-P. de Roever and K. Engelhardt. *Data Refinement: Model-Oriented Methods and Their Comparison*. Cambridge University Press, 1999.

[GM86]   N. Gehani and A. McGettrick, editors. *Software Specification Techniques*. Addison-Wesley, 1986.

[LZ77]   B. Liskov and S. Zilles. An introduction to formal specifications of data abstractions. In R. T. Yeh, editor, *Current Trends in Programming Methodology, Software Specification and Design*, volume 1, chapter 1, pages 1–32. Prentice Hall, 1977.

[Mil71] R. Milner. An algebraic definition of simulation between programs. In *Proceedings of the Second International Joint Conference on Artificial Intelligence*, pages 481–9. The British Computer Society, London, 1971. Also Technical Report CS-205, Computer Science Department, Stanford University, February 1971.

[Mit91] J. C. Mitchell. On the equivalence of data representations. In V. Lifschitz, editor, *Artificial Intelligence and Mathematical Theory of Computation: Papers in Honor of John McCarthy*, pages 305–30. Academic Press, 1991.

[OT95]   P. W. O'Hearn and R. D. Tennent. Parametricity and local variables. *J. ACM*, 42(3):658–709, May 1995.

[Red98] U. S. Reddy. Objects and classes in ALGOL-like languages, 1998. Presented at the Fifth International Workshop on Foundations of Object-Oriented Languages, January 17–18, 1998, San Diego, CA. Avaliable here: `http://pauillac.inria.fr/~remy/fool/program.html`.

[Rey81] J. C. Reynolds. *The Craft of Programming*. Prentice Hall International, 1981.

[Ten94] R. D. Tennent. Correctness of data representations in ALGOL-like languages. In A. W. Roscoe, editor, *A Classical Mind, Essays in Honour of C. A. R. Hoare*, chapter 23, pages 405–17. Prentice Hall International, 1994.

Chapter 6

Data Representation: Additional Examples

In this chapter we discuss a variety of useful data representations, including extensions to the SparseSet interface discussed in Chapter 5, other representations of sets, and other mathematical structures (sequences, partial functions, ordered sets, directed graphs, and partially ordered sets). Our aim is to demonstrate the utility of abstract-model specifications and representation invariants in design, development, and verification of data representations.

6.1 Traversing a Sparse Set

Professor Higgins wants to be able to print out a class list for his course in computational metaphysics. With the database interface used in Chapter 5, this can be done only by iterating through all the *potential* members of the set and testing their membership in CompMetaphys, as follows:

```
Entry StudentNum;
for (StudentNum = low; StudentNum <= high; StudentNum++)
  if (CompMetaphys.contains(StudentNum))
    printf("%i\n", StudentNum);
```

where low and high are, respectively, the smallest and largest possible student numbers. Of course, this is rather inefficient if, as assumed, the number of student numbers is very much larger than the number of students in the course. In other applications, a set might contain elements that are float values or strings or complex structures, and exhaustive enumeration of the universe would be completely impractical. What is needed is a way to iterate through the *actual* elements of a sparse set (in any order); this kind of iterative process is termed a *traversal* (of a data structure).

6.1.1 USING A CHOICE FUNCTION

There are several ways to augment the sparse-set interface to support traversals. The simplest is to add the following new operations to the interface:

```
Entry choice(void); /* returns any element of S (nonempty) */
bool empty(void);   /* S == {}? */
```

Function choice (which is named after the axiom of choice in set theory) is to return *any* of the current members of the set. Of course, this function cannot return a result if the set is empty. We must therefore adopt S != {} as a pre-condition to choice. A bool function empty has been added to the interface to allow application programs to test whether a set is nonempty *before* calling choice.

A class list would then be generated by an application program as follows:

```
while (!CompMetaphys.empty())
{ Entry StudentNum;
  StudentNum = CompMetaphys.choice();
  printf("%i\n", StudentNum);
  CompMetaphys.exclude(StudentNum);
}
```

Notice that after a student number is "chosen" and processed, it is removed from the set so that it will not be chosen subsequently. Of course, the loop as a whole then has the (perhaps undesired) "side effect" of emptying the set!

If the application requires that the set contents be preserved, the members may be *saved* and then *restored* to the set after traversal. A simple implementation of this idea is to use a recursive traversal function instead of a loop, as in the following:

```
void ClassList(void)
{ if (!CompMetaphys.empty())
  { Entry StudentNum;
    StudentNum = CompMetaphys.choice();
    printf("%i\n", StudentNum);
    CompMetaphys.exclude(StudentNum);
    ClassList();
    CompMetaphys.include(StudentNum);
  }
}
```

The student number chosen is saved in a local variable and re-included into the set after the remaining set members are processed by the recursive call. (If an interface function insert as discussed in Exercise 5.8 is available, it can be used here and will be more efficient than include.) Set entries that have been traversed are in effect saved on the run-time stack built into the implementation of functions.

Here are implementations of the two new operations that are compatible with the representation used in Program 5.2:

```
Entry choice(void) /* returns any element of S (nonempty) */
{ if (n==0) error("the set is empty");
  return A[0];
}

bool empty(void) /* S == {}? */
{ return n==0; }
```

EXERCISE 6.1 What is the advantage in choosing A[0] (rather than, say, A[n-1]) in the implementation of function choice? How should choice be implemented if the representation uses a search cache, as in Program 5.7?

EXERCISE 6.2 Implement a bool function AllAcceptable that uses the augmented sparse-set interface and would allow Professor Higgins to test whether *all* student numbers currently in the database satisfy a given bool function acceptable(StudentNum). The set traversal should be terminated as soon as an unacceptable element has been encountered; the set of student numbers represented by the database should not be permanently changed.

EXERCISE 6.3 Implement a function RemoveUnacceptable that uses the augmented sparse-set interface and would allow Professor Higgins to remove from the database all student numbers that fail to satisfy a given bool function acceptable(StudentNum).

EXERCISE 6.4 Use a sparse set with the augmented interface to implement an application program that processes a long text and determines a database that may subsequently be used to output a list (in any order) of all the words that occur in the text. Each such word should be output only once. Assume that a word consists of consecutive alphabetic characters (a to z), ignoring upper/lowercase distinctions.

6.1.2 IN-PLACE TRAVERSAL

For many applications, traversing a set by successively saving the entries and then restoring them, as was done in Section 6.1.1, would be unacceptably inefficient because of all the time-consuming copying that must be done. In this section, we discuss operations to support "in-place" traversals.

The basic idea is to augment the representation of a sparse set so that, during a traversal, a subset of "untraversed" elements is maintained. For example, the partially filled array implementation of Sections 5.3 and 5.6 may be augmented by a counter variable nu to record the number of untraversed entries. During a traversal, the array may be considered as being partitioned as follows:

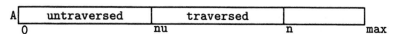

so that segment A[0:nu-1] represents the not-yet-traversed elements, and A[nu:n-1] represents the elements already traversed. A traversal is initiated by setting nu to n:

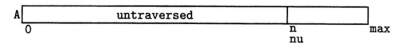

and terminates when nu has been reduced to 0:

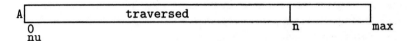

The traversal is in place because only the counter nu is changed during a traversal; the array entries are not copied or re-arranged.

The following are new `SparseSet` interface operations to support this kind of traversal:

```
void traverse(void)
bool HasNext(void)
Entry next(void)
```

The `traverse` operation initializes the traversal. So long as `HasNext` returns true, there are more elements to traverse; `next` returns one of the not-yet-traversed elements and adjusts the representation to allow subsequent `next` operations to return the remaining untraversed set members. Here is typical application code to traverse a sparse set using these operations:

```
CompMetaphys.traverse();
while (CompMetaphys.HasNext())
{ Entry StudentNum;
  StudentNum = CompMetaphys.next();
  printf("%i\n", StudentNum);
}
```

EXERCISE 6.5 Show how an application program might use these new in-place traversal operations to achieve the effect of the following operations on `SparseSet` variables S and T:

(a) S = S ∪ T;   (i.e., add the members of T to S);

(b) S = S − T;   (i.e., remove the members of T from S).

We may obtain an abstract model of a sparse set that also supports in-place traversal by augmenting the assumed set S by an additional set U of untraversed elements of S; initially, U is empty. A traversal is initiated by (conceptually) assigning S to U; then each call of `next` has the effect of choosing and removing one element of U, and returning it to the application program, as in the following:

```
{ Entry x = U.choice();
  U.exclude(x);
  return x;
}
```

The `HasNext` operation simply tests whether U is nonempty. However, we must *also* consider the effect of the existing interface operations `include` and `exclude` on the new abstract-model component U.

The array implementation we have been considering would naturally support insertion of new elements to the *traversed* subset, rather than to the untraversed subset; the latter would be more natural if the array were partitioned as follows:

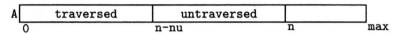

However, if the sparse set were to be implemented using a hash table, new elements might get inserted unpredictably into *either* the traversed subset *or* the untraversed subset. In representations that use linked structures, insertion or removal of an arbitrary component might interfere with the traversal, leading to dangling references or infinite loops. Even in our simple array-based implementations, removal of an arbitrary entry may have the unexpected effect of moving an entry from the traversed segment to the untraversed segment, or vice versa. For these reasons, we do *not* want to allow arbitrary insertions or removals from the sparse set *during* a traversal. We therefore add the precondition U == {} to operations include and exclude; moreover, U should not be affected by calls of these operations.

The simple array implementation of Program 5.2 may be modified to support the new traversal operations by introducing a variable nu to contain the number of *untraversed* elements:

```
# define max 255
Entry A[max+1];
int n = 0;
int nu = 0;   /* number of untraversed elements */
int i;        /* search index */
```

The new traversal operations may then be implemented as follows:

```
void traverse(void) { nu = n; }

bool HasNext(void) { return nu > 0; }

Entry next(void)
{ if (nu == 0) error("no more untraversed elements");
  nu--;
  return A[nu];
}
```

where the following array diagram portrays the partitioning of the array:

A	untraversed		traversed		
0		nu		n	max

In a robust implementation, the new pre-conditions to include and to exclude would be verified by testing the value of nu.

EXERCISE 6.6 Show how to implement the new traversal operations using the following array partitioning:

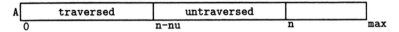

EXERCISE 6.7 Although it is usually impractical to allow a sparse set to be changed arbitrarily using include or exclude operations during a traversal, removal of the element chosen by next *is* normally possible and is a very useful feature. Consider adding the following interface operation to allow removal of the most recently traversed set element: void remove(void) .

(a) Suppose S and T are SparseSet variables; show how to use the new traversal operations (including remove) in application code to achieve the effect of S = S ∩ T; (i.e., to remove from S any elements that are not also members of T).

(b) Augment the abstract model described earlier to support the proposed remove operation.

(c) Augment the array-based representation of traversible sparse sets described earlier to support the proposed remove operation.

(d) Investigate how the remove operation could be implemented with other approaches to sparse-set representation.

6.1.3 ORDERED TRAVERSALS

Professor Higgins is dissatisfied with the class lists being produced because the student numbers are not listed in any useful order. So Eliza redesigns the interface to the data-representation module so that the choice operation, which may return an *arbitrary* set member, is replaced by

    Entry smallest(void); /* returns the smallest element of S */

A traversal using smallest in place of choice allows the set members to be processed in increasing (i.e., sorted) order. A sparse set that supports such ordered traversals will be termed an *ordered* sparse set. It will be assumed that values of type Entry may be compared using a complete ordering relation < (i.e., for any pair of distinct entries x and y, either x<y or y<x).

An obvious approach to implementation of an ordered sparse set in an array is to store the set members in *sorted* order. This approach makes it easy to implement smallest and iterative traversals in sorted order and allows binary search to be used; on the other hand, include and exclude will be very inefficient because array segments must be shifted left or right to preserve the ordering. Successive include operations implement an *insertion sort* of the set members.

EXERCISE 6.8 Why in this approach to implementation would it be advantageous to maintain the entries sorted in *decreasing* (rather than *increasing*) order?

A less obvious approach is to store the set members in *arbitrary* order, as before. Then include, exclude, and smallest may require a linear search (but no array shifting). Successive exclude operations on smallest members or iterative traversal in sorted order implement a *selection sort* of the sparse set.

EXERCISE 6.9 How should the implementation be designed so that a second search is not needed in the sequence e = S.smallest(); S.exclude(e);?

An implementation that allows fairly efficient implementations of all the operations is to maintain the array of set members as a *heap* with the smallest value at the root (i.e., so that A[i] < A[2*i] and A[i] < A[2*i+1] whenever the subscripts are in the range 1:n). Then A[1] is the smallest member, and operations include and exclude may be implemented to preserve the heap structure efficiently. An ordered traversal of the sparse set is essentially a *heapsort* of the array.

EXERCISE 6.10 Implement ordered sparse-set representations using each of the suggested strategies; in each case, state a representation invariant.

EXERCISE 6.11 Which of the sparse-set implementations of Exercise 5.12 may be augmented to support reasonably efficient *ordered* traversal operations?

EXERCISE 6.12 Use an ordered sparse set to implement a program that processes a long text and then outputs an alphabetically ordered "index" of all the words that occur (at least once) in the text. Use the same definition of a word as in Exercise 6.4.

6.2 Sparse Arrays

Professor Higgins is *still* dissatisfied with the course lists being generated. He wants the *names* of the students, as well as the student numbers, to appear in the course lists. It would not be acceptable simply to replace student numbers by student names: it may happen that more than one student has the same name, whereas student numbers are unique identifiers (or *keys*) for students.

6.2.1 INTERFACE

Eliza is beginning to realize that Professor Higgins seems to demand new features fairly frequently. She decides to design the database to support *arbitrary* "attribute" fields for each record in the database. She proposes the following modifications to the database interface:

- changing the include operation to take an additional parameter a of type Attr (i.e., attribute; initially, a student name, as a string):

```
void include(Entry e, Attr a);
/* post-cond: contains(e), key e maps to attribute a */
```

and

- adding the following function, which allows the application program to retrieve the attribute currently associated with e in the database:

```
Attr retrieve(Entry e);
/* returns the attribute of key e */
/* pre-cond: contains(e) */
```

Notice that by redefining type Attr, it will be possible to store and retrieve other kinds of information in and from records in the database.

If we assume the variable definitions

```
Entry StudentNum;
Attr StudentName;
```

some typical code fragments in an application program might be as follows:

- to enroll a student in the course,

```
if (CompMetaphys.contains(StudentNum))
  printf("This student has already been enrolled.\n");
else
  CompMetaphys.include(StudentNum, StudentName)
```

- to print out the name of a student in the course,

```
if (!CompMetaphys.contains(StudentNum))
  printf("This student is not currently enrolled.\n");
else
  printf("%s\n", CompMetaphys.retrieve(StudentNum));
```

- to change the name of a student in the course,

```
if (!CompMetaphys.contains(StudentNum))
  printf("This student is not currently enrolled.\n");
else
{ printf("Changing the name for %i ", StudentNum);
  printf("from %s ", CompMetaPhys.retrieve(StudentNum));
  printf("to %s.\n", StudentName);
  CompMetaphys.include(StudentNum, StudentName);
}
```

6.2.2 SPECIFICATION

What is a suitable abstract model for the expanded database? As a first approximation, one might try to view it as a (mathematical) *function* from the set of keys (student numbers) to the set of attributes (student names). In mathematics, if A and B are any sets, a *function* from A to B is a correspondence that associates to *every* member of A exactly *one* member of B; set A is termed the *domain* of the function, and B is its *co-domain* (or "range"). For example, the "squaring" function on the set of integers associates to every integer n the number n^2. The usual representation of a function from A to B in set theory is as a set of ordered pairs (a, b) such that $a \in A$, $b \in B$, and there is exactly one such pair for each element of A.

EXERCISE 6.13 How many functions are there from *A* to *B* if *A* is a one-element set? If *B* is a one-element set? If *B* is ∅ and *A* is nonempty? If *A* is ∅ and *B* is nonempty? If both *A* and *B* are ∅?

But our database can't realistically be viewed as a function on the set of *all* possible student numbers: it is only the relatively small subset of students actually enrolled in the course who must have their names recorded in the database. For the vast majority of student numbers, no student name need be recorded, nor even exist.

In mathematics, a function on a *subset* of a set *A* is termed a *partial function* on *A*. We will use the notation* $f: A \dashrightarrow B$ (with a "dashed" arrow) to indicate that *f* is a partial function from *A* to *B*, and *dom f* for the *domain (of definition)* of *f* (i.e., the subset of *A* for which *f* is defined).

The concept of a partial function is exactly what we need to model our augmented database: it may be viewed abstractly as a partial function F: Entry $\dashrightarrow$ Attr, where Entry is the type of all possible student numbers, Attr is the type of student names, and *dom* F is the subset of student numbers for the students currently enrolled in the course.

The basic operations for the database may then be specified as follows:

contains(e)	is interpreted as	e ∈ *dom* F
include(e, a)	is interpreted as	F(e) = a;
exclude(e)	is interpreted as	F = F − (e, F(e));
retrieve(e)	is interpreted as	F(e) (provided e ∈ *dom* F)

The assignment notation F(e) = a may be regarded as a convenient abbreviation for F = (F | e ↦ a), where (F | e ↦ a) denotes the (partial) function G that is like F except that e ∈ *dom* G and G(e) = a (cf. Section 4.2). Initially, we want *dom* F = {} (i.e., F should initially be the partial function such that F(e) is undefined for *every* e of type Entry).

6.2.3 IMPLEMENTATION

The closest data-structure analogue to the set-theoretic concept of partial function is the *array*. For example, the variable A defined by

```
Attr A[n];
```

is capable of storing *one* value A[i] of type Attr for *every* value i in the range 0:n-1, but any A[i] could also be "garbage" (i.e., effectively undefined). But an Attr array in C could not realistically be used as an implementation of the course database if *all* student numbers could be array indices: there are far too many possible student numbers. The crucial property of our database that allows an efficient representation is that the partial function it represents is defined for only a *sparse* subset of the set of *all* student numbers. A data structure

---

*The notations $f: A \rightarrowtail B$ and $f: A \rightharpoonup B$ (with a "broken" arrow head) are also in use.

that implements a partial function $f: A \dashrightarrow B$ such that *dom f* is a sparse sub-set of *A* will be termed a *sparse array*. They are also called maps, directories, dictionaries, symbol tables, and association lists.

It is usually possible to adapt any implementation of a sparse *set* to a repre-sentation of a sparse *array* (having the sparse set as its domain of definition) by adding variables for storing the attributes associated with set entries. For ex-ample, the implementations of Section 5.3 and 5.6 may be modified as shown in Program 6.1 to use an array B of attribute values in parallel with the ex-isting array A of "keys." When an entry is removed, the attribute value B[n] at position n as well as the key value A[n] at that position must be moved to position i. Note that function include must assign to the attribute variable B[i] corresponding to an entry A[i] even when it is an *existing* entry (and not merely when it is a *new* entry).

6.2.4 VERIFICATION

To document and verify the implementation, we need a representation invari-ant that relates the abstract model (partial function F) to its representation by variables A, B, n, and i. By simply changing S in the representation invariant for the sparse-set implementation of Program 5.7 to dom F, we obtain the fol-lowing three assertions:

- `ForAll (Entry e) e in A[0:n-1] iff e in dom F`

which asserts that the entries in A[0:n-1] represent the domain of definition of F;

- `|A[0:n-1]| == n`

which asserts that the entries in A[0:n-1] are distinct; and

- `0 <= i <= n && A[i] != A[0:i-1]`

which asserts the invariant properties of the cache variable i. To these, we need to add only the following:

- `ForAll (j=0, j<n) B[j] == F(A[j])`

which specifies the relation between the entries in B[0:n-1] and the values of partial function F.

EXERCISE 6.14 Verify that the conjunction of the assertions proposed here is an appro-priate representation invariant for the operations defined in Program 6.1.

EXERCISE 6.15 Read about struct objects in C and develop a SparseArray class that uses a single array of struct values rather than two parallel arrays. State a representa-tion invariant.

Program 6.1

```
class SparseArray
{ private:

  /* map f: Entry - - -> Attr */
  # define max 255
  Entry A[max+1];
  Attr B[max];
  int n;
  int i;

  void find(Entry x)
  {
    :
    ASSERT(i <= n && A[i] == x && x != A[0:i-1] )
  }

  public:

  SparseArray(void)   /* dom f = {} */
  { n=0; i=0; }

  bool contains(Entry e)   /* e in dom f? */
  { find(e); return i<n; }

  void include(Entry e, Attr a)   /* f(e) = a */
  { find(e);
    if (i==n)
    { if (n==max) error("the domain of this map is too large");
      n++;
    }
    B[i] = a;
  }

  void exclude(Entry e)   /* f = f - (e,f(e)) */
  { find(e);
    if (i<n)
    { n--;
      A[i] = A[n]; B[i] = B[n];
    }
  }

  Attr retrieve(Entry e)   /* f(e) */
  { ASSERT( e in dom f )
    find(e);
    if (i==n) error("this entry is not in the domain of the map");
    return B[i];
  }
};
```

EXERCISE 6.16 Modify the sparse-set implementations of Exercise 5.12 so that each implements a sparse array. State appropriate representation invariants.

EXERCISE 6.17 Discuss various ways to allow *traversals* through (the domain of) a sparse array. For each method you discuss, provide application code that would use the interface operations to print out a class list of student numbers and corresponding student names.

EXERCISE 6.18 Using a sparse array, augment the program you wrote in Exercise 6.12 so that it also outputs the total number of occurrences of each word in the text.

EXERCISE 6.19 Modify the program you wrote for Exercise 6.18 so that, instead of the number of occurrences of each word, it lists the set of line numbers of all the lines in which the word occurs. (A word might appear more than once in the same line.)

EXERCISE 6.20 Modify the program you wrote for Exercise 6.19 so that it lists the line number of all the lines in which any word occurs, together with the number of occurrences of the word in that line.

EXERCISE 6.21 Discuss the similarities and differences between a bag (Exercise 5.9) and a sparse array whose attributes are integers > 0.

6.3 Sequences

Many familiar data structures may be modeled as *sequences*. In mathematics, a sequence is simply an n-tuple $\langle x_0, x_2, \ldots, x_{n-1} \rangle$ of entries in a definite order. The entries need not be distinct or sorted; unlike the *set* $\{x_0, x_2, \ldots, x_{n-1}\}$, the position i of each entry x_i is significant. Various kinds of sequences are termed lists, n-tuples, streams, stacks, queues, deques, vectors, sequential files, and strings. In this section, we will write

- *nil* for the empty sequence (no components);
- $s \frown t$ for the concatenation of sequences s and t (in that order);
- *first s* for the first component of s (s must be nonempty);
- *rest s* for the sequence that results from deleting the first component of s (nonempty).

For example, the following might be the interface supported by a typical *stack* of entries of type Entry:

```
bool empty(void);
void push(Entry e);
Entry pop(void);
```

If we model a stack t by a sequence S (of components of type Entry), the interface operations may be specified as follows:

t.empty()	is interpreted as	$S = nil$
t.push(e);	is interpreted as	$S = \langle e \rangle \frown S;$
e = t.pop();	is interpreted as	$e = first\ S;\ \ S = rest\ S;$

EXERCISE 6.22 Assume the maximum depth of the stack is max and implement the stack interface using an array. State and verify a suitable representation invariant.

EXERCISE 6.23 Implement the stack interface using a singly linked list. State and verify informally a suitable representation invariant.

EXERCISE 6.24 In some applications, it is convenient to be able to refer directly to the top of stack t as a variable, as in

```
t.top++;
```

which should be equivalent in overall effect to

```
{ int i = t.pop();
  i++;
  t.push(i);
}
```

Revise the interface for stacks to allow this extension and adapt the implementation you gave in Exercise 6.22. State and verify a suitable representation invariant.

EXERCISE 6.25 Specify the desired behavior of the following interface for a *queue* of entries of type Entry:

```
int length(void);
void insert(Entry e);
Entry remove(void);
```

Implement the interface and verify your implementation using a suitable invariant.

It is not normally appropriate to *traverse* structures like stacks and queues. A sequence-based structure that *does* support traversals is the *sequential file*. Initially, the sequence is created by successively appending components. Then the structure may be put into "reading" mode and traversed, possibly only partially. After any number of such traversals, it may be re-initialized to be empty and put back into "writing" mode.

The following interface for a sequential file uses the same names for the operations as the file operations in PASCAL:

```
void write(Entry e);
void reset(void);
Entry read(void);
bool eof(void);
void rewrite(void);
```

We may give a formal specification using the following abstract declarations:

```
enum { writing, reading } mode;
sequence f, g;
```

with initialization

```
mode = writing; f = nil; g = nil;
```

During a traversal (while mode = reading), f and g will be, respectively, the traversed and not-yet-traversed subsequences. The interface operations are then interpreted as follows:

`write(e);`	is interpreted as	$f = f \frown \langle e \rangle$;
`reset();`	is interpreted as	`mode = reading;` $g = f$; $f = nil$;
`e = read();`	is interpreted as	$e = first\ g$; $f = f \frown \langle e \rangle$; $g = rest\ g$;
`eof()`	is interpreted as	$g == nil$
`rewrite();`	is interpreted as	`mode = writing;` $f = nil$; $g = nil$;

where `mode == writing` is a pre-condition to the `write` operation, and

> `mode == reading && !eof()`

is a pre-condition to the `read` operation.

Typical application-program code fragments are as follows:

- to create a sequential file `f`,

```
f.rewrite();
while (...)
{ Entry e;
  e = ... ;
  f.write(e);
}
```

- to traverse sequential file `f`,

```
f.reset();
while (!eof())
{ Entry e;
  e = f.read();
  ...e... ;
}
```

EXERCISE 6.26 Code implementations of the sequential-file interface using (a) an array; (b) a singly linked list; and (c) an operating-system file. In each case, provide an appropriate representation invariant.

6.4 Bit-String Representation of Sets

For sets that are *not* sparse, a completely different approach to representation is needed.

6.4.1 SMALL SETS OF SMALL INTEGERS

If the universe under consideration may be "normalized" to consist of integers within a range such as `0:n-1`, sets may be represented by `bool` vectors of length n. Each component represents the presence or absence of one possible member of the set. For example, up to eight values of type `bool` may typically be packed into a single `unsigned char` variable (and more, if necessary, in an `unsigned int` or `unsigned long int`). This kind of representation is termed a *bit string*. For example, the set $\{0, 1, 3, 4, 6\}$ might be represented in an `unsigned char` variable as follows:

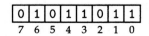

(using 1 for `true` and 0 for `false`). The empty set $\emptyset$ would be represented as

0	0	0	0	0	0	0	0
7	6	5	4	3	2	1	0

Note that once the representation size is decided, the same amount of storage space is used no matter how many actual members a set has.

The following table shows how various set-theoretic notations and operations may be implemented in C when this representation method is used:

$\emptyset$	`0`
$\{i\}$	`1<<i`
$i \in s$	`(s & 1<<i) != 0`
$s \cup t$	`s	t`
$s \cap t$	`s & t`
$s - t$	`s & ~t`
$s \subseteq t$	`s & t == s`
$s \subset t$	`(s & t == s) && (s != t)`

The "bitwise" `&`, `|`, and `~` operations make it possible to do union, intersection, and subtraction operations very efficiently, without using traversal loops.

It is often convenient when using bit-string representations of sets in C to define a `Set` type as follows:

```
typedef unsigned long int Set
```

and to define macros (or functions) such as the following:

```
# define contains(s, i) ((s & (1 << i)) != 0)
# define include(s, i) (s = s | (1 << i))
# define exclude(s, i) (s = s & ~(1 << i))
```

EXERCISE 6.27 How would the bit-string representation of the set $\{0, 1, 3, 4, 6\}$ be constructed?

EXERCISE 6.28 Explain how to traverse the members of a set s that is represented by a bit string.

EXERCISE 6.29 Another representation for nonsparse sets of integers in the range $0:n-1$ is to use a `bool` array `B[n]`. What are the advantages and disadvantages of this representation?

Program 6.2 on page 140 gives a nice example of how bit string-represented sets may be used effectively. The program is required to read two "sentences" of text and output each letter that appears in *both* of the sentences, where a sentence is defined to be any text terminated by a period, exclamation mark, or question mark. The library functions `isalpha` and `tolower` are described in

Program 6.2

```
typedef unsigned long int Set;

# define contains(s, i) ((s & (1 << i)) != 0)
# define include(s, i) (s = s | (1 << i))
# define exclude(s, i) (s = s & ~(1 << i))

int toInt(char ch) { return ch - 'a'; }

void OutputSet(Set s)
/* Traverses bit-string set s and outputs each member. */
{ ... }

Set LettersInSentence(void)
/* Reads a sentence and returns the set of all letters in it.
   Uppercase letters are mapped to lowercase.
*/
{ Set s = 0;
  int c = getc(stdin);
  while (c != '.' && c != '!' && c != '?' && c != EOF)
  { if (isalpha(c))
      include(s, toInt(tolower(c)));
    c = getc(stdin);
  }
  return s;
}

int main(void)
{ Set s1, s2, both;
  s1 = LettersInSentence();
  s2 = LettersInSentence();
  both = s1 & s2;
  OutputSet(both);
  return 0;
}
```

Section A.7.2. The function `toInt` subtracts the value of `'a'` from the letter to normalize the value into a sufficiently low range. No searching is necessary because bitwise intersection is used.

EXERCISE 6.30 Complete Program 6.2 by coding function `OutputSet`.

EXERCISE 6.31 Modify function `LettersInSentence` so that it defines and uses a set $\{\,'.\,',\,'!\,',\,'?\,'\}$ of sentence-terminating punctuation characters. Assume the ASCII character set.

6.4.2 LARGE SETS OF INTEGERS

Program 6.3 is a pseudo-code formulation of a classical algorithm known as the *sieve of Eratosthenes*. It determines all *prime* numbers (i.e., positive integers greater than 1 that are evenly divisible only by 1 and themselves) up to some maximum n. Initially, all positive integers greater than 1 (up to some maximum) are put into the sieve set; then all multiples of prime numbers (starting

Program 6.3

```
int n = ...;
Set sieve; /* { primes < n } <= sieve */

void sift(int p)   /* removes multiples of p from sieve */
{ int mp;
  mp = p*p;
  while (mp < n)
  { sieve = sieve - {mp};
    mp = mp + p;
  };
}

int main(void)
{ int p;
  sieve = { int i | 2 <= i < n};
  p = 2;
  while (p*p < n)
  INVAR( p prime && no multiples of primes < p in sieve )
  { sift(p);
    FACT( p prime implies Exists(prime q) p < q < p*p )
    do
      p++;
    while (p !in sieve);
  }
  ASSERT( ForAll (i=0, i<n) i in sieve => i is prime )
    :
  return 0;
}
```

with 2) are successively "sifted" out of the sieve until only prime numbers remain. Termination of the inner do loop is assured by the number-theoretic fact that, if p is any prime, there exists another prime that is larger than p but less than p^2.

For example, suppose $n = 32$; then the successive states of variable p and the sieve set are as follows:

p	sieve
2	2 3 4 5 6 7 8 9 10 11 12 13 14 15 16 17 18 19 20 21 22 23 24 25 26 27 28 29 30 31
3	2 3 5 7 9 11 13 15 17 19 21 23 25 27 29 31
5	2 3 5 7 11 13 17 19 23 25 29 31
7	2 3 5 7 11 13 17 19 23 29 31

At this point, p*p is greater than n, and the algorithm terminates. All the remaining sieve elements are primes.

EXERCISE 6.32 Explain why it is not necessary in sift to consider multiples of p *smaller* than p*p. (This answer will also explain why the outer loop in the main function may terminate when p*p $\geq$ n.)

EXERCISE 6.33 In Program 6.3, all even numbers are removed from the sieve in the first execution of the outer loop. Improve the efficiency by treating the integer 2 as a special case (i.e., use the sieve for *odd* numbers only).

How should the Set variable sieve be represented? The representations for *sparse* sets are not applicable here: although the set eventually becomes relatively sparse, it is initially almost "full." But a simple bit-string representation wouldn't be very useful because the largest integer that could be stored might in some implementations be as small as 31 and is unlikely to be larger than 127.

A representation suitable for a *large* set like sieve is an *array* of bit strings, as in the following:

```
typedef unsigned long int bitstring;
bitstring A[ArrayLimit];
```

The representation invariant is that A[i] records the membership information for integers in the range from i*BitLimit to (i+1)*BitLimit - 1, where BitLimit, the number of bits in a bit string, is implementation dependent but is always CHAR_BIT * sizeof(bitstring), where CHAR_BIT is normally 8 and is defined officially for each implementation in the limits library. Here is an interface suitable for our application:

```
bool contains(int i);     /* i in S? */
void include(int i);      /* S = S + {i}; */
void exclude(int i);      /* S = S - {i}; */
void complement(void);    /* S = ~S; */
```

Except for complement, these basic operations are the same as those used with *sparse* sets. The complement operation may be used to initialize the sieve efficiently.

EXERCISE 6.34 Rewrite Program 6.3 to use the operations of this interface.

The first three operations of the interface may be implemented for this representation as follows:

```
bool contains(int i)   /* i in S? */
{ return (A[i/BitLimit] & (1 << (i % BitLimit))) != 0; }

void include(int i)    /* S = S + {i}; */
{ A[i/BitLimit] = A[i/BitLimit] | (1 << (i % BitLimit)); }

void exclude(int i)    /* S = S - {i}; */
{ A[i/BitLimit] = A[i/BitLimit] & ~(1 << (i % BitLimit)); }
```

The operation i % b yields the remainder when i is divided by b.

EXERCISE 6.35 Implement the complement operation for this representation. Would it be feasible to augment the sparse-set interface to include a complement operation?

EXERCISE 6.36 Augment the large-set interface to allow traversal of the set; implement the new operations.

EXERCISE 6.37 Redo Exercise 6.33 using a large-set representation.

6.5 Reachability in a Directed Graph

The following diagram portrays an example of what is termed a *directed graph*,
a mathematical structure that arises in many applications:

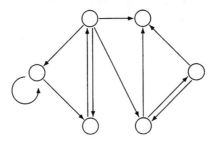

There is a set of *nodes* or *vertices* (drawn as circles) and *edges* between them. The
edges are *directed* (i.e., each edge goes *from* a node *to* a node, and there may or
may not be another edge in the reverse direction). There may be an edge from
a node to itself. If there is an edge from node i to node j, we say that j is *adjacent
to* i.

The edges of a finite directed graph may be modeled mathematically as a
function *adj* (abbreviation for "adjacent") from the set of nodes to sets of nodes,
as follows: for any node i, node $j \in adj(i)$ if and only if there is an edge from i
to j; that is, $adj(i)$ is the set of all nodes adjacent to node i.

For example, if the nodes of the example directed graph are numbered as
follows:

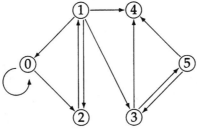

the corresponding *adj* function is as follows:

i	$adj(i)$
0	$\{0,2\}$
1	$\{0,2,3,4\}$
2	$\{1\}$
3	$\{4,5\}$
4	$\{\}$
5	$\{3,4\}$

Various representations of an *adj* function are possible. Here are two obvious representations if the nodes are numbered $0, 1, 2, \ldots, n - 1$:

- an array of n bit string-represented sets;

- an array of *n* sparse sets.

EXERCISE 6.38 Suppose that the node labels for a directed graph are drawn from a very large set, such as strings, rather than integers $0, 1, 2, \ldots, n - 1$. What would be an appropriate representation of the *adj* function?

In the remainder of this section, we will consider the following algorithmic problem: given the *adj* function of a finite directed graph and a "start" node *s*, determine the set of all nodes *reachable* from *s* in the graph, that is, the set of nodes *n* such that there exists a directed path (of any length, including 0) from *s* to *n*:

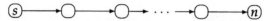

Trivially, *s* is reachable from itself, and every $i \in adj(s)$ is reachable from *s*, but also $j \in adj(i)$ is reachable from *s* if $i \in adj(s)$, and so on.

The basic procedure for determining the set R of nodes reachable from a starting node s is to initialize R to $\{s\}$ and then repeatedly to choose some appropriate node n in R and update R by the nodes adjacent to n:

    R = R ∪ *adj*(n);

The invariant properties of R are then as follows:

- $s \in R$

- ForAll (node i) $i \in R$ implies i reachable from s

But what is an "appropriate" node n to choose? And how do we ensure that this procedure terminates? The algorithm must certainly avoid indefinitely choosing the *same* node, and an efficient algorithm would avoid choosing the same node more than once.

To avoid infinite iteration and inefficiency, the algorithm must keep track of which nodes have not yet been "processed"; then, it will be possible to avoid choosing the same node for processing more than once.

Suppose that we introduce a set variable U to keep track of the subset of reachable nodes that are *unprocessed*; that is, the following assertions are also to be invariants of the main loop:

- $U \subseteq R$

- ForAll (node i) $i \in (R-U)$ implies adj(i) $\subseteq R$

The second assertion states that, if node i is reachable but *not* in U, all nodes adjacent to i have already been added to R.

The reachability algorithm is then as follows, where Node is a defined type of node labels:

```
R = {s}; U = {s};
while (U != ∅)
{ Node n;
   n = U.choice(); U.exclude(n);
   for (m ∈ adj(n))
      if (m ∉ R) { R = R ∪ {m}; U = U ∪ {m}; }
}
```

EXERCISE 6.39 Explain why this algorithm will always terminate.

EXERCISE 6.40 Assume that nodes are labeled $0, 1, 2, \ldots, n-1$ and that n, the number of nodes, is sufficiently small to allow a bit-string representation; show how to implement the reachability algorithm using bit-string representations of sets R and U. Try to avoid traversing the set $adj(n)$ by using bit-string operations.

EXERCISE 6.41 Implement the reachability algorithm using sparse-set representations of R and U. If the SparseSet interface supports an insert operation (of a *new* element, as in Exercise 5.8), how many include calls may be replaced by more efficient calls to insert?

There is also a way to represent R and U *jointly*, rather than as unrelated sets. The use of a subset U that is being traversed may remind the reader of the abstract model used for in-place set traversals in Section 6.1.2. Is it possible to represent both set R and subset U in the *same* array? The key difference between a conventional sparse-set traversal and the reachability algorithm considered here is that, in the latter, it is essential to be able to add entries to the "unprocessed" subset. This constraint precludes some sparse-set representations, such as a hash table; however, a partially filled array representation is feasible if the array is partitioned into segments as follows:

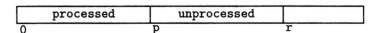

where r is the number of nodes known to be reachable and $p \le r$ is the number of those nodes already processed. The "unprocessed" array segment acts essentially as a queue of nodes, with new entries inserted at position r and entries chosen for processing (in place!) at position p.

EXERCISE 6.42 Implement the reachability algorithm using the joint array-based representation of R and U just described.

6.6   Sorting a Partially Ordered Set

The following diagram portrays some course-prerequisite requirements:

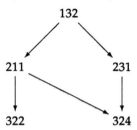

Here the numbers are course names and $a \rightarrow b$ means that course a is a pre-requisite to course b; we say that a precedes b and b is a successor of a. This kind of structure is known as a *partially ordered set* (or *poset*) and arises in many applications.

A binary relation $\rightarrow$ on a set S is termed a *(strict) partial order* if it is both

- transitive (i.e., if $a \rightarrow b$ and $b \rightarrow c$ then $a \rightarrow c$) and

- irreflexive (i.e., for no a is $a \rightarrow a$).

In the preceding diagram, arrows have been omitted when they may be inferred from transitivity; for example, $132 \rightarrow 322$ because $132 \rightarrow 211 \rightarrow 322$, but the arrow from 132 to 322 has been omitted in the diagram.

EXERCISE 6.43 If $\rightarrow$ is any strict partial order, show that it is asymmetric; that is, if $a \rightarrow b$, it is not the case that $b \rightarrow a$.

EXERCISE 6.44

(a) For any strict partial order $\rightarrow$, define a relation $\leq$ by $a \leq b$ if and only if $a \rightarrow b$ or $a = b$; show that $\leq$ satisfies the following conditions:

- transitivity;
- reflexivity (i.e., $a \leq a$); and
- antisymmetry (i.e., if $a \leq b$ and $b \leq a$ then $a = b$).

(b) Show that if $\leq$ is *any* binary relation satisfying the preceding three conditions, the relation $<$ defined by $a < b$ if and only if $a \leq b$ and $a \neq b$ is a strict partial order.

Suppose that S is a set of n items and $\rightarrow$ is a strict partial order on S. A *(topological) sort* of the poset $(S, \rightarrow)$ is an enumeration $s_0, s_1, \ldots, s_{n-1}$ of (all) the elements of S such that, whenever $s_i \rightarrow s_j$ in the partial order, s_i precedes s_j in the enumeration (i.e., a complete ordering of S that respects the partial ordering). In general, a poset may be sortable in more than one way.

In our prerequisite example, a calendar describing the courses in the order specified by any sort of the poset would not describe a course before any of its prerequisites. For example, 132, 211, 322, 231, 324 is a sort of the preceding example poset, as is 132, 231, 211, 324, 322, but 211, 132, ... is not. In this example, the course names themselves taken in numerical order also give a sort, but this property can't be relied upon in general because the elements of S might be arbitrary data.

6.6.1 THE MAIN PROGRAM

A variant of selection sort may be used to sort any finite poset. An element $m \in S$ is *minimal* in poset $(S, \rightarrow)$ if there is no $s \in S$ such that $s \rightarrow m$. There may be several minimal elements in a poset, but any finite poset has at least one minimal element; furthermore, if any minimal element is removed, what remains is still a poset. So the following algorithm may be used to sort $(S, \rightarrow)$:

while S is nonempty,
- choose and remove a minimal element m from S;
- output m.

Program 6.4 inputs the description of any small poset $(S, \rightarrow)$ and then uses the preceding algorithm to output a sort. Poset is assumed to have been defined as a class with the following interface:

```
void precedes(Entry x, Entry y); /* make x -> y */
bool empty(void);       /* S == {}? */
Entry minimal(void); /* a minimal element of S (nonempty) */
void ExcludeMinimal(Entry m);    /* S = S - {m}, m minimal */
```

Program 6.4

```
Poset p;
void ConstructPoset(void)
{ int x, y;
  char ch;
  printf("Enter pairs x y such that x precedes y: \n");
  while (!eof())
  { if (scanf("%i%i\n", &x, &y) != 2) error("input failure");
    printf("%i -> %i\n", x, y);
    p.precedes(x, y);
  }
}

void SortPoset(void)
{ int m;
  while (!p.empty())
  { m = p.minimal();
    p.ExcludeMinimal(m);
    printf("%i", m);
    if (!p.empty()) printf(", ");
  }
  putchar('\n');
}

int main(void) { ConstructPoset(); SortPoset(); return 0; }
```

The user defines the ordering by entering pairs x y, meaning x → y. It isn't necessary to enter relationships that may be inferred by transitivity (such as 132 → 322 in our example), but it is not erroneous to do so.

6.6.2 THE POSET CLASS: A SIMPLE IMPLEMENTATION

A simple implementation of the Poset class uses an *array* A to record, for each item $a \in S$, the set of remaining successor nodes (of those entered using precedes), and a count NumPredecessors of the number of predecessors remaining (of those entered using precedes). This is achieved by defining A to be an array of Attr values, where Attr is defined to be a struct type as follows:

```
struct
{ Set successors;
  int NumPredecessors;
}
```

For example, the defined components of the array for our example poset would be as follows:

	successors	NumPredecessors
132	{211,231}	0
211	{322,324}	1
231	{324}	1
322	{}	1
324	{}	2

For efficiency, a set Min of all *minimal* elements in the poset is also maintained: when the NumPredecessors field for entry b (i.e., the number of predecessors of b) goes to zero (because all items a such that $a \rightarrow b$ have already been removed), b is added to the set of minimal elements. For our example, the initial value of Min would be the singleton set {132} because it is the only item that initially has no predecessors. Without Min, it would be necessary to traverse the poset to find minimal entries.

A Poset class that uses this representation is shown in Program 6.5. Function precedes is responsible for adding its arguments x and y to S if they are new items, possibly adding y to the set of successors for x, and incrementing the number of predecessors for y, and excluding y from the subset of minimal elements. If x is a new item, it is included in Min.

Function ExcludeMinimal is responsible for removing its argument m from S and from Min and for decrementing the predecessor counts of all successor items e. This is done by traversing the set of successors of m; it is not necessary to restore this set after traversal because m is being removed from the poset. If the NumPredecessors count of any such item e gets reduced to zero, e is added to the subset of minimal elements.

Program 6.5

```
class Poset
{ private:

  Set S;    /* the set of entries in the poset */

  typedef struct
  { Set successors;
    int NumPredecessors;
  } Attr;

  Attr A[SetLimit];
  Set Min;  /* the subset of minimal entries */

  public:

  Poset(void) { S = 0; Min = 0; }

  void precedes(int x, int y)  /* make x -> y */
  { if (!contains(S, x))
    { include(S, x);
      A[x].successors = 0;
      A[x].NumPredecessors = 0;
      include(Min, x);
    }
    if (!contains(S, y))
    { include(S, y);
      A[y].successors = 0;
      A[y].NumPredecessors = 0;
    }
    if (!contains(A[x].successors, y))
    { include(A[x].successors, y);
      A[y].NumPredecessors++;
    }
    exclude(Min, y);
  } /* end precedes */

  bool empty(void) { return (S == 0); }

  int minimal(void) { return choice(Min); }

  void ExcludeMinimal(int m) /* S = S - {m}; (m minimal) */
  { exclude(Min, m);
    exclude(S, m);
    while (A[m].successors != 0)
    { int e = choice(A[m].successors);
      exclude(A[m].successors, e);
      A[e].NumPredecessors--;
      if (A[e].NumPredecessors == 0)
        include(Min, e);
    } /* end successor loop */
  } /* end ExcludeMinimal */

}; /* end Poset */
```

For example, after the first call of ExcludeMinimal, the value of S has become {211,231,322,324}, Min is {211,231}, and array A is as follows:

	successors	NumPredecessors
132	{}	0
211	{322,324}	0
231	{324}	0
322	{}	1
324	{}	2

Note that there are now *two* minimal elements in S to choose between.

EXERCISE 6.45 What will happen if the user enters a prerequisite "loop," such as $a \rightarrow b$ and $b \rightarrow a$? Implement a more robust approach that produces a good error message and then aborts execution.

EXERCISE 6.46 Does the implementation work correctly if $a \rightarrow b$ is entered more than once?

6.6.3 THE POSET CLASS: A MORE FLEXIBLE IMPLEMENTATION

If the number of possible entries is sufficiently small, the Set objects used in Program 6.5 may be represented by bit strings or arrays of bit strings. But in many applications, the number of possible entries is too large to allow a bit-string implementation. It is then necessary to replace the Set objects by sparse sets and the array variable by a sparse array with keys of type Entry and attributes of type Attr, now redefined to be

```
struct
{ SparseSet successors;
  int NumPredecessors;
}
```

where SparseSet is assumed to be an existing class of sparse-set objects (with elements of type Entry). We also assume a suitable SparseArray class (with at least operations contains, include, retrieve, exclude, empty, and choice).

The revised Poset class is given in Program 6.6. The first implementation was used as a prototype. Operations on bit string-represented sets have been replaced by corresponding sparse-set operations. Similarly, updates of array components have been replaced by code that retrieves the appropriate attribute from the sparse array, updates a local copy, and finally stores the updated attribute back into the sparse array. For example, A[e].NumPredecessors-- in ExcludeMinimal is replaced by the sequence

```
eAttr = A.retrieve(e);
eAttr.NumPredecessors--;
A.include(e, eAttr);
```

Program 6.6

```
class Poset
{ private:

  SparseSet Min; /* elements of type Entry */
  SparseArray A; /* keys of type Entry; attributes of type Attr */

  public:

  void precedes(Entry x, Entry y)  /* make x --> y */
  { Attr xAttr, yAttr;
    if (!A.contains(x))
    { xAttr.NumPredecessors = 0;
      Min.include(x);
    }
    else xAttr = A.retrieve(x);
    if (!A.contains(y))
      yAttr.NumPredecessors = 0;
    else yAttr = A.retrieve(y);
    if (!xAttr.successors.contains(y))
    { xAttr.successors.include(y);
      yAttr.NumPredecessors++;
    }
    A.include(x, xAttr);
    A.include(y, yAttr);
    Min.exclude(y);
  } /* end precedes */

  bool empty(void) { return A.empty(); }

  Entry minimal(void) { return Min.choice(); }

  void ExcludeMinimal(Entry m) /* S = S - {m}; (m minimal) */
  { Attr mAttr = A.retrieve(m);
    Min.exclude(m);
    A.exclude(m);
    while (!mAttr.successors.empty())
    { Entry e = mAttr.successors.choice();
      Attr eAttr;
      mAttr.successors.exclude(e);
      eAttr = A.retrieve(e);
      eAttr.NumPredecessors--;
      A.include(e, eAttr);
      if (eAttr.NumPredecessors == 0)
        Min.include(e);
    } /* end successor loop */
  } /* end ExcludeMinimal */

}; /* end Poset */
```

There is no need to represent set S itself because that information is available by using `A.contains(...)`.

EXERCISE 6.47 Consider Program 6.7, which uses bit string-represented sets to schedule exams in parallel sessions, avoiding conflicts that would require a student to attend more than one exam in a session.

For example, if the input is

```
101, 102, 104, 106, 110;
103, 105, 106, 109;
102, 106, 107, 108, 109, 110;
101, 103, 105, 107, 110;
101, 102, 106, 108, 111.
```

where each line gives the list of courses taken by one of the students, the output is

```
Schedule together courses 101 109
Schedule together courses 102 103
Schedule together courses 104 105 108
Schedule together courses 106
Schedule together courses 107 111
Schedule together courses 110
```

Array variable `conflict` is determined in function `ReadData` as follows: c1 is to be in `conflict[c2]` if and only if, for some student, both c1 and c2 are in the set of courses taken by that student. (As a result, c is in `conflict[c]` for every course c, but this is harmless.) The extension `for (num in S)...` has been used for set traversal in two places (cf. Exercise 6.28).

Re-write this program so that NC (the upper limit for course numbers) is allowed to be larger than `CHAR_BIT*sizeof(unsigned long int)`.

6.7 Additional Reading

See [Hoa72a] for a detailed discussion of a large-set representation similar to that described in Section 6.4.2. The treatment of directed-graph reachability is based on [Rey81, Section 5.1]. Topological sorting is used as an example (of linked data representations) in [Knu68, Wir76]. Exam timetabling (Exercise 6.47) is discussed in [Hoa72b, Wir76].

We have not discussed formal reasoning about *linked* representations; see [ORY01] for recent work in this area. A rigorous treatment of "underdetermined" operations such as `choice()` is given in [Den98].

REFERENCES

[Den98]   E. W. K. C. Denney. *A Theory of Program Refinement*. PhD thesis, University of Edinburgh, Laboratory for Foundations of Computer Science, 1998. Available here: `http://www.dcs.ed.ac.uk/home/lfcsreps/`.

[HJ89]   C. A. R. Hoare and C. B. Jones, editors. *Essays in Computing Science*. Prentice Hall International, 1989.

Program 6.7

```c
typedef unsigned long int Set;
# define contains(A, s) ((A & (1 << s)) != 0)
# define include(A, s) (A = A | (1 << s))
# define exclude(A,s) (A = A & ~(1 << s))
# define NC CHAR_BIT * sizeof(Set) /* course numbers < NC */

Set conflict[NC];
Set unscheduled; /* courses with exams to be scheduled */

void ReadData(void) /* Read data, determine conflict and unscheduled */
{ int c, num;
  unscheduled = 0;
  for (num=0; num < NC; num++) conflict[num] = 0;
  do /* read registration data for students, separated by ; */
  { Set registration;
    registration = 0;
    do /* read course numbers, separated by , */
    { if (scanf("%i", &num) != 1) error("input failure");
      include(registration, num);
      c = getc(stdin);
    } while ( c == ',');
    for (num in registration)
      conflict[num] = conflict[num] | registration;
    unscheduled = unscheduled | registration;
  } while (c == ';');
}

void ScheduleExams(void)
{ Set session; /* courses with exams scheduled together */
  int num;
  while (unscheduled != 0)
  { session = 0;
    printf("Schedule together courses");
    for (num in unscheduled)
      if ((conflict[num] & session) == 0)
      { printf(" %i", num);
        include(session, num);
      }
    putchar('\n');
    unscheduled = unscheduled & ~(session);
  }
}

int main(void) { ReadData(); ScheduleExams(); return 0; }
```

[Hoa72a] C. A. R. Hoare. Proof of a structured program: 'The sieve of Eratosthenes'. *Computer Journal*, 15(4):321–5, 1972. Reprinted in [HJ89], pages 117–32.

[Hoa72b] C. A. R. Hoare. Notes on data structuring. In O.-J. Dahl, E. W. Dijkstra, and C. A. R. Hoare, *Structured Programming*, pages 83-174. Academic Press, 1972.

[Knu68] D. E. Knuth. *Fundamental Algorithms*, volume 1 of *The Art of Computer*

Programming. Addison-Wesley, 1968.

[ORY01]   Peter O'Hearn, John Reynolds, and Hongseok Yang. Local reasoning about programs that alter data structures. In *Proceedings of 15th Annual Conference of the European Association for Computer Science Logic: CSL 2001*, volume 2142 of *Lecture Notes in Computer Science*, pages 1–19, Paris, France, 2001. Springer-Verlag.

[Rey81]   J. C. Reynolds. *The Craft of Programming*. Prentice Hall International, 1981.

[Wir76]   N. Wirth. *Algorithms + Data Structures = Programs*. Prentice Hall, 1976.

Part C

Language Recognizers

Introduction to Part C

We now consider specification and construction techniques tailored to a particular application domain: code that is intended to test whether arbitrary input strings may be matched by a specific "pattern." The pattern itself is essentially the specification for such a program, and a variety of *specialized* notations and implementation techniques have been developed to allow convenient expression and realization of such specifications. Although the methods are specialized to the application, the key principles of formal methods—distinguishing between specification and realization, adopting appropriate formalized notation for specifications, and using systematic or verifiable methods of program construction—are still relevant. Chapter 7 introduces the basic concepts, and Chapters 8 to 11 discuss various styles of pattern specification and how they may be systematically transformed and realized.

Additional Reading

Many books cover this material, usually from either a primarily theoretical perspective [HU79, MAK88, LP98] or a compiler-oriented one [ASU86]; [Gou88, AU92, HMU01] are closest to the approach adopted here.

REFERENCES

[ASU86] A. V. Aho, R. Sethi, and J. D. Ullman. *Compiler Design: Principles, Techniques, and Tools.* Addison-Wesley, 1986.

[AU92] A. V. Aho and J. D. Ullman. *Foundations of Computer Science.* W. H. Freeman, 1992.

[Gou88] K. J. Gough. *Syntax Analysis and Software Tools.* Addison-Wesley, 1988.

[HMU01] J. E. Hopcroft, R. Motwani, and J. D. Ullman. *Introduction to Automata Theory, Languages, and Computation.* Addison-Wesley, 2001.

[HU79] J. E. Hopcroft and J. D. Ullman. *Introduction to Automata Theory, Languages, and Computation.* Addison-Wesley, 1979.

[LP98] H. R. Lewis and C. H. Papadimitriou. *Elements of the Theory of Computation,* 2nd edition. Prentice Hall, 1998.

[MAK88] R. N. Moll, M. A. Arbib, and A. J. Kfoury. *An Introduction to Formal Language Theory.* Springer Verlag, 1988.

Chapter 7

Basic Concepts

Recognizing patterns in strings is ubiquitous in computing. For example, a programming-language compiler has to recognize whether input programs match the "pattern" defined by the syntax rules of the programming language. Many important software tools, such as text editors, command interpreters, and formatters, require the capability to recognize patterns in strings. In fact, any program that reads textual input from its users must implicitly test the well-formedness of that input. In the following chapters, we introduce some of the interesting concepts and techniques that may be used to address this class of applications.

7.1   Strings

In computing, the term *string* is normally understood to refer to finite sequences of characters drawn from a character set such as ASCII. We will find it convenient to generalize this concept slightly by allowing string components to be drawn from an *arbitrary* finite set, termed the *alphabet* or the *vocabulary*.

DEFINITION 7.1 If Σ is any finite set, a *string over* Σ is any finite sequence of elements of Σ.

Strings may also be termed *words* or *sentences*. String components (i.e., elements of Σ) might be termed, depending on the context, *characters, tokens, symbols, atoms,* or *generators*. If Σ is the ASCII character set, a string over Σ is exactly what is normally considered to be a string. But if we are discussing the syntax of a programming language, the relevant vocabulary might be a set of *lexical tokens*, ignoring, at this level of abstraction, the substructure of multiple-character tokens such as <=.

Usually, the elements of an alphabet Σ will be represented by single-character symbols, such as a, b, c, $\ldots$, or 0 and 1, and we will write strings as follows: abc, aaa, a, 0101, 0, and so on, without quotation marks, commas, brackets, or other unnecessary syntactic baggage. This means that a single-component string is not distinguished notationally from the character itself, but it will always be clear from context which interpretation is intended.

We consider the *empty* sequence of characters to be a string, termed the *empty* string. We use the symbol ε to denote the empty string, implicitly assuming that ε is not an element of the alphabet.

If s and t are arbitrary strings over some alphabet Σ, we write $s \cdot t$ or st for the string obtained by *concatenating* (joining up) s and t (in that order). We will usually omit an explicit concatenation operator; this convention is similar to the use of an implicit multiplication operator in elementary algebra. Because concatenation is an associative operation, we may write stu rather than $(st)u$ or $s(tu)$, and mix strings and tokens, as in sct when $c \in \Sigma$. The following properties hold for any string s: $\varepsilon s = s = s\varepsilon$ (i.e., ε is the identity for string concatenation).

If n is any nonnegative integer, and s is a string, we will use s^n as an abbreviation for the concatenation of n copies of s; that is, for

$$\underbrace{s\, s \cdots s}_{n \text{ factors}}$$

In particular, for *any* string s, $s^1 = s$, and $s^0 = \varepsilon$.

If $s = c_0 c_1 \cdots c_{n-1}$ is a string over Σ, we use s^R to denote the *reversal* of s (i.e., the string $c_{n-1} \cdots c_1 c_0$). Of course, $(s^R)^R = s$ for all strings s, $a^R = a$ for all tokens $a \in \Sigma$, and $\varepsilon^R = \varepsilon$. A string that is equal to its own reversal ($s^R = s$) is called a *palindrome*.

If a string w may be obtained as a concatenation $x \cdot y \cdot z$ of strings x, y, and z (any of which may be ε), we say x is a *prefix* of w, z is a *suffix* of w, and y is a *substring* of w. Note that any string w is trivially a prefix, a suffix, and a substring of itself, and ε is a trivial prefix, suffix, and substring of any string.

7.2   Formal Languages

The set of *all* strings (including ε) over an alphabet Σ is denoted Σ^* and is termed the *closure* of Σ. For many applications, it is necessary to define particular *subsets* of Σ^*.

DEFINITION 7.2 If Σ is any finite set, a *(formal) language over* Σ is any well-defined set of strings over Σ.

Here are some examples of languages:

- if Σ is the ASCII character set, the set of all legal identifiers for some programming language;

- if $\Sigma = \{I, V, X, L, C, D, M\}$, the set of all well-formed Roman numerals, such as MXLIV;

- if $\Sigma = \{0, 1\}$, the set of all strings with an *even* number of 1s:

$$\{\varepsilon, 0, 00, 11, 000, 011, 101, 110, \dots\}$$

The empty string ε might or might not be an element of a particular language; but the empty *language*, which we denote by $\emptyset$ or $\{\}$, is a *subset* of every language; that is, if L is a language (over any alphabet), $\emptyset \subseteq L$. A language may consist of a *finite* set of strings; however, most of the languages we need to consider will be *infinite* (i.e., not finite).

The three key problems that will be addressed in our study of formal languages are as follows.

(a) Specification: we will develop formalized notations for giving rigorous definitions of specific formal languages of interest (particularly infinite languages, whose elements we cannot simply list explicitly).

(b) Realization: we will describe systematic methods for programming *recognizers* for the formal languages of interest (i.e., programs to decide whether any given input string is, or is not, an element of the language).

(c) Classification: we will organize the space of all formal languages into a hierarchy of classes that correspond to specification and realization complexities and establish equivalences between classes of languages defined in different ways.

For example, a programmer needs both a *specification* of the syntax of a programming language and a compiler that (correctly) *realizes* that specification; to implement the compiler, the compiler writer may need to know that the programming language lies within a certain *class* of formal languages.

Because formal languages are *sets* (of strings), we may define them using conventional set-theoretic notation, such as "set formers" of the form $\{s \in \Sigma^* \mid P(s)\}$, where $P(s)$ is a property that characterizes all the strings s in the intended language over Σ. For example, the language of all palindromes over an alphabet Σ may be defined as follows: $\{s \in \Sigma^* \mid s = s^R\}$. We may also use familiar operations on sets (or define new operations on sets of strings) to construct languages from simpler ones. In the following section, we discuss the most important of these operations.

7.3   Basic Operations on Languages

7.3.1   UNION

If S and T are formal languages, the *union* of S and T consists of all strings that are in S or in T or in both. We could use the traditional notation $S \cup T$, but more often we will use the notation $S + T$. The notation $S \mid T$ will also be used. Sometimes the operation is called *alternation*.

We adopt the following notational convention: if a single string s is used where a *language* is expected, the language is taken to be the singleton language $\{s\}$. This convention also applies to the empty string ε, and to single-token strings, such as $a, b, c, 0, 1$, and the like. For example, if s and T is a language, $s + T$ is an abbreviation for $\{s\} + T$ and $\varepsilon + 1$ is an abbreviation for $\{\varepsilon\} + \{1\}$.

For arbitrary languages R, S and T, the following properties hold.

Commutativity: $S + T = T + S$

Associativity: $R + (S + T) = (R + S) + T$

Identity: $\varnothing + S = S = S + \varnothing$

Idempotence: $S + S = S$

A consequence of associativity is that it is not ambiguous to omit parentheses when forming n-ary unions: $S_0 + S_1 + \cdots + S_{n-1}$.

EXERCISE 7.1 Verify the preceding properties directly from the definitions of union and the empty set.

EXERCISE 7.2 Define operations of language *intersection* and *complementation*, and list their most important properties.

7.3.2   CONCATENATION

We have already considered the operation of concatenation on *strings*; we may also define a concatenation operation on *languages* (sets of strings): if S and T are formal languages, the concatenation $S \cdot T$ or ST consists of all strings that may be obtained by concatenating a string in S with a string in T (in that order). Because of our convention on "promotion" of strings to single-element languages, if s is a string and T is a language, sT denotes the set of all strings that may be formed by concatenating s and an element of T, and similarly for aT if a is a token.

The following properties hold for arbitrary formal languages R, S, and T.

Associativity: $R(ST) = (RS)T$

Identity: $\varepsilon S = S = S\varepsilon$

Zero: $\emptyset S = \emptyset = S\emptyset$

Left Distributivity: $R(S + T) = RS + RT$

Right Distributivity: $(R + S)T = RT + ST$

EXERCISE 7.3 Verify the preceding properties directly from the definitions.

The operation of language concatenation is sometimes termed the language *product*, and it does have many of the properties of numerical multiplication; however, in general, concatenation is *not* commutative: ST may not be the same as TS.

If n is any nonnegative integer, and S is a language, we will use S^n as an abbreviation for

$$\underbrace{S\,S \cdots S}_{n \text{ factors}}$$

In particular, for *any* language S, $S^1 = S$, and $S^0 = \varepsilon$, because ε is the identity for language concatenation.

If $S = \{ab, bc\}$ and $T = \{c, d\}$, the following are some of the languages that may be defined by concatenation:

- $ST = \{abc, abd, bcc, bcd\}$
- $TS = \{cab, cbc, dab, dbc\}$
- $bT = \{bc, bd\}$
- $Sd = \{abd, bcd\}$
- $S^2 = \{abab, abbc, bcab, bcbc\}$
- $T^3 = \{ccc, ccd, cdc, cdd, dcc, dcd, ddc, ddd\}$

EXERCISE 7.4 Is the following true for all $n \geq 0$: $\emptyset^n = \emptyset$?

7.3.3 CLOSURE

We have already explained that Σ^*, the *closure* of alphabet Σ, is the set of all strings over Σ. We may extend this operation to any *language* S as follows:

$$S^* = \{s_0 s_1 \cdots s_{n-1} \mid \text{for all } 0 \leq i < n, s_i \in S\} = \varepsilon + S + S^2 + S^3 + \cdots$$

That is, S^* is the set of all strings composed by concatenating any finite number (including zero) of strings in S. The n substrings s_i are all required to be elements of S but do *not* have to be equal. Both $\emptyset^*$ and ε^* are the language whose only element is the empty string; however, for any other language S, even a finite one, S^* is an *infinite* language. For example, if $S = \{ab, c\}$,

$$S^* = \{\varepsilon, ab, c, abc, cab, abab, cc, ababab, abcab, cabab, \ldots\}$$

Many languages of interest may be defined from vocabulary tokens and ε using union, concatenation, and closure. Here are some examples; in each case, the alphabet is $\{0, 1\}$. We assume the following precedence hierarchy, from highest to lowest: closure, concatenation, and union.

- All strings that end in a 1: $(0 + 1)^*1$.

- All strings with exactly one 1: 0^*10^*.

- All strings with at most one 1: $0^*(\varepsilon + 1)0^*$.

- All strings with at least one 1: $(0 + 1)^*1(0 + 1)^*$.

- All strings with an even number of 1s: $(0 + 10^*1)^*$.

EXERCISE 7.5 Suppose $\Sigma = \{0, 1\}$. Show how to define the following languages over Σ using only ε, tokens 0 and 1, and the operations of union, concatenation, and closure.

(a) All strings that begin with 0 and end with 1.

(b) All strings except the empty string.

(c) All strings that have at least two 1s.

(d) All strings of even length.

(e) All strings such that all odd-numbered (first, third, fifth, ...) character positions are 0s.

(f) All strings that have 010 as a suffix.

(g) All strings that have 010 as a substring.

(h) All strings such that every run of 1s is of even length; for example, 011000111100, but not 0110010.

7.3.4 RECURSION

Language closure involves a form of *iteration*; languages may also be defined using *recursion* (i.e., definition of a language in terms of itself). For example, consider the following: $B = \varepsilon + 0B1$; this is an *equation* with "unknown" B. The equation may be interpreted as saying that B is a language such that

- the empty string ε is an element of B;

- for any $b \in B$, $0b1$ is also in B; and

- these are the only elements of B.

It is easily verified that if the set $\{0^i 1^i \mid i \geq 0\} = \{\varepsilon, 01, 0011, 000111, \ldots\}$ of all "balanced" strings over $\{0, 1\}$ is substituted for B in $B = \varepsilon + 0B1$, the equation is satisfied; that is, the right-hand side ($\varepsilon + 0B1$) denotes the same set of strings as B:

$$
\begin{aligned}
\varepsilon + 0B1 &= \varepsilon + 0\{0^i 1^i \mid i \geq 0\}1 \\
&= \varepsilon + \{0^i 1^i \mid i > 0\} \\
&= 0^0 1^0 + \{0^i 1^i \mid i > 0\} \\
&= \{0^i 1^i \mid i \geq 0\} \\
&= B
\end{aligned}
$$

EXERCISE 7.6 Show that neither of the languages $\{0^i 1^i \mid i > 0\}$ or $0^* 1^*$ satisfy the equation.

As another example, the language $P = \{s \in \Sigma^* \mid s = s^R\}$ of all *palindromes* over $\Sigma = \{0, 1\}$ (i.e., strings equal to their own reversal) may be defined by the equation $P = \varepsilon + 0 + 1 + 0P0 + 1P1$. This equation says that

- ε, 0, and 1 are all elements of P;

- if $p \in P$, so is cpc, for any $c \in \Sigma$; and

- these are the only elements of P.

EXERCISE 7.7 Verify that the set of all palindromes over $\{0, 1\}$ satisfies the equation for P.

EXERCISE 7.8 (a) Verify that the language $\{0^i 10^j \mid i, j \geq 0\}$ satisfies the following equation: $L = 1 + 0L + L0$. (b) Also, verify that the language $\{0^i 1^i \mid i \geq 0\}$ does *not* satisfy the equation.

FACT 7.1 In general, if F is any language transformer (i.e., function from languages to languages) defined using only ε, vocabulary tokens, and the operations of union and concatenation, the equation $L = F(L)$ may be solved as follows. If $L_0 = \varnothing$ and, for $j = 0, 1, 2, \ldots$, $L_{j+1} = F(L_j)$, the language $L = \bigcup_{j \geq 0} L_j$ satisfies the equation $L = F(L)$. Furthermore, L is the *smallest* solution; that is, if L' is any language such that $F(L') = L'$, then $L \subseteq L'$.

For example, if $F(L) = \varepsilon + 0L1$, we get

$$L_0 = \emptyset$$
$$L_1 = \varepsilon + 0\emptyset 1 = \{\varepsilon\}$$
$$L_2 = \varepsilon + 0\varepsilon 1 = \{\varepsilon, 01\}$$
$$L_3 = \{\varepsilon, 01, 0011\}$$
$$L_4 = \{\varepsilon, 01, 0011, 000111\}$$
$$\vdots$$

It is now evident (and may be proved by mathematical induction) that, for all $j \geq 0$, $L_j = \{0^i 1^i \mid 0 \leq i < j\}$, and so $L = \bigcup_{j \geq 0} L_j = \{0^i 1^i \mid i \geq 0\}$.

EXERCISE 7.9 Determine the L_j when $F(L) = \varepsilon + 0 + 1 + 0L0 + 1L1$.

EXERCISE 7.10 Describe informally or using set-former notation $\{\cdots \mid \cdots\}$ the language L defined by each of the following equations:

(a) $L = 1 + 0L0$

(b) $L = 1 + 0L$

(c) $L = 1 + L$

(d) $L = L$

(e) $L = \varepsilon + (L)L$ (The left and right parentheses here are vocabulary tokens.)

(f) $L = \varepsilon + 0L0 + 1L1$

(g) $L = \,! + 0L0 + 1L1$

(h) $L = \varepsilon + 0L1 + 1L0 + LL$

EXERCISE 7.11 If S denotes some language, what language is defined by the equation $L = \varepsilon + SL$?

EXERCISE 7.12 Consider the following equation (over the real numbers):

$$x = \tfrac{1}{2}\left(x + \tfrac{a}{x}\right)$$

where a denotes a positive real number and x is the unknown, ranging over real numbers.

(a) Show that the substitution $x = \sqrt{a}$ satisfies the equation.

(b) Use the sequence $x_0 = 1$ and $x_{j+1} = \tfrac{1}{2}(x_j + \tfrac{a}{x_j})$ to calculate the first five approximations to $\sqrt{a}$ for any positive real number a, such as $a = 2.00$. (This is known as *Newton's method* for computing better and better approximations to $\sqrt{a}$.)

The iterative solution scheme described earlier may be generalized to treat n mutually recursive equations in n language variables. For example, if $n = 2$, the equations

$$L = F(L, M)$$
$$M = G(L, M)$$

(where F and G are defined using union and concatenation only) have smallest solutions $L = \bigcup_{j\geq 0} L_j$ and $M = \bigcup_{j\geq 0} M_j$, where $L_0 = M_0 = \emptyset$ and, for $j = 0, 1, 2, \ldots,$

$$L_{j+1} = F(L_j, M_j)$$
$$M_{j+1} = G(L_j, M_j)$$

7.4 Classes of Languages

Languages may be *classified* by the set of operations necessary to define them. For example, a language definable from alphabet elements using only (binary) union and concatenation must be a *finite* language. Furthermore, if we also allow $\emptyset$ and ε as primitives, *every* finite language may be defined using only union and concatenation. This approach may also be applied to characterize larger classes of language.

DEFINITION 7.3 A formal language definable using only union, concatenation, and closure from alphabet elements, ε, and $\emptyset$ is termed a *regular language*, and a language description of this form is termed a *regular expression*.

It is clear that any finite language is regular, but there are infinite regular languages as well.

There are also many languages of interest that are *not* regular. We will later prove that the set $\{0^i 1^i \mid i \geq 0\}$ of all "balanced" strings over $\{0, 1\}$ is *not* a regular language. But we have seen that this language may be defined using *recursion* (and concatenation and union). This fact motivates the following definition.

DEFINITION 7.4 A formal language definable using only union, concatenation, and recursion from alphabet elements and ε is termed a *context-free language*, and a language description of this form is termed a *context-free grammar*.

The origin of this terminology will be explained in Chapter 10.

There are also languages that are not context-free; it will later be proved that the set $\{a^i b^i c^i \mid i \geq 0\}$ is not a context-free language. We therefore have the following small complexity hierarchy of classes of languages, determined by the principles of construction needed to define them.

$$\text{finite} \subset \text{regular} \subset \text{context-free} \subset \text{unrestricted}$$

All the inclusions shown are proper (i.e., the relation $\subset$ means $\subsetneq$ and not $\subseteq$). In this book, we will be focusing our attention primarily on the classes of regular and context-free languages.

7.5 Additional Reading

The regular and context-free classes of languages were introduced in [Kle56, Cho56]. The treatment of equations as recursive definitions of languages is discussed in [MAK88, chapter 6]; a thorough treatment of language equations may be found in [Lei99].

REFERENCES

[Cho56]   N. Chomsky. Three models for the description of language. *IRE Trans. on Information Theory*, 2(3):113–24, 1956.

[Kle56]   S. C. Kleene. Representation of events in nerve nets and finite automata. In C. E. Shannon and J. McCarthy, editors, *Automata Studies*, pages 3–42. Princeton University Press, 1956.

[Lei99]   E. L. Leiss. *Language Equations*. Springer Verlag, 1999.

[MAK88]   R. N. Moll, M. A. Arbib, and A. J. Kfoury. *An Introduction to Formal Language Theory*. Springer Verlag, 1988.

Chapter 8

State-Transition Diagrams

> The behavior of the computer at any moment is determined by the symbols
> which he is observing and his "state of mind" at that moment.
>
> Alan M. Turing*

One of the most basic paradigms in computing is that of a device being, at any
time, in one or other of a set of possible *states* or *modes*, with the "current" state
changing in response to inputs or to actions by external agents. For example,
this paradigm underlies imperative computation: each state records the values
of program variables, and the state is changed by the effect of assignments and
input statements in the program being executed.

In this chapter, we use this paradigm as a convenient framework for describing formal languages and implementing recognizers for them.

8.1 Basic Definitions

Figure 8.1

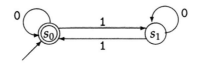

Consider Figure 8.1, which gives an example of what is termed a *state-
transition diagram*. It is essentially a finite directed graph (a set of nodes with
directed edges between them), with the edges labeled by elements from an alphabet; here, the alphabet is $\{0, 1\}$. To allow the nodes to be identified, they

---

*In [Tur36].

have been given distinctive labels (s_0, s_1) in Figure 8.1, but node labels play no official role whatsoever.

The nodes of a state-transition diagram are termed *states*, and the idea is that they represent the possible states of a *finite state automaton*, a mechanism that, at any time, is in one of a finite set of states, and whose state changes in predetermined ways in response to a sequence of tokens. The edges in the diagram represent the state changes possible; the label on an edge is the input token that causes the state to change in that way.

In any state-transition diagram, there must be exactly one state that is specially designated by a short unlabeled arrow to be the *starting* or *initial* state; in the diagram in Figure 8.1, it is the state labeled s_0. Normally, one or more of the states are designated to be *accepting* states by use of a double-circle. In the diagram in Figure 8.1, state s_0 is an accepting state; the other state, labeled s_1, is not an accepting state.

DEFINITION 8.1 A string $c_1 c_2 c_3 \cdots c_n$ is said to be *accepted* by a state diagram if there is a directed path from the starting state to an accepting state such that the sequence of edge labels for the path is $c_1, c_2, \ldots, c_n$:

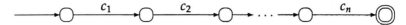

For example, the following directed path shows that the string 1010 is accepted by Figure 8.1:

Note that the same state may be visited more than once in such an accepting path, and that states designated as accepting states may be "intermediate" states in such a path. The empty string ε is accepted by a state-transition diagram if the starting state is also an accepting state.

As a convenient abbreviation, we may allow an edge of a state-transition diagram to be labeled by a list $c_1, c_2, \ldots, c_n$ of $n > 1$ characters. This kind of edge should be considered to be an abbreviation for n edges between the same nodes, each labeled by one of the c_i; that is,

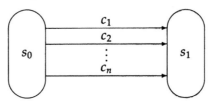

should be considered as equivalent to

The following definition gives us a way of regarding state-transition diagrams as *specifications* of formal languages.

DEFINITION 8.2 The set of all strings accepted by a state-transition diagram is said to be the language *accepted* (or *recognized*) by the state-transition diagram.

Here are some examples.

- The language accepted by the diagram in Figure 8.1 is the set of all strings over $\{0, 1\}$ with an *even* number of 1s.

- Suppose that in some programming language an identifier consists of a letter, followed by any number of letters or digits. If *letter* stands for a, b, ..., z, A, B, ..., Z and *digit* stands for 0, 1, ..., 9, the following state-transition diagram accepts the set of legal identifiers:

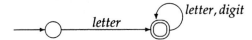

- An "unsigned real number" in standard PASCAL must contain a decimal part, an exponent part, or both; a state-transition diagram that recognizes this language is given in Figure 8.2, where, again, *digit* stands for 0, 1, ..., 9. Here are some strings in this language:

  ```
  3.1415926535
  6.023E+23
  6.625E-34
  0.0
  1E0
  ```

Figure 8.2

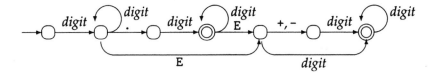

EXERCISE 8.1 Consider the language of identifiers that obey the following rules.

- The first character must be a letter.
- The remaining characters, if any, may be letters, digits, or the underscore character (_), provided that an underscore is not the last character and is not followed immediately by another underscore.

(a) Show that this is a regular language.

(b) Design a state diagram that recognizes the language.

8.2   Software Realization

In this section, we begin to study the construction of software *recognizers* for
languages defined by state-transition diagrams; the constructed recognizer essentially emulates the automaton described by the state diagram. We will only
consider simple examples here, but because the construction process is systematic and may even be mechanized, the techniques are also applicable to large
and complex applications.

Suppose that we have a state-transition diagram with edge labels drawn
from some alphabet; the input for the recognizer is, conceptually, any finite
string over that alphabet, and the output is to be an indication of whether the
string is or is not accepted by the state-transition diagram. We do *not* want to
store the entire string in memory because the string may be of arbitrary length.
The automaton we are simulating must read the string just once from left to
right, but we cannot assume that the vocabulary we are dealing with coincides
with, say, the ASCII character set of conventional textual input.

Our solution to these problems is to define, for any vocabulary Σ, a suitable
function gettoken as part of the following interface:

```
typename vocab;        /* vocabulary, augmented by EOS */
const vocab EOS;       /* end-of-string pseudo-token */
vocab gettoken(void);  /* returns next token */
```

In other words, we assume that a programmer-defined type vocab defines the
vocabulary, that each call of gettoken returns the next input token in this
vocabulary, and that the end of the input string is indicated by the pseudo-
token EOS. Notice that it is not possible to "back up" to a previous token in the
string.

For example, the gettoken function in Program 8.1 reads ASCII 0s and 1s
(terminated by an end-of-line) from standard input and implements an input
sequence of ZERO or ONE values (terminated by an EOS or end-of-string value).
If there are illegal characters in the input, the execution is aborted.

Program 8.1

```
typedef enum { ZERO, ONE, EOS } vocab;

vocab gettoken(void)
{ int c;
  c = getc(stdin);
  if (c == '0') return ZERO;
  else if (c == '1') return ONE;
  else if (c == '\n') return EOS;
  else error("illegal character");
}
```

We now consider the recognizer itself. Given a state diagram, we want the recognizer code to emulate the automaton represented by the state diagram. If the input string (as accessed through a suitable gettoken function) is *not* in the language, the recognizer is to output the following message:

```
String not accepted.
```

and then return. If the string *is* in the language, nothing should be output. In effect, the state diagram is a specification for the recognizer code.

Program 8.2

```
int main(void)
{ typedef enum { S0, S1 } state;
  state s = S0;
  vocab t = gettoken();
  while (t != EOS)
  {   switch (s)
      {  case S0:
             if (t == ONE) s = S1; break;
         case S1:
             if (t == ONE) s = S0; break;
      } /* end state switch */
      t = gettoken();
  } /* end input string loop */
  if (s != S0)
      printf("String not accepted.\n");
  return 0;
}
```

For example, Program 8.2 is recognition code for the even-parity language accepted by the state-transition diagram in Figure 8.1. The recognizer code begins with the definition of a vocab variable t and a state variable s. In this example, we need only two states, here called S0 and S1. The value of t is the current token, and the value of s represents the state of the emulated automaton. After initializing s, a loop is entered; the loop repeatedly changes the value of s and reads the next token until the end of the string is reached. Then a message is output if the final state is *not* an accepting state.

Notice that the code is essentially determined by the state diagram and may be directly or even mechanically generated from it.

EXERCISE 8.2 Design a state-transition diagram for the language of all strings over {0, 1} that have an *odd* number of 1s. Then implement a recognizer for this language based on the state diagram.

Program 8.3

```c
typedef enum { LETTER, DIGIT, ... , EOS } vocab;

vocab gettoken(void)
{   int c = getc(stdin);
    if (isalpha(c)) return LETTER;
    else if (isdigit(c)) return DIGIT;
    else ...
    else if (c == '\n') return EOS;
    else error("illegal character");
}

int main(void)
{   typedef enum { FIRST, REST, DEAD } state;
    state s = FIRST;
    vocab t = gettoken();
    while (t != EOS)
    {   switch (s)
        {   case FIRST:
                if (t == LETTER) s = REST;
                else s = DEAD;
                break;
            case REST:
                if (t != LETTER && t != DIGIT) s = DEAD;
                break;
            case DEAD:
                break;
        } /* end state switch */
        t = gettoken();
    } /* end input string loop */
    if (s != REST)
        printf("String not accepted.\n");
    return 0;
}
```

Program 8.3 consists of a `gettoken` function for a vocabulary of the form {LETTER, DIGIT,...} and a recognizer of the identifiers described in Section 8.1. In this example, the recognizer must deal with "unacceptable" input tokens. In the starting state (here called FIRST), only a LETTER token is acceptable, and in the REST state, only a LETTER or DIGIT is acceptable. We have dealt with this issue by introducing an additional (nonaccepting) DEAD state, which was not in the original state-transition diagram; after assigning DEAD to s, the rest of the input will be read, with the state s remaining at DEAD. It is as if the original state diagram had been "completed" by adding a third state and additional transitions, as follows, where Σ is the entire vocabulary:

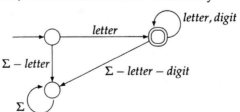

Program 8.4

```
typedef enum { DIGIT, E, POINT, PLUS, MINUS, EOS } vocab;

vocab gettoken(void)
{   int c = getc(stdin);
    if (isdigit(c)) return DIGIT;
    switch (c)
    {   case 'e':
        case 'E':       return E;
        case '.':       return POINT;
        case '+':       return PLUS;
        case '-':       return MINUS;
        case '\n':      return EOS;
        default:        error("illegal character");
    }
}

int main(void)
{   # define DEAD 7
    typedef int state;
    state s = 0;
    vocab t = gettoken();
    while (t != EOS)
    {   if (t == DIGIT)
        {   switch (s)
            {   case 0: case 1: s = 1; break;
                case 2: case 3: s = 3; break;
                case 4: case 5: case 6: s = 6; break;
                case DEAD: break;
            }
        }
        else if (t == E && (s == 1 || s == 3))
            s = 4;
        else if (t == POINT && s == 1)
            s = 2;
        else if ((t == PLUS || t == MINUS) && s == 4)
            s = 5;
        else
            s = DEAD;
        t = gettoken();
    } /* end input string loop */
    if (s != 3 && s != 6)
        printf("String not accepted.\n");
    return 0;
}
```

The final example (Program 8.4) is code to recognize unsigned real numbers, as described by the state-transition diagram in Figure 8.2. The states in the diagram have simply been numbered $0, 1, \ldots, 6$, and then a state 7 acts as a DEAD state. For this example, it is convenient to organize the recognizer so that it branches first on the current input token t and then, as necessary, on the current state s. Note that there are *two* accepting states in this example.

EXERCISE 8.3 Write a recognizer for the language of identifiers of Exercise 8.1; it should be based on your state diagram.

EXERCISE 8.4 The following gives a slightly more efficient realization of the recognizer code of Program 8.2:

```
int main(void)
{ vocab t;

 S0: t = gettoken();
     switch (t)
     {   case ZERO: goto S0;
         case ONE:  goto S1;
         case EOS:  return 0;
     }

 S1: t = gettoken();
     switch (t)
     {   case ZERO: goto S1;
         case ONE:  goto S0;
         case EOS:  printf("String not accepted.\n");
                    return 0;
     }
}
```

Note that there is no explicit state variable; the current state for the emulated automaton is determined by whether the current execution point is in the S0 code section or the S1 section. Re-implement the recognizer of Program 8.4 in this style.

8.3 Nondeterminism

It might be thought from the examples of Section 8.2 that implementing a recognizer for the language described by a state-transition diagram would always be straightforward. However, the state-transition diagrams so far considered have been *deterministic*; that is, at most one edge may be followed out of any node for any input token. But this need not always be true; there may be edges from a state to *distinct* states labeled by the *same* input token:

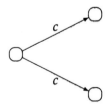

According to the definition of string acceptance, a string must be accepted if it is spelled out by *any* path from the starting state to an accepting state. It should be clear that nondeterminism in a state-transition diagram makes it more challenging to code a recognizer for the language in a conventional programming language, which may only follow one thread of control at a time, particularly if we do not want to allow backing up the input.

As an example illustrating why it is not desirable simply to *disallow* nondeterminism in state-transition diagrams, consider the problem of describing the set of all strings over $\Sigma = \{a, b, \ldots, z\}$ that end in man, such as alderman and chairman.

EXERCISE 8.5 Give an example string that shows that the following (deterministic) state-transition diagram is *incorrect* as a description of the language. The edge label $\Sigma - m$ refers to all alphabet tokens *except* m, and similarly for $\Sigma - a$ and $\Sigma - n$.

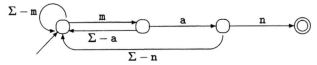

We will later give a *correct* deterministic state-transition diagram for the language of strings that end in man; however, it will turn out to be much more complicated than the *nondeterministic* diagram in Figure 8.3, the correctness of which is immediately obvious.

Figure 8.3

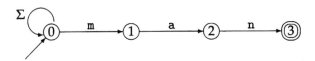

EXERCISE 8.6 In what way is the state-transition diagram in Figure 8.3 *not* deterministic?

EXERCISE 8.7 Design (possibly nondeterministic) state-transition diagrams that recognize the languages of Section 7.3.3.

We will describe *two* implementation methods for nondeterministic state-transition diagrams. The basic idea in both approaches is to emulate a *deterministic* automaton whose state at any time is the *set* of diagram states that a nondeterministic automaton *might* be in.

In the first approach, the necessary state sets are determined dynamically; the pseudo-code in Program 8.5 on page 178 illustrates this approach. Type state consists of four values, representing the four nodes in the state-transition diagram. Variable A of an assumed type StateSet acts as the state variable for the deterministic recognizer; it invariantly contains the *set* of diagram states that a nondeterministic automaton *might* be in (after reading this far in the input string).

Program 8.5

```
typedef enum{ S0, S1, S2, S3 } state;

int main(void)
{ vocab t = gettoken();
  StateSet A;  /* set of possible diagram states */
  A.include(S0);
  while (t != EOS)
  {   StateSet NewA;
      /* traverse A and construct NewA: */
      for (state s in A)
      {   switch (s)
          {   case S0:
                NewA.include(S0);
                if (t == 'm')
                    NewA.include(S1);
                break;
              case S1:
                if (t == 'a')
                    NewA.include(S2);
                break;
              case S2:
                if (t == 'n')
                    NewA.include(S3);
                break;
              case S3:
                break;
          } /* end state switch */
      } /* end traversal of A */
      A = NewA;
      t = gettoken();
  } /* end input string loop */
  if (S3 !in A)
      printf("String not accepted.\n");
  return 0;
}
```

Updating A takes place as follows. The `for (state s in A) ...` loop is used to traverse the elements of A. An `include` method is used to add diagram states to a temporary `StateSet` variable `NewA` if they are reachable from one of the states in A by an edge labeled by the current input token. In the case of diagram state S0 and input token m, there are *two* possible transitions, and so both diagram states S0 and S1 are added to `NewA`. When the traversal of the states in A is finished, `NewA` is assigned to A.

At the end of the string, the string is accepted if *any* of the diagram states in A are accepting states. Note that the *empty* state set plays the role of a "dead" state in this approach.

EXERCISE 8.8 Use a class of traversible sparse sets as discussed in Section 6.1 to implement the `StateSet` variables in this recognizer code.

The method of implementing nondeterminism just described is adequate in applications in which the recognition code will be deleted immediately after use, such as text editors. However, when performance is very important, such as the scanner phase of a compiler, it is possible to improve the efficiency by *precalculating* the sets of states that might be used, rather than calculating them dynamically as the input is being read.

For any set S of diagram states and input token $x \in \Sigma$, there should be an x-labeled transition from S to the set T of all diagram states t for which there is a transition

$$\text{\textcircled{s}} \xrightarrow{\quad x \quad} \text{\textcircled{t}}$$

in the state-transition diagram for some $s \in S$. This rule essentially determines how the state sets are computed in Program 8.5. The difference now is that we determine all such transitions independently of an input string by considering *every* possible input token.

Consider again the nondeterministic state-transition diagram in Figure 8.3:

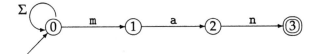

We start with the singleton state set $\{0\}$. For any token *except* m, the only possible transition from state 0 in the original state diagram is to state 0; however, for token m, there is a transition from state 0 to state 0 *and* to state 1. These transitions give us the following edges out of the state set $\{0\}$:

$$\Sigma - m \;\text{\textcircled{0}} \xrightarrow{\quad m \quad} \boxed{0, 1}$$

The preceding step has introduced a new state set $\{0, 1\}$ and so we consider transitions out of it. For token m, there is a transition from state 0 to state 1 and from state 0 to itself, but no additional transitions from state 1:

$$\boxed{0, 1} \xrightarrow{\quad m \quad} \boxed{0, 1}$$

For token a, there is a transition from state 1 to state 2 and a transition from state 0 to itself:

$$\boxed{0, 1} \xrightarrow{\quad a \quad} \boxed{0, 2}$$

For every other token, there is only a transition from state 0 to itself:

$$\boxed{0, 1} \xrightarrow{\quad \Sigma - m - a \quad} \boxed{0}$$

Combining, we get the following edges out of state set $\{0, 1\}$:

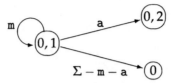

The preceding step has introduced a new state set $\{0, 2\}$. Here are the transitions out of this state set:

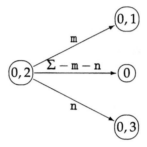

Finally, here are the transitions out of the new state set $\{0, 3\}$:

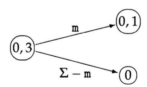

The construction process now terminates because there are no new state sets to consider; note that termination is inevitable because a finite set of diagram states has only a *finite* number of subsets. A state set is considered to be *accepting* if any of its elements is an accepting state in the original state-transition diagram. In this example, $\{0, 3\}$ is the only accepting state set.

The result of this process is the *deterministic* state-transition diagram in Figure 8.4, in which the states are labeled by *sets* of the states of the original nondeterministic diagram. Though the state-transition diagram is surprisingly complex, it *is* deterministic, and so it may easily be realized directly, as we demonstrated in Section 8.2. Recognizer code is given in Program 8.6. This recognizer is more efficient than that in Program 8.5 because all the state sets have been precomputed.

To summarize, we have described an algorithm that, given any nondeterministic state-transition diagram, constructs a deterministic diagram that is *equivalent* to it, in the sense that it recognizes the same language. The deterministic diagram may then be realized directly using the techniques of Section 8.2.

Figure 8.4

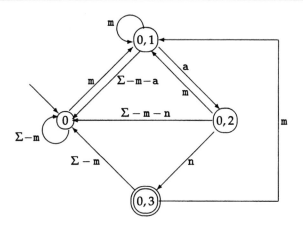

Program 8.6

```
typedef enum { S0, S01, S02, S03 } state;
state s = S0;
vocab t = gettoken();
while (t != EOS)
{   switch (s)
    {   case S0:
            if (t == 'm') s = S01;
            break;
        case S01:
            if (t == 'a') s = S02;
            else if (t != 'm') s = S0;
            break;
        case S02:
            if (t == 'n') s = S03;
            else if (t == 'm') s = S01;
            else s = S0;
            break;
        case S03:
            if (t == 'm') s = S01;
            else s = S0;
            break;
    } /* end state switch */
    t = gettoken();
} /* end input string loop */
if (s != S03)
    printf("String not accepted.\n");
return 0;
```

EXERCISE 8.9 Use the technique of Exercise 8.4 to construct an even more efficient recognizer that does not have an explicit state variable such as s.

EXERCISE 8.10 Here are some of the relational operators in PASCAL:

    <   >   <=   >=   =   <>

The following nondeterministic state-transition diagram recognizes this language.

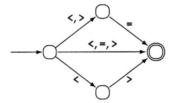

(a) Code a recognizer for this language; it should determine state sets dynamically.

(b) Construct an equivalent deterministic state-transition diagram.

(c) Code a recognizer based on the deterministic diagram.

EXERCISE 8.11

(a) Construct a (nondeterministic) state diagram for the following operators in C:

    + ++ - -- < << > >> <= >= ! != == = += -= -> <<= >>=

(b) Construct an equivalent deterministic diagram and code a recognizer based on this diagram.

EXERCISE 8.12 A float constant in C is described as consisting of an integer part, a decimal point, a fraction part, an e or E, an optionally signed integer exponent and an optional type suffix (one of f, F, l, or L). The integer and fraction parts both consist of of a sequence of digits. Either the integer part or the fraction part (not both) may be missing; either the decimal point or the e and the exponent (not both) may be missing.

(a) Construct a nondeterministic state diagram that accepts exactly the language of float constants in C.

(b) Construct an equivalent deterministic state diagram and code a recognizer based on this diagram.

EXERCISE 8.13 Suppose $\Sigma = \{0, 1\}$.

(a) Give three examples of strings over Σ that are *not* accepted by the following (non-deterministic) state-transition diagram:

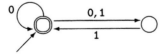

(b) Program a recognition procedure that directly implements this diagram, using as its states *sets* of diagram states. Assume the same interface as the preceding examples.

(c) Construct an equivalent *deterministic* state-transition diagram and code a corresponding recognition procedure.

8.4 State-Transition Diagrams with ε Transitions

It is sometimes convenient to allow "spontaneous" transitions between states of a state-transition diagram, representing changes of state *without* an input token being read. This may be indicated in a state-transition diagram by using the empty-string symbol ε as an edge label. For example, the following state-transition diagram has three ε transitions; it recognizes the language of "unsigned real constants" as in the last example of Section 8.1 but makes it more evident that a decimal part and a sign in an exponent are optional:

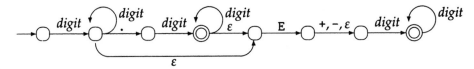

For any state-transition diagram *with* ε transitions, a new transition diagram equivalent to the original one but *without* ε transitions may be constructed as follows.

1. Construct a state-transition diagram that is like the original one, but without any of the ε transitions; also remove any state (including all outgoing transitions) that, in the original diagram, has only ε transitions going in. The starting state is not removed.

2. Add transitions to the new diagram as follows: whenever, in the original diagram, there is a chain of one or more ε transitions starting at a state s, followed by a "real" transition labeled by a token $x \in \Sigma$, to a state t, as in

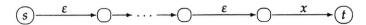

   add the transition  to the new state-transition diagram.

3. If, in the original state-transition diagram, there is a chain of ε transitions from a state s to an *accepting* state, as in

   then state s should be an accepting state in the new state-transition diagram.

For example, if this procedure is applied to the preceding example, the result of the first step is the following (disconnected) diagram:

Three ε transitions and a state with only ε transitions going in have been removed. Then three new transitions are added by the second step, giving the
following diagram, which is exactly the same as the diagram in Figure 8.2:

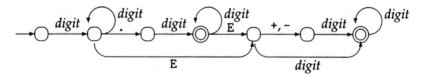

In this example, no accepting states were reachable by ε transitions, and so the
final step of the algorithm has no effect.

EXERCISE 8.14 Use the procedure described in this section to construct state-transition
diagrams without ε transitions equivalent to the following:

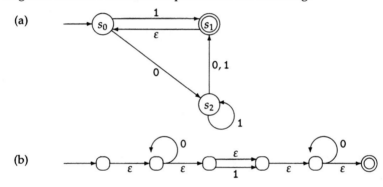

EXERCISE 8.15 Consider generalizing state diagrams by allowing edge labels to be arbitrary *strings* (or finite nonempty sets of strings) over the alphabet. For any such generalized state diagram, show how to construct an equivalent conventional state diagram.

8.5   Reactive Systems*

We have used state-transition diagrams to specify language recognizers. But
this is only one class of applications for this formalism. More generally, state-
transition diagrams (i.e., finite state automata) model *reactive systems*: devices
or computational processes that operate continuously and react determinis-
tically and virtually instantaneously to input signals.   This computational
paradigm should be distinguished not only from the familiar input-to-output
style of computation, but also from more complex *interactive* computational
processes, such as operating systems, databases, and the internet, which are
not primarily input driven.

---

*The material in this section is not referred to in the rest of this book.

Examples of reactive systems include calculators, digital wristwatches, video games, process controllers, user interfaces, device drivers, and communication protocols. The language recognizers we have been considering are very simple examples of reactive systems, possibly producing an output signal of nonacceptance at the end of a sequence of input signals.

As a slightly more complex example of a reactive system, suppose that a process is required to generate output 0 as soon as it has received both of two independent input signals, designated A and B; the process should return to its initial state without generating any output as soon as it receives an R signal.

This system may be described using a state-transition diagram. We need to define a vocabulary in which the tokens represent presence or absence of the three possible input signals and the output. Hence the tokens will have the form of quadruples as follows: $(\pm A, \pm B, \pm R, \pm 0)$, where each $\pm$ here is to be replaced by *either* + (the input is present or the output is generated) *or* − (the input is absent or the output is not generated). We will also allow $\pm$ itself to be used in transition labels, meaning that the relevant component may be either + or −.

The reactive system may now be described more precisely by the state-transition diagram given in Figure 8.5. Note that there is no accepting state because the process is supposed to continue indefinitely.

Unfortunately, this state-transition diagram is rather incomprehensible because of the complexity of the tokens and the large number of transitions, even

---

Figure 8.5

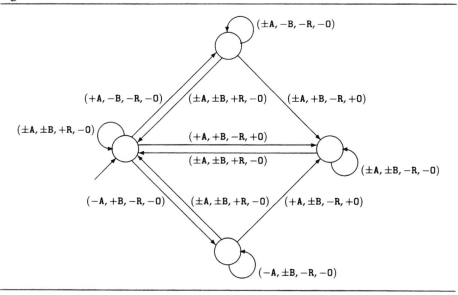

for this simple example. And even worse, there is a scalability problem; if the process were required to wait in the same way for *three* input signals, the number of states would increase to 8 and the number of transitions would be close to 64. For describing formal languages, higher-level formalisms, such as regular expressions, are available, but these are not suitable for specifying more complex reactive systems.

To address these problems, various higher level approaches have been developed for programming reactive systems; programs in these languages are *compiled* into state-transition diagrams or executable code or even chip designs.

One approach is to allow state-transition diagrams to be *composed* in various ways, allowing modular descriptions of complex systems. For example, the reactive system discussed earlier is described in a structured graphical form known as SYNCCHARTS in Figure 8.6. The notation A? labels a transition that is to be followed if there is an A input, and the same is true for B? and R?. The notation O! labels a transition that generates an O output. The dotted line indicates orthogonal product of the two subdiagrams it separates. The loop labeled R? indicates immediate pre-emption.

Figure 8.6

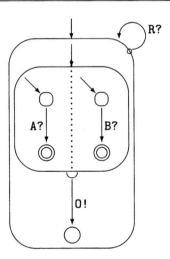

EXERCISE 8.16 Modify the diagram of Figure 8.6 so that the process waits until three inputs, A, B, and C, have all occurred before generating output O.

Program 8.7

```
module ABRO;
  input A, B, R;
  output O;
  loop
    [ await A || await B ];
    emit O
  each R
end module
```

Another approach is to use programming languages that have been specifically designed for programming reactive systems. For example, the reactive process discussed earlier may be coded in the language ESTEREL as shown in Program 8.7. The first line names the module; the next two lines are declarations of input and output signals, respectively; and the next four lines describe the cyclic process of waiting for both input signals A and B, followed by output of O, and re-initialization by input R.

EXERCISE 8.17 Modify the ABRO program so that the process waits until three inputs, A, B, and C, have all occurred before generating output O.

EXERCISE 8.18 Draw the state-transition diagram corresponding to the following modification of the ABRO program:

```
module ABRO;
  input A, B, R;
  output O;
  loop
    [ await A || await B ];
    emit O;
    await R
  end loop
end module
```

A more substantial example of ESTEREL coding is given in Program 8.8 on page 188, which has been adapted from [BB+89]. This is a program for a simple reflex-testing game. After the machine is turned on, a player starts the game by inserting a COIN, starts a reflex-testing sequence by pushing the READY button, and stops the reflex test by pushing the STOP button. The device signals that it is ready to test the user's reflexes by lighting a GO lamp and gives the reflex times in a numerical DISPLAY; furthermore, it signals that the game is over by lighting a GAME_OVER lamp, that a wrong button has been pushed by ringing a BELL, and that the user has tried to cheat (or has abandoned the game) by lighting a TILT lamp.

Program 8.8

```
module REFLEX_GAME :
  constant LIMIT_TIME, MEASURE.NUMBER, PAUSE_LENGTH : integer;
  function RANDOM():integer;
  input MS, COIN, READY, STOP;
  relation MS # COIN # READY, COIN # STOP, READY # STOP;
  output DISPLAY(integer), RING_BELL, GO_ON, GO_OFF,
         GAME_OVER_ON, GAME_OVER_OFF, TILT_ON, TILT_OFF;
  % overall initializations
  emit DISPLAY(0); emit GO_OFF; emit GAME_OVER_ON; emit TILT_OFF;
  % loop over a single game
  every COIN do
    emit DISPLAY(0); emit GO_OFF;
    emit GAME_OVER_OFF; emit TILT_OFF;
    % exception handling
    trap ERROR in
      var TOTAL_TIME:=0 : integer in
        repeat MEASURE.NUMBER times
          % waiting for READY
          do
            do every STOP do emit RING_BELL end
            upto READY
          watching LIMIT_TIME MS timeout exit ERROR end;
          trap END_MEASURE in
            [ every READY do emit RING_BELL end
            ||
              % random delay
              do await RANDOM() MS
              watching STOP timeout exit ERROR end;
              emit GO_ON;
              % waiting for STOP
              do
                var TIME:=0 : integer in
                  do every MS do TIME:=TIME+1 end
                  upto STOP;
                  emit DISPLAY(TIME);
                  TOTAL_TIME := TOTAL_TIME + TIME
                end
              watching LIMIT_TIME MS timeout exit ERROR end;
              emit GO_OFF;
              exit END_MEASURE
            ]
          end
        end;
        % final display
        await PAUSE_LENGTH MS do
          emit DISPLAY(TOTAL_TIME / MEASURE.NUMBER)
        end
      end
    handle ERROR do emit TILT_ON; emit GO_OFF end;
    % end of the game
    emit GAME_OVER_ON
  end
end module
```

We cannot here explain every feature of this code, but the following hints may be helpful. Three integer constants and a random number-generating function are provided by the environment. The MS signal comes from an external timer every millisecond. The relation statement is a hint to the compiler that certain combinations of inputs cannot occur together; this helps the compiler produce smaller and more efficient code.

This program may be compiled by ESTEREL compilers into compact and efficient code that realizes a state-transition diagram with six states and 169 transitions.

8.6 Additional Reading

Finite state automata (state-transition diagrams) originated in [MP43, Huf54, Moo56]. Nondeterministic finite state automata were introduced in [RS59]. Implementation aspects are covered in [Gou88, AU92] and also in books on compilers, such as [ASU86]. The man example is from [AU92].

Reactive systems are discussed in [HP85, Hal92, HP98, Ber00]. Modular approaches to state-transition diagrams are described in [Har87, Hal92, Mar91, vdB94, And96, ABD98, HP98]. The ESTEREL language for programming reactive systems is described in [BG92]. The reflex-game example is from [BB+89]. An amusing and relevant fable about a familiar reactive system may be found here:

> http://www.spectrum.ieee.org/INST/apr98/after5.html

REFERENCES

[ABD98]   C. André, H. Boufaïed, and S. Dissoubray. SyncCharts: Un modèle graphique synchrone pour systèmes réactifs complexes. In *Real-Time Systems 1998*, pages 175–93, Paris, January 1998. Teknea.

[And96]   C. André. Representation and analysis of reactive behaviors: a synchronous approach. In *IEEE-SMC, Proceedings CESA '96 (Computational Engineering in System Applications)*, pages 19–29, Lille, France, July 1996. Also available here: http://www-mips.unice.fr/~andre/synccharts.html.

[ASU86]   A. V. Aho, R. Sethi, and J. D. Ullman. *Compiler Design: Principles, Techniques, and Tools*. Addison-Wesley, 1986.

[AU92]   A. V. Aho and J. D. Ullman. *Foundations of Computer Science*. W. H. Freeman, 1992.

[BB+89]   R. Bernhard, G. Berry, F. Boussinot, G. Gonthier, A. Ressouche, J.-P. Rigault, and J.-M. Tanzi. Programming a reflex game in ESTEREL v3, 1989. Available here: http://www.inria.fr/meije/esterel.

[Ber00]   G. Berry. The foundations of ESTEREL. In G. Plotkin, C. Stirling, and M. Tofte, editors, *Proof, Language and Interaction: Essays in Honour of Robin Milner*, pages 425–54. The MIT Press, 2000.

[BG92]   G. Berry and G. Gonthier. The ESTEREL synchronous programming
           language: Design, semantics, implementation. *Science of Computer
           Programming*, 19:87–152, 1992.
[Gou88]   K. J. Gough. *Syntax Analysis and Software Tools*. Addison-Wesley, 1988.
[Hal92]   N. Halbwachs. *Synchronous Programming of Reactive Systems*. Kluwer, 1992.
[Har87]   D. Harel. Statecharts, a visual approach to complex systems. *Science of
           Computer Programming*, 8:231–74, 1987.
[HP85]   D. Harel and A. Pnueli. On the development of reactive systems. In K. Apt,
           editor, *Logics and Models of Concurrent Systems*, pages 477–98.
           Springer-Verlag, 1985.
[HP98]   D. Harel and M. Politi. *Modeling Reactive Systems with Statecharts*.
           McGraw-Hill, 1998.
[Huf54]   D. A. Huffman. The synthesis of sequential switching circuits. *J. Franklin
           Institute*, 257:3–4, 161–90, and 275–303, 1954.
[Mar91]   F. Maraninchi. The ARGOS language: Graphical representation of automata
           and description of reactive systems. In *IEEE Workshop on Visual Languages*,
           Kobe, Japan, October 1991.
[Moo56]   W. F. Moore. Gedanken experiments on sequential machines. In
           C. E. Shannon and J. McCarthy, editors, *Automata Studies*, pages 129–53.
           Princeton University Press, 1956.
[MP43]   W. S. McCulloch and W. Pitts. A logical calculus of the ideas immanent in
           nervous activity. *Bulletin Math. Biophysics*, 5:115–33, 1943.
[RS59]   M. O. Rabin and D. Scott. Finite automata and their decision problems. *IBM
           J. Research and Development*, 3(2):115–25, 1959.
[Tur36]   A. M. Turing. On computable numbers, with an application to the
           Entscheidungsproblem. *Proceedings of the London Mathematical Society, series 2*,
           42:230–65, 1936. A correction, *ibid.*, 43:544–6, 1937.
[vdB94]   M. von der Beek. A comparison of STATECHART variants. In *Formal
           Techniques in Real Time and Fault Tolerant Systems*, volume 863 of *Lecture
           Notes in Computer Science*, pages 128–48. Springer-Verlag, 1994.

Chapter 9

Regular Languages

In Chapter 8, state-transition diagrams were presented as descriptions of formal languages from which recognizers could easily be implemented. We will show in this chapter that the languages describable by state-transition diagrams are exactly the *regular* languages (Definition 7.3), that is, languages definable from vocabulary tokens, ε, and $\varnothing$, using only union, concatenation, and closure.

9.1   From Regular Expressions to State Diagrams

We first show that, for *any* regular language, there is a state-transition diagram that recognizes it; furthermore, we may construct it systematically from the regular expression that describes the language. When this construction is combined with the realization techniques discussed in the preceding chapter, we obtain a systematic (and even mechanizable) way of implementing recognizers for regular languages. In effect, the state diagram becomes a convenient *intermediate representation* between the regular expression and the recognizing code.

We begin by presenting state-transition diagrams that recognize the languages described by the three *primitive* forms of regular expression:

- for any $x \in \Sigma$:

- for ε:

- for $\varnothing$:

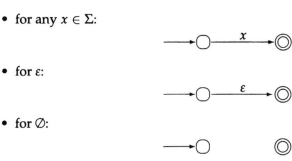

Table 9.1

1. There is exactly one accepting state, which is not the starting state.

2. There are no transitions into the starting state.

3. There are no transitions out of the accepting state.

Each of these forms of state-transition diagrams has the three properties listed in Table 9.1. These properties will be preserved by the constructions to be described subsequently for union, concatenation, and closure and will ensure that these constructions are correct in general. If it is desired to apply one of the constructions to an *arbitrary* state diagram, the diagram may first be transformed into an equivalent diagram with the three properties by introducing a new starting state with ε transitions *to* the former starting state and a new unique accepting state with ε transitions *from* any former accepting states.

We now consider regular expressions that use the operations of union, concatenation, and closure. We suppose that S and T are regular expressions and that

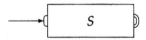

represents a state-transition diagram with the properties of Table 9.1 recognizing the language S. Similarly, suppose that

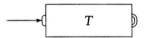

represents a state-transition diagram with the properties of Table 9.1 recognizing language T.

A state-transition diagram recognizing $S + T$ may be constructed by merging the two starting states into a single state and similarly merging the two accepting states. In other words, the relevant states are considered to be the same, so that any edges into or out of one are regarded as being into or out of both of them. The two "merged" states become the starting state and the accepting state, respectively, of the composite state-transition diagram. This construction may be portrayed as a "parallel" connection, as follows:

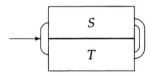

Note that because we have assumed that there are no edges *into* the starting states of the diagrams for S and T, and no edges *out of* the accepting states, there are in general no transitions from the S part of the composite diagram into the T part, nor vice versa; furthermore, the composite diagram also has the properties of Table 9.1.

As a simple example of this construction, a state diagram for $\varepsilon + 1$ may be constructed using the diagram for ε, the diagram for token 1, and the construction for the union operation as follows:

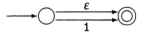

Similarly, a state-transition diagram recognizing the concatenation S T may be constructed by merging the accepting state of the diagram for S with the starting state of the diagram for T; the starting state of the diagram for S becomes the starting state of the composite diagram, and the accepting state of the diagram for T becomes the accepting state of the composite diagram. The resulting composite diagram may be portrayed as the following "series" connection:

Because we have assumed that the diagrams for S and for T have the properties of Table 9.1, there are no edges from the T part of the composite diagram into the S part; and again, the composite diagram also has the properties of Table 9.1.

For example, the following is a state diagram recognizing the language described by $(\varepsilon + 1)0$:

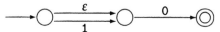

Finally, we want to be able to construct a state diagram to recognize the language S^*. The first step is to merge the starting state and the accepting state of the state diagram for S. We portray the resulting state diagram as follows, as if it had been "folded back" on itself:

For example, here is the result of merging the starting and accepting states of the diagram for $(\varepsilon + 1)0$:

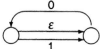

However, it would not be correct in general to make the merged state either the starting state or the accepting state of the new state diagram: the diagram might then not have the properties of Table 9.1. We may avoid this problem by adding a new starting state and a new accepting state, with ε transitions to and from the merged state:

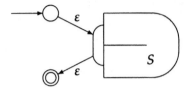

The resulting state diagram recognizes S^* and has the properties of Table 9.1.

For example, the following state diagram recognizes the language described by 0^* and has the desired properties:

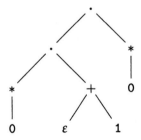

We now have everything we need to construct systematically a state diagram for any given regular expression. Consider, for example, the following regular expression: $0^*(ε + 1)0^*$, which defines the language of strings over the alphabet $\{0, 1\}$ with at most one 1. The hierarchical structure of a regular expression such as this may be displayed by a tree with

- operators · (for concatenation), + (for union), and * (for closure) at the *internal* nodes and

- tokens, ε, or ∅ at the *leaves,*

as in the following:

We now work up the tree, starting with state diagrams for the leaves and combining state diagrams at the internal nodes using the appropriate general construction. The state diagram obtained at the root of the tree corresponds to the original regular expression. For this example, we put the diagrams for 0^* and $ε + 1$ in sequence and then attach another copy of the diagram for 0^* to get the following:

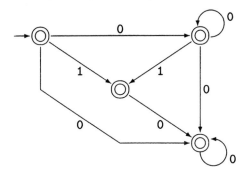

which recognizes the language defined by the regular expression.

When the complete diagram has been constructed, it is possible to elimi-nate ε transitions, as explained in Section 8.4; the resulting state-transition dia-gram is as follows:

This is not the simplest possible state-transition diagram for this language. There are techniques available for *minimizing* state-transition diagrams, but we will not discuss them in this book.

Although the process described is completely general, it may be worth-while in practice to simplify a regular expression using properties of the opera-tions *before* constructing the state diagram. For example, consider the following regular expression:

$$0^*01^*1 + 00^*11^* + 10^*11^*$$

It may be simplified as follows:

$$
\begin{aligned}
0^*01^*1 + 00^*11^* &+ 10^*11^* \\
= \quad 00^*11^* + 00^*11^* + 10^*11^* &\quad \ldots 0^*0 = 00^*, 1^*1 = 11^* \\
= \quad (0 + 1)0^*11^* &\quad \ldots \text{right distributivity}
\end{aligned}
$$

from which a state diagram is more easily constructed.

EXERCISE 9.1 Using the procedure described in this section, construct a state diagram that recognizes the language described by the regular expression $(01 + 010)^*$. Then construct an equivalent *deterministic* state diagram.

EXERCISE 9.2 Construct state-transition diagrams for the languages described in Section 7.3.3, using the procedure described in this section. How do your diagrams compare to those you constructed in Exercise 8.7?

9.2   From State Diagrams to Regular Expressions

In this section, we show that the language recognized by any state-transition diagram may be described by a regular expression.

In this section only, we will use *generalized* state-transition diagrams in which the edges may be labeled by general *regular expressions*, not just tokens or finite sets of tokens. These diagrams will be intermediate representations between conventional state-transition diagrams and regular expressions.

Suppose that we are given a state-transition diagram; because a list of tokens $x_1, x_2, \ldots, x_n$ may be replaced by the regular expression $x_1 + x_2 + \cdots + x_n$, we may assume without loss of generality that there is at most one edge between any two states. Furthermore, we may assume that there is exactly one accepting state, which is not the starting state. If there are *no* accepting states in the original state-transition diagram, the language is described by the regular expression $\emptyset$. If there are *several* accepting states, we may change them to be nonaccepting and introduce a new unique accepting state to which there are ε transitions from them, and similarly if the starting state is an accepting state.

Our strategy now is to select for elimination any state u that isn't the starting state or the accepting state. Suppose that the diagram has

- edges *to* state u from states $s_i \neq u$, labeled by regular expressions S_i, respectively;

- edges *from* u to states $t_j \neq u$, labeled by regular expressions T_j, respectively; and

- a "loop" from u to itself, labeled by regular expression U (which may be $\emptyset$ if there is no such loop).

Note that the s_i and the t_j need not be distinct in general. Finally, for every such s_i and t_j, let the edge from s_i to t_j be labeled by regular expression X_{ij}:

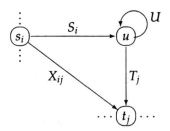

If there is *no* edge from s_i to t_j, such an edge should be added and labeled $\emptyset$.

Then state u and all edges into or out of u may be eliminated from the diagram as follows: for every pair of states s_i and t_j as in the preceding diagram, the regular expression X_{ij} on the edge from s_i to t_j should be replaced by $X_{ij} + S_i \cdot U^* \cdot T_j$; the additional term here (i.e., $S_i \cdot U^* \cdot T_j$) represents all possible sequences of transitions from s_i to t_j that move to u, loop around u any number of times (including zero), and then move to t_j:

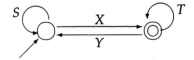

$$X_{ij} + S_i \cdot U^* \cdot T_j$$

The state-elimination procedure described in the preceding paragraphs may then be applied to any of the remaining nonstarting and nonaccepting states, and this process continues until the only states left are the starting state and the accepting state.

Suppose that the edges are now labeled as follows:

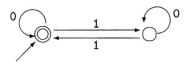

If some of these edges don't actually exist, we may add them and take the labels to be $\emptyset$. Then the language accepted by the state-transition diagram is described by the following regular expression:

$$S^* \cdot X \cdot (T + Y \cdot S^* \cdot X)^*$$

This completes the construction process.

As an example, consider the following state-transition diagram, which recognizes the language of strings over $\{0, 1\}$ with an even number of 1s:

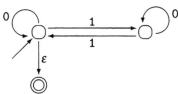

Because the starting state is an accepting state, we make it nonaccepting and introduce a new accepting state, adding an ε transition to it from the starting state:

We now eliminate the only state that is neither the starting state nor the accepting state. There is a single edge to it from the starting state, and a single edge from it to the starting state. Let s_1 and t_1 both refer to the starting state, and let S_1 and T_1 both be 1, and U and X_{11} both be 0; then the state may be eliminated if the loop on the starting state is relabeled $X_{ij} + S_i \cdot U^* \cdot T_j$, which, in this case, is $0 + 10^*1$. This procedure gives the following reduced (generalized) state diagram:

$$0 + 10^*1$$

The only remaining states are the starting state and the accepting state. The regular expression for the language accepted by the state-transition diagram is $S^* \cdot X \cdot (T + Y \cdot S^* \cdot X)^*$, where S is $0 + 10^*1$, X is ε, and both Y and T are $\emptyset$; consequently, the regular expression is

$$(0 + 10^*1)^*\varepsilon(\emptyset + \emptyset(0 + 10^*1)^*\varepsilon)^*$$

This expression simplifies to $(0 + 10^*1)^*$ because $\emptyset$ is the identity for union, ε is the identity for concatenation, $\emptyset$ is the zero for concatenation, and $\emptyset^* = \varepsilon$.

In summary, we have shown that the class of languages described by regular expressions and the class recognized by state-transition diagrams are exactly the same (the *regular* languages), and that we may systematically convert from one formalism to the other. In particular, a recognizer for a regular language may be systematically implemented by first constructing an equivalent state diagram and then using the techniques of Chapter 8.

EXERCISE 9.3 Use the procedure described in this section to construct regular expressions for the languages accepted by the following state-transition diagrams:

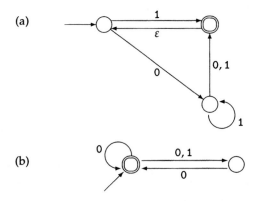

9.3 Additional Operations on Regular Languages

The basic operations on regular languages are union, concatenation, and closure, but additional useful operations may be defined.

9.3.1 OPTIONS

If S is a regular expression, the expression $\varepsilon + S$ is used when a string matching S is *optional*; often the notation $[S]$ is used for this.

EXERCISE 9.4 Design a construction that, given a state-transition diagram that recognizes the language S and has the properties of Table 9.1, produces a state-transition diagram that recognizes the language $[S]$ and has the properties of Table 9.1.

9.3.2 POSITIVE CLOSURE

If S is a regular expression, the expression $S \cdot S^* = S + SS + SSS + \cdots$ describes the language whose elements are obtained by concatenating one or more elements of S. The notation S^+ is used for this operation, and the language is termed the *positive closure* of S.

EXERCISE 9.5 Is it true in general that $S^+ = S^* - \{\varepsilon\}$?

EXERCISE 9.6 Design a construction that, given a state-transition diagram that recognizes the language S and has the properties of Table 9.1, produces a state-transition diagram that recognizes the language S^+, has the properties of Table 9.1, and is simpler than a diagram based on $S \cdot S^*$.

9.3.3 COMPLEMENT

If S is a language over vocabulary Σ, the notation $\overline{S}$ denotes the *complement* of S, that is, the language

$$\{s \in \Sigma^* \mid s \notin S\}$$

We may prove that, if S is a regular language, so is $\overline{S}$, by constructing a state diagram that recognizes it, given a state-transition diagram that recognizes S. Suppose, without loss of generality, that there is a state-transition diagram recognizing S that is deterministic, and that, for each state and for each vocabulary token, there is exactly one outgoing edge labeled by that token; if necessary a "dead" state may be added. Then a state-transition diagram that recognizes $\overline{S}$ is obtained from the one that recognizes S by making all accepting states nonaccepting, and vice versa.

EXERCISE 9.7 If S is the language of all strings over $\{0, 1\}$ that have an *odd* number of 1s, construct a state-transition diagram that recognizes this language by modifying the diagram in Figure 8.1.

EXERCISE 9.8 Draw a deterministic state diagram that recognizes all strings over $\{0, 1\}$ that *don't* end with the consecutive substring 001.

9.3.4 INTERSECTION

If S and T are regular expressions over the same vocabulary Σ, their *intersection* $S \cap T = \{s \in \Sigma^* \mid s \in S \text{ and } s \in T\}$ is also a regular language. This is because

$$S \cap T = \overline{\overline{S} + \overline{T}}$$

and the class of regular languages is closed under complement and union.

EXERCISE 9.9 Prove that the intersection of regular languages S and T is regular by giving a general construction of a state diagram for $S \cap T$ from state diagrams for S and T.

9.3.5 REVERSAL

For any language S, we may define its *reversal* $S^R = \{s \mid s^R \in S\}$, where s^R denotes the reversal of string s.

EXERCISE 9.10 Show that, if S is a regular language, so is S^R.

9.4 Nonregular Languages

In this section we describe a technique that can be used to show that languages are *not* regular. At first sight, it might seem to be very difficult to prove that there is *no* state-transition diagram or regular expression, of any complexity, that recognizes the language. The technique is based on a proof that all infinite regular languages have a certain property, so that if an infinite language does *not* have the property, it is not a regular language. The property in question is expressed in the following proposition.

PROPOSITION 9.1 (PUMPING LEMMA) If a state-transition diagram having n states accepts some string x of length $m \geq n$, then there exist strings p, q, and r satisfying all the following:

- $x = pqr$

- $q \neq \varepsilon$

- The string pq is of length $\leq n$.

- All strings of the form $pq^k r$ for any $k \geq 0$ are also accepted by the state-transition diagram.

This proposition is termed the *pumping lemma* because the assumed string $x = pqr$ may be "pumped up" to longer and longer acceptable strings $pq^k r$ by repeating the inner part q of the string; also, pqr may be "pumped down" once, by setting $k = 0$.

Proof. Let the accepted string x be $c_1 c_2 c_3 \cdots c_m$, where all the c_i are vocabulary elements; consequently, there must be a directed path of the form

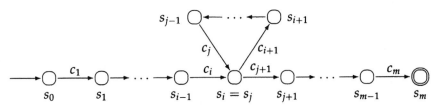

through the state-transition diagram. The states named $s_0, s_1, \ldots, s_m$ in the preceding diagram need not be distinct; in fact, because, by assumption, $m \geq n$ and the diagram has only n states, some state in the sequence *must* be the same as a preceding state in the sequence. Let s_j be the first such duplicated state so that $s_j = s_i$ for $i < j \leq n$. The requirements listed in the statement of the proposition are then met by taking $p = c_1 c_2 \cdots c_i$, $q = c_{i+1} \cdots c_j$, and $r = c_{j+1} \cdots c_m$. The string pr (i.e., the case $k = 0$) is accepted because of the path

and strings $pq^k r$ for $k > 0$ are accepted because of the paths that go round the loop k times in the following:

$\square$

For example, consider the following state-transition diagram, which has two states:

The diagram accepts the string 11; for this string, $p = \varepsilon$, $q = 11$, $r = \varepsilon$, and all strings of the form $(11)^k$ are accepted by the state-transition diagram. The diagram also accepts 1010; for this string, $p = 1$, $q = 0$, $r = 10$, and all strings of the form $10^k 10$ are accepted by the state-transition diagram.

The most important applications of this result are to show that certain languages are *not* regular.

EXAMPLE 9.1 The language $\{0^i 1^i \mid$ for all $i \geq 0\}$ is *not* a regular language.

Proof. We use the method of proof by contradiction; that is, we assume that the language *is* regular and then show that this inevitably leads to a contradiction, proving that the language is *not* regular.

If the language were regular, it would be the language recognized by some state-transition diagram. Let n be the number of states in this state-transition diagram, and consider the following string: $0^n 1^n$; this is in the language being considered and has length $> n$.

According to the pumping lemma, the string $0^n 1^n$ may be written as pqr for strings p, q ($\neq \varepsilon$), and r, such that all strings $pq^k r$ for $k \geq 0$ must also be accepted by the state-transition diagram; furthermore, pq will be of length $\leq n$. But, because the string starts with n 0s, q must consist of 0s *only* (and is not empty); this means that, for any $k \neq 1$, $pq^k r$ has the form $0^m 1^n$ for $m \neq n$. Such a string would *not* be in the language being considered because the numbers of 0s and 1s do not agree, and it should not be accepted by the state-transition diagram. This is a contradiction, and so the assumption that the language is regular is not tenable.

If we let L be the language under consideration and n be the number of states in the hypothetical recognizing state diagram, the structure of the proof is as follows:

```
Exists(x)  x ∈ L &&
  ForAll(p)(q)(r)  x = pqr && q ≠ ε && length pq ≤ n implies
    Exists(k)  k ≠ 1 && pq^k r ∉ L
```

In other words, you are required to come up with a *particular* string x that is in the language but for which *every* allowed decomposition into substrings p, q, and r leads to a contradiction. You are not allowed to choose a particular decomposition that happens to be problematical. On the other hand, it is sufficient to show that *some* choice of a $k \neq 1$ results in a string not in the language (and, consequently, establishes a contradiction).

EXAMPLE 9.2 Is the following language regular: $\{0^i 0^i \mid$ for all $i \geq 0\}$?

First, let us try to prove that the language is *not* regular using the pumping lemma.

Assume that the language is regular; hence, it must be the language recognized by some state-transition diagram. Let n be the number of states in this state-transition diagram, and consider the following string: $0^n 0^n$; this is in the language being considered and has length $> n$.

According to the pumping lemma, the string $0^n 0^n$ may be written as pqr for strings p, q ($\neq \varepsilon$), and r, such that all strings $pq^k r$ for $k \geq 0$ must also be accepted by the state-transition diagram; furthermore, pq will be of length $\leq n$. Because the string starts with at least n 0s, q must consist of 0s (and is not empty); this means that, for any $k \neq 1$, $pq^k r$ has the form $0^i 0^n$ for $i \neq n$.

But we may *not*, based on the information we have, conclude that this string is *not* in the language: it may be that $i + n = 2 \cdot j$ (i.e., is an even number) and so the string $pq^k r$ would have the form $0^j 0^j$, which clearly *is* in the language. So it seems that we are unable to *force* a contradiction using the string $0^n 0^n$!

Of course, this failure does not mean that the language *is* regular: it may be that we just didn't choose a suitable string. But, on further consideration, it becomes apparent that the language in question is in fact described by the regular expression $(00)^*$, and this observation *proves* that the language is in fact regular.

EXERCISE 9.11 For each of the following sets of strings over $\{0, 1\}$, determine whether it is a regular language; if so, give a state-transition diagram or regular expression that describes the language, and if not, prove it.

(a) $\{0^i 10^i \mid \text{for all } i \geq 0\}$

(b) $\{0^i 1^j \mid \text{for all } i, j \geq 0\}$

(c) $\{0^i 1^j \mid \text{for all } i > j \geq 0\}$

EXAMPLE 9.3 The language consisting of all strings over $\{0, 1\}$ with the same number of 0s and 1s is *not* a regular language.

Proof. By contradiction. If this language were regular, so would be its intersection with the regular language $0^* 1^*$; however, the intersection of these languages is the language that was proved in Example 9.1 *not* to be regular. This is a contradiction, and so the assumption that the language is regular is not tenable.   □

EXERCISE 9.12 Determine whether the language $\{0^i 1^j \mid \text{for all } i \neq j\}$ is regular. If it is regular, give a state-transition diagram or regular expression that describes the language. If it is not regular, prove it.

EXERCISE 9.13 Can the pumping lemma be used to prove that a language is regular? Explain your answer.

EXERCISE 9.14 Prove that a state-transition diagram with n states accepts an infinite language if and only if it accepts a string of length l with $n \leq l < 2n$.

9.5   Other Formalisms

9.5.1   REGULAR GRAMMARS

In Chapter 10, a more powerful class of language-description formalisms called
context-free grammars will be discussed. A certain restricted subclass of such
grammars, termed *regular* grammars, describe regular languages; furthermore,
any regular language may be described by a regular grammar. These facts are
primarily of theoretical interest, as regular grammars are too clumsy to be of
much use in practice.

9.5.2   PATTERNS IN SOFTWARE TOOLS

Many kinds of programs need to find "patterns" in text and to re-arrange
the components in some appropriate way; regular expressions are often used
to describe such patterns. For example, many utilities in UNIX–like operating systems are based on regular expressions; these include text editors (ed,
vi, emacs), file-searching tools (grep), scripting languages (AWK, PERL, TCL,
PYTHON), lexical-analyzer generators (lex), stream-processing utilities (sed,
cut, paste), dialogue editors (expect), and so on. Regular expressions are also
used in many programming environments, such as Delphi. The techniques
described in Chapter 8 (or optimizations of those techniques) are used to implement regular expression-based pattern matching.

The characters |, *, +, and ? are typically used as *metacharacters*, denoting
union, closure, positive closure, and option, respectively; escape conventions
allow these characters to be interpreted as themselves. Often, some convenient abbreviations and extensions to standard regular expressions are also
supported.

- The metacharacter . matches any character *except* the "new-line" character; the exception prevents unintended matches *across* a line boundary.

- "Character classes," such as [0123456789], match any single character
  from among those within the brackets; this example could also be abbreviated as [0-9]. Another example is [a-zA-Z]. The character-class
  notation is particularly useful when, for efficiency reasons, the general
  union operation is *not* supported.

- There may be ways to match the empty string at the *beginning* or at the
  end of a line, or of a word.

- There may be ways to get the effects of S^n, $\bigcup_{i \geq n} S^i$, or $\bigcup_{n \leq i \leq m} S^i$ for any
  regular expression S.

9.5.3 Syntax Diagrams

Syntax diagrams are often used to specify the syntax of programming languages. When they are restricted to being nonrecursive, the languages described are regular languages. For example, the following is a syntax diagram for unsigned real numbers in Pascal:

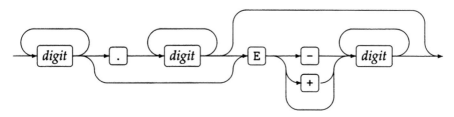

Note that, in this notation, vocabulary tokens are used to label the *nodes* and that the edges are unlabeled, whereas the opposite is true for state-transition diagrams.

9.6 Additional Reading

The equivalence between regular expressions and state-transition diagrams was first shown in [Kle56]. Applications of regular expressions are treated in detail in [Fri97]. An efficient algorithm for minimizing state diagrams is given in [Hop71].

References

[Fri97] J. E. F. Friedl. *Mastering Regular Expressions*. O'Reilly, 1997.

[Hop71] J. E. Hopcroft. An *n* log *n* algorithm for minimizing the states in a finite automaton. In Z. Zohavi and A. Paz, editors, *International Symposium on the Theory of Machines and Computations*, pages 189–96. Academic Press, 1971.

[Kle56] S. C. Kleene. Representation of events in nerve nets and finite automata. In C. E. Shannon and J. McCarthy, editors, *Automata Studies*, pages 3–42. Princeton University Press, 1956.

Chapter 10

Context-Free Languages

In this chapter, we study formalisms that allow languages to be defined using union, concatenation, and *recursion*; the effect of language closure may be obtained as a special case of recursion. A definition of a formal language that uses only union, concatenation, and recursion (in addition to alphabet tokens and the empty string) is known as a *context-free grammar*.

10.1   Backus-Naur Formalism

One of the best-known notations for context-free grammars was first used to describe the syntax of the programming language ALGOL 60; it is now known as Backus-Naur formalism (BNF). For example, the language of palindromes over {0, 1} is defined by the BNF rules of Table 10.1. Each line is termed a *production*. It is possible to combine productions with the same left-hand side using the union operation (conventionally represented in context-free grammars by the | operator), as in Tables 10.2 or 10.3 on page 208.

Table 10.1
___

⟨*palindrome*⟩ ::= ⟨*empty*⟩

⟨*palindrome*⟩ ::= 0

⟨*palindrome*⟩ ::= 1

⟨*palindrome*⟩ ::= 0 ⟨*palindrome*⟩ 0

⟨*palindrome*⟩ ::= 1 ⟨*palindrome*⟩ 1

⟨*empty*⟩ ::=

Table 10.2

⟨*palindrome*⟩ ::= ⟨*empty*⟩ | 0 | 1 | 0 ⟨*palindrome*⟩ 0 | 1 ⟨*palindrome*⟩ 1

⟨*empty*⟩ ::=

Table 10.3

⟨*palindrome*⟩ ::= ⟨*empty*⟩
            | 0
            | 1
            | 0 ⟨*palindrome*⟩ 0
            | 1 ⟨*palindrome*⟩ 1

⟨*empty*⟩ ::=

The ⟨· · ·⟩ forms are termed (syntactic) *metavariables* or *syntactic categories*. Traditionally, all these must be "defined" by being used as the left-hand side of one or more of the productions. But we will find it convenient to allow some of the metavariables to remain "undefined" (i.e., treated as tokens). Those that appear on the left of one or more productions will be termed *nonterminal symbols*; these are essentially language-valued *variables*. Those that do not appear on the left-hand side of any production and all other symbols (except | and ::=) are termed *terminal symbols*. A sequence of terminal symbols is termed a *terminal string*.

It should be clear how BNF productions may be interpreted as (mutually recursive) equations defining languages, as in Section 7.3.4. A more "operational" interpretation, which is useful for discussing *recognizers*, is given in Section 10.2.

EXERCISE 10.1 Does the following grammar define the empty language?
     ⟨*empty*⟩ ::=
If not, how may the empty language be defined by a BNF grammar?

EXERCISE 10.2 Define each of the following languages over $\{0, 1\}$ using BNF productions:

  (a) $\{0^i 1^i \mid i \geq 0\}$
  (b) $\{0^i 10^i \mid i \geq 0\}$

As another example, Table 10.4 gives a BNF grammar for simple algebraic expressions over a set of operators. In this grammar, the symbols ⟨*var*⟩ (variable) and ⟨*con*⟩ (constant) are terminal symbols. The productions specify that

Table 10.4

$$
\begin{aligned}
\langle exp \rangle \quad &::= \quad \langle con \rangle \\
&\mid \quad \langle var \rangle \\
&\mid \quad \langle exp \rangle \; \langle op \rangle \; \langle exp \rangle \\
&\mid \quad (\, \langle exp \rangle \,) \\[6pt]
\langle op \rangle \quad &::= \quad + \mid - \mid * \mid /
\end{aligned}
$$

an expression is either a constant, a variable, a binary operation with two subexpressions as operands, or a parenthesized expression; note that, in the latter, the parentheses are terminal symbols (i.e., expected to appear in the input string), rather than BNF metacharacters such as ::= and |. For example, here are some terminal strings in the language $\langle exp \rangle$:

$$
\begin{aligned}
&\langle con \rangle \\
&(\langle con \rangle) \\
&\langle var \rangle \\
&\langle var \rangle + \langle con \rangle \\
&\langle con \rangle * \langle var \rangle \\
&(\langle var \rangle + \langle con \rangle) \,/\, \langle var \rangle \\
&\langle var \rangle - (\langle var \rangle - \langle var \rangle)
\end{aligned}
$$

Finally, the productions in Table 10.5 give a grammar that defines a language $\langle statement \rangle$ consisting of (some of) the forms of statement in the programming language C. In this grammar, $\langle var \rangle$ (variable) and $\langle exp \rangle$ (expression) are terminal symbols.

Table 10.5

$$
\begin{aligned}
\langle statement \rangle \quad &::= \quad ; \\
&\mid \quad \langle var \rangle = \langle exp \rangle \; ; \\
&\mid \quad \text{if } (\, \langle exp \rangle \,) \; \langle statement \rangle \; \text{else } \langle statement \rangle \\
&\mid \quad \text{while } (\, \langle exp \rangle \,) \; \langle statement \rangle \\
&\mid \quad \{ \; \langle sequence \rangle \; \} \\[6pt]
\langle sequence \rangle \quad &::= \quad \langle empty \rangle \mid \langle statement \rangle \; \langle sequence \rangle \\[6pt]
\langle empty \rangle \quad &::=
\end{aligned}
$$

A context-free grammar for the extended subset of C used for the programs in this book may be found in Section A.13.

EXERCISE 10.3 Augment the grammar of Table 10.5 to allow for do . . . while loops.

EXERCISE 10.4 What languages are defined by the following grammar?

$\langle neutral \rangle ::= \langle empty \rangle \mid + \langle neg \rangle \langle neutral \rangle \mid - \langle pos \rangle \langle neutral \rangle$

$\langle neg \rangle ::= - \mid + \langle neg \rangle \langle neg \rangle$

$\langle pos \rangle ::= + \mid - \langle pos \rangle \langle pos \rangle$

$\langle empty \rangle ::=$

EXERCISE 10.5 If all the productions in a context-free grammar are *either* of the form $\langle N \rangle ::= a$ where a is a terminal symbol or ε, *or* of the form $\langle N \rangle ::= a \langle M \rangle$ where a is a terminal symbol or ε and $\langle M \rangle$ is a nonterminal, it is termed a *regular* grammar.* Design a regular grammar for the language of all strings over $\{0, 1\}$ with an even number of 1s.

10.2   Derivations

BNF productions may be interpreted as replacement rules, which may be used to *generate* terminal strings.

DEFINITION 10.1 If s and s' are strings of symbols (both terminal and nonterminal) and s' may be obtained from s by replacing one instance of a nonterminal symbol in s by the sequence of symbols in one of the productions for that nonterminal, we say that s *immediately generates* s', or that s' is *immediately derivable from* s, written $s \Rightarrow s'$.

Of course, this definition is to be interpreted in the context of a specific set of productions. In the case of an *empty* production, such as the productions for nonterminal $\langle empty \rangle$ in the example grammars, the nonterminal should be replaced by the empty string ε, that is to say, the nonterminal should simply be deleted.

Some of the immediate-generation relationships specified by the productions in Table 10.1 (or Tables 10.2 or 10.3) are given in Table 10.6. Note that, in general, there may be several nonterminal symbols in string s, of which exactly one is chosen for "expansion." Unlike the conventional interpretation of inference rules in logic, multiple instances of the *same* metavariable in s need not be replaced by the *same* production right-hand side in s'.

The origin of the term "context-free" may now be explained. In some forms of grammar, the productions may have left-hand sides that are not single nonterminals. The effect is to impose contextual constraints on the applicability of the production. With a context-free grammar, no contextual criteria must be satisfied to expand a nonterminal symbol.

---

*It may be proved that the language defined by any regular grammar is a regular language, and that every regular language is definable by a regular grammar.

Table 10.6

$$
\begin{array}{rcl}
\langle empty \rangle & \Rightarrow & \varepsilon \\
\langle palindrome \rangle & \Rightarrow & \langle empty \rangle \\
\langle palindrome \rangle & \Rightarrow & 0 \\
\langle palindrome \rangle & \Rightarrow & 1 \\
\langle palindrome \rangle & \Rightarrow & 0\langle palindrome \rangle 0 \\
\langle palindrome \rangle & \Rightarrow & 1\langle palindrome \rangle 1 \\
0\langle palindrome \rangle 0 & \Rightarrow & 0\langle empty \rangle 0 \\
0\langle palindrome \rangle 0 & \Rightarrow & 01\langle palindrome \rangle 10 \\
0\langle palindrome \rangle 0 & \Rightarrow & 010 \\
0\langle palindrome \rangle 0 & \Rightarrow & 000 \\
0\langle empty \rangle 0 & \Rightarrow & 00 \\
0\langle palindrome \rangle 0\langle palindrome \rangle 0 & \Rightarrow & 010\langle palindrome \rangle 0 \\
0\langle palindrome \rangle 0\langle palindrome \rangle 0 & \Rightarrow & 0\langle palindrome \rangle 010
\end{array}
$$

DEFINITION 10.2 If s and s' are symbol strings, we say that s *generates* s', or that s' is *derivable from* s (according to the set of BNF productions under consideration), written $s \Rightarrow^* s'$, if either $s' = s$, $s \Rightarrow s'$, or there exist $n > 0$ "intermediate" strings $s_1, s_2, \ldots, s_n$ such that $s \Rightarrow s_1 \Rightarrow \cdots \Rightarrow s_n \Rightarrow s'$. The sequence of strings, each immediately derivable from its predecessor, is termed a *derivation* (of s' from s).

The "generates" relation is, therefore, the reflexive and transitive closure of the "immediately generates" relation.

For example, the following derivation shows that 101101 may be derived from $\langle palindrome \rangle$:

$$
\begin{array}{rcl}
\langle palindrome \rangle & \Rightarrow & 1\langle palindrome \rangle 1 \\
& \Rightarrow & 10\langle palindrome \rangle 01 \\
& \Rightarrow & 101\langle palindrome \rangle 101 \\
& \Rightarrow & 101\langle empty \rangle 101 \\
& \Rightarrow & 101101
\end{array}
$$

EXERCISE 10.6 For each step in the preceding derivation, identify which production is being used.

The *language* generated by nonterminal $\langle N \rangle$ (according to the set of BNF productions under consideration) is then the set of all *terminal* strings generated by $\langle N \rangle$. This is, of course, the same language that would be defined for

$\langle N \rangle$ by the iterative equation-solution scheme discussed in Section 7.3.4. For example, the languages generated by $\langle empty \rangle$ and $\langle palindrome \rangle$ in Table 10.1 are $\{\varepsilon\}$ and the set of all palindromes over $\{0, 1\}$, respectively.

10.3   Parse Trees

For many applications, a context-free grammar is used to determine not only a *language* (set of strings) but also the *phrase structure* of the strings in the language. The phrase structure of a string in a language defined by a context-free grammar may be portrayed by means of what is termed a *parse tree* (or derivation tree). If the string is generated by a nonterminal symbol $\langle N \rangle$, the root node is labeled $\langle N \rangle$, and its subtrees represent the components of the production $\langle N \rangle ::= s_1 s_2 \cdots s_n$ used for that nonterminal-symbol instance in the derivation of the string, as in the following:

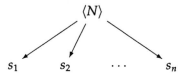

If the production is "empty," the representation

may be used. The same principles apply to all internal nodes, so that the "frontier" of the tree (the sequence of leaves from left to right) consists of nodes labeled by the successive terminal symbols of the string, perhaps interspersed by occurrences of ε.

For example, $(\langle var \rangle + \langle con \rangle) * \langle var \rangle$ is a string in the language generated by $\langle exp \rangle$ according to the grammar of Table 10.4; its parse tree is given in Figure 10.1. Note that operators such as $*$ and $+$ appear as labels of terminal nodes in this kind of tree, not in internal nodes.

EXERCISE 10.7 Show by giving a simple example that different derivations may result in the same parse tree.

10.4   Ambiguity

If the phrase structure of strings is significant, the grammar in use must not ascribe more than one parse tree to any string in the language; a grammar that does so is termed *ambiguous*. The grammar of Table 10.4 for expressions is ambiguous; for example, both of the parse trees in Figure 10.2 are valid for the

Figure 10.1

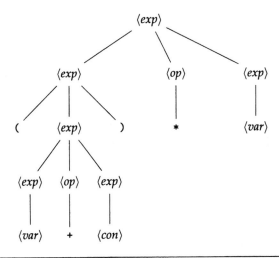

string ⟨var⟩ – ⟨var⟩ – ⟨var⟩. Because subtraction is *not* an associative operation, these would in general give different results if the expression grammar were used for a calculator or programming language. Most programming languages assume that the – operator "associates to the left," and so the tree on the left is the "correct" one, but the tree on the right is also valid for the given grammar.

Figure 10.2

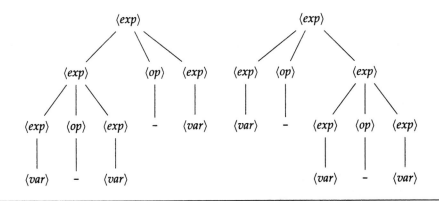

EXERCISE 10.8 Give two parse trees ascribed to the string ⟨*var*⟩ + ⟨*var*⟩ * ⟨*var*⟩ by the grammar of Table 10.4. Which would be the correct one according to the usual conventions for operator precedence?

These problems may be addressed by redesigning the grammar for expressions to take account of syntactic associativity and precedence of operators. The grammar given in Table 10.7 is appropriate if the operators * and / have higher precedence than + and – and all operators associate to the left. The partitioning of the operators into "addition" operators and "multiplication" operators and the introduction of the new syntactic categories ⟨*term*⟩ and ⟨*factor*⟩ ensure the desired precedence. The use of "left-recursive" productions, as in

   ⟨*exp*⟩ ::= ⟨*exp*⟩ · · ·

and

   ⟨*term*⟩ ::= ⟨*term*⟩ · · ·

ensures left-associativity.

Table 10.7

   ⟨*exp*⟩ ::= ⟨*term*⟩ | ⟨*exp*⟩ ⟨*addop*⟩ ⟨*term*⟩

   ⟨*addop*⟩ ::= + | –

   ⟨*term*⟩ ::= ⟨*factor*⟩ | ⟨*term*⟩ ⟨*multop*⟩ ⟨*factor*⟩

   ⟨*multop*⟩ ::= * | /

   ⟨*factor*⟩ ::= ⟨*con*⟩ | ⟨*var*⟩ | (⟨*exp*⟩)

We will later show that this grammar for expressions is in fact unambiguous. For example, the *only* parse tree for the string ⟨*var*⟩ + ⟨*var*⟩ * ⟨*var*⟩ using the grammar of Table 10.7 is given in Figure 10.3.

EXERCISE 10.9 Draw the parse tree ascribed to each of the following strings by the grammar of Table 10.7:

   (a) ⟨*var*⟩ – ⟨*var*⟩ – ⟨*var*⟩

   (b) (⟨*var*⟩ – ⟨*var*⟩) – ⟨*var*⟩

   (c) ⟨*var*⟩ – (⟨*var*⟩ – ⟨*var*⟩)

   (d) (⟨*var*⟩ + ⟨*var*⟩) * ⟨*var*⟩

EXERCISE 10.10 Augment or modify the grammar of Table 10.7 to allow for *unary* use of the addition operators, as in –⟨*var*⟩ + ⟨*con*⟩.

Figure 10.3

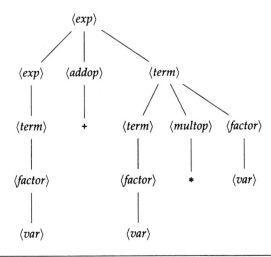

EXERCISE 10.11 Augment or modify the grammar of Table 10.7 to allow for use of **
as an exponentiation operator; it is to have the highest precedence and associate to the
right.

EXERCISE 10.12

(a) What language is generated by the following context-free grammar:

$\langle S \rangle ::= \langle empty \rangle \mid 0\ \langle S \rangle \mid \langle S \rangle\ 1$

$\langle empty \rangle ::=$

(b) Is the language a regular language?

(c) Show that the grammar is ambiguous.

(d) Give an unambiguous grammar for the language.

EXERCISE 10.13 Is the following simpler grammar for statements satisfactory? Explain
your answer.

$\langle statement \rangle ::=\ ;$
        $\mid\ \langle var \rangle = \langle exp \rangle\ ;$
        $\mid$ **if** ($\langle exp \rangle$) $\langle statement \rangle$ **else** $\langle statement \rangle$
        $\mid$ **while** ($\langle exp \rangle$) $\langle statement \rangle$
        $\mid\ \langle statement \rangle\ \langle statement \rangle$
        $\mid$ { $\langle statement \rangle$ }
        $\mid\ \langle empty \rangle$

$\langle empty \rangle\ \ ::=$

The heuristic techniques we have demonstrated for designing an unambiguous grammar for expressions cannot work for *all* ambiguous context-free grammars.

FACT 10.1 The language $\{a^i b^j c^k \mid i = j \text{ or } j = k\}$ is context-free but does not have an unambiguous grammar.

Such languages are described as being *inherently ambiguous*. Fortunately, inherently ambiguous languages rarely arise in practice.

Even more discouraging (and surprising) is the following.

FACT 10.2 There cannot be a *general* algorithm for determining whether an arbitrary context-free grammar is ambiguous.

This fact does not merely state that we do not currently *have* such an algorithm; it asserts that such an algorithm cannot exist! This state of affairs will be discussed in some detail in Chapter 12.

The good news is that it is usually possible to design provably unambiguous grammars for most context-free languages of practical interest. Furthermore, recognizers for such grammars are more efficient than recognizers based on techniques suitable for *arbitrary* context-free languages. Recognizers for context-free languages will be discussed in Chapter 11.

10.5 Push-Down Automata

In Chapters 8 and 9, we saw that a language is regular if and only if it is the language accepted by a state-transition diagram. In this section, we describe a comparable machine model of language recognition that allows a similar correspondence to be established with the class of all context-free languages. The automata are termed *push-down automata* and are essentially finite state automata of the kind described by state-transition diagrams, but they also have available a "push-down store" or stack of unbounded depth.

We will describe push-down automata using state-transition diagrams in which the edge labels have been augmented by stack instructions. If c stands for a vocabulary token, d for a stack token (possibly drawn from a different or partially overlapping vocabulary of tokens), and w for a string of stack tokens, edge labels have the form $c, d \mapsto w$. A transition of this form may be made if the current input string token is c and the token at the top of the stack is d; the effect is to read the input token and replace the top of the stack by the components of w, with the leftmost component of w becoming the new top of the stack.

We allow edge labels with $c = \varepsilon$, in which case the state changes without reading an input token, possibly changing the stack. We also allow $d = \varepsilon$, in which case the state changes and a stack-token string is pushed into the stack as explained earlier, but without matching or popping a stack token. In particular, this convention makes it possible for the initial stack to be *empty*.

An input string is accepted if there is a directed path from the starting state to an accepting state whose sequence of input tokens spells out the string *and* the stack, initially empty, may be manipulated by the stack instructions in the edge labels as indicated earlier, and is again empty after reading the string.

EXAMPLE 10.1 The following push-down automaton recognizes the language $\{0^i 1^i \mid i \geq 0\}$ of all balanced strings over $\{0, 1\}$:

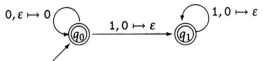

The automaton pushes 0s into the stack as it reads them; after the 0s, it reads 1s, popping 0s off the stack, verifying that the numbers of 0s and 1s are the same. If there are too many 0s, the stack is not emptied. If there are too many 1s, there will not be a matching stack token, and the automaton must "die."

The following table traces the behavior of this push-down automaton as it processes the input string 000111:

state	input	stack
q_0	000111	ε
q_0	00111	0
q_0	0111	00
q_0	111	000
q_1	11	00
q_1	1	0
q_1	ε	ε

EXAMPLE 10.2 The following push-down automaton recognizes the language

$$\{w! w^R \mid w \in \{0, 1\}^*\}$$

of "centered" palindromes; these palindromes have an exclamation mark at their central position.

$0, \varepsilon \mapsto 0$
$1, \varepsilon \mapsto 1$ q_0 $!, \varepsilon \mapsto \varepsilon$ q_1 $0, 0 \mapsto \varepsilon$
$1, 1 \mapsto \varepsilon$

In the starting state, input tokens 0 and 1 are read and pushed into the stack; when the ! token is read, the automaton changes state and begins matching input tokens against stack tokens, which are of course popped from the stack in reverse order. The string is accepted if the entire stack is emptied. The following table traces the processing of input string 110!011:

state	input	stack
q_0	110!011	ε
q_0	10!011	1
q_0	0!011	11
q_0	!011	011
q_1	011	011
q_1	11	11
q_1	1	1
q_1	ε	ε

Note that the top of the stack is at the left.

In general, a push-down automaton may be *nondeterministic* (i.e., may allow more than one transition for some configuration).

EXAMPLE 10.3 The following push-down automaton recognizes the language

$$\{ww^R \mid w \in \{0,1\}^*\}$$

of all even-length palindromes over $\{0,1\}$:

This automaton resembles the preceding one, but in state q_0 it may *either* push the next input symbol into the stack (and stay in state q_0) *or* change state using an ε transition. This nondeterminism is needed because there is no way for the automaton to recognize the "center" of the input string.

EXERCISE 10.14 Design a push-down automaton that recognizes the language of *all* palindromes over $\{0,1\}$.

EXERCISE 10.15 Design a push-down automaton that recognizes the language of all strings over $\{+,-\}$, with the number of + signs equal to the number of − signs.

For *any* context-free language for which we have a context-free grammar, we may construct a push-down automaton that recognizes the language. Only two states are needed; let the two states be called q_0 (the initial state) and q_1 (the only accepting state). There is to be one transition from q_0 to q_1 as follows: $\varepsilon, \varepsilon \mapsto \langle S \rangle$, where $\langle S \rangle$ is the nonterminal symbol for the language; this initial transition sets up the automaton to begin recognizing an instance of S. Then, for each possible input token (terminal symbol) c, there is to be a transition from q_1 to itself if the current input token matches the current top-of-stack token: $c, c \mapsto \varepsilon$. Finally, for each production $\langle N \rangle ::= c_0 c_1 \cdots c_{n-1}$ of the grammar, there is to be a transition from q_1 to itself of the form $\varepsilon, \langle N \rangle \mapsto c_0 c_1 \cdots c_{n-1}$. The result is, schematically, as follows:

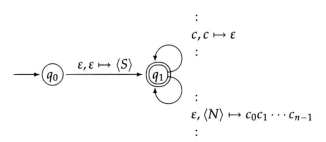

Notice that the stack vocabulary includes all the nonterminal symbols of the grammar, as well as all the terminal symbols. When the automaton accepts a string, it has emulated a derivation of the string according to the grammar; furthermore, the automaton does not accept any string that cannot be so derived.

For example, from the following grammar for balanced strings:

$\langle B \rangle ::= \langle empty \rangle \mid 0 \langle B \rangle 1$

$\langle empty \rangle ::=$

the push-down automaton constructed is as follows:

$$0, 0 \mapsto \varepsilon$$
$$1, 1 \mapsto \varepsilon$$

$$\varepsilon, \varepsilon \mapsto \langle B \rangle$$

$$\varepsilon, \langle B \rangle \mapsto \langle empty \rangle$$
$$\varepsilon, \langle B \rangle \mapsto 0 \langle B \rangle 1$$
$$\varepsilon, \langle empty \rangle \mapsto \varepsilon$$

The following table traces the behavior of this automaton on the input string 000111:

state	input	stack
q_0	000111	ε
q_1	000111	$\langle B \rangle$
q_1	000111	$0\langle B \rangle 1$
q_1	00111	$\langle B \rangle 1$
q_1	00111	$0\langle B \rangle 11$
q_1	0111	$\langle B \rangle 11$
q_1	0111	$0\langle B \rangle 111$
q_1	111	$\langle B \rangle 111$
q_1	111	111
q_1	11	11
q_1	1	1
q_1	ε	ε

The construction just described shows that every context-free language may be recognized by a (possibly nondeterministic) push-down automaton with only two states. What about the other direction? One might think that by using more than two states it would be possible to recognize languages that are not context-free, but this is not the case.

FACT 10.3 The language accepted by any push-down automaton is a context-free language.

This fact may be proved by showing how to construct a context-free grammar to emulate any given push-down automaton; the construction will not be described here.

10.6 Non-Context-Free Languages*

The following result may be used to prove that certain languages are *not* definable by any context-free grammar.

PROPOSITION 10.1 (PUMPING LEMMA FOR CONTEXT-FREE LANGUAGES)
Suppose that a language is recognized by a context-free grammar with n nonterminal symbols and that m is the maximum number of symbols in any production. If the grammar generates any string s of length greater than m^{n+1}, there exist strings $u, v, w, x,$ and y such that

- $s = u\,v\,w\,x\,y$

- $v \neq \varepsilon$ or $x \neq \varepsilon$

- the string vwx has length $\leq m^{n+1}$

- all strings of the form $uv^k wx^k y$ for every $k \geq 0$ are also generated.

Proof. The idea behind the proof is that if a generated string is sufficiently long, its parse tree must be sufficiently tall that there is a path from the root to a terminal symbol in which some nonterminal symbol $\langle N \rangle$ appears more than once. The subtree rooted at the first such occurrence of $\langle N \rangle$ may be replaced by the subtree rooted at the second occurrence, or vice versa, and so on, to yield

---

*The material in this section is not referred to in the rest of this book.

other generated strings. That is, the parse tree

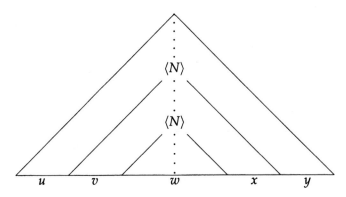

may be pumped *down* ($k = 0$) to get

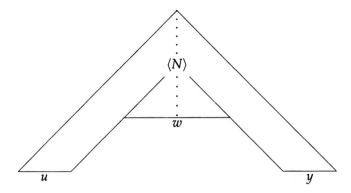

or pumped *up* once ($k = 2$) to get

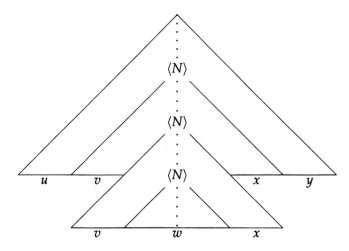

and so on.

The critical length m^{n+1} is determined as follows. For a parse tree of height 1, the number of leaves is m or fewer because m is the length of the longest production. For a parse tree of height 2, the number of leaves is m^2 or fewer. In general, if the height of a parse tree is h, the length of the frontier is at most m^h. If a generated string has length $> m^{n+1}$, it must therefore have a parse tree of height at least $n + 1$. This means that there is a path from the root to the frontier of length at least $n + 1$, and this path must have at least $n + 1$ occurrences of nonterminal symbols because only the lowest symbol on this path is terminal; however, n is assumed to be the number of nonterminals in the grammar, so there must be at least one duplicate on the path.

The string vwx may be forced to be small enough by choosing the "deepest" occurrence of duplicated nonterminals.   □

EXAMPLE 10.4 The language $\{a^i b^i c^i \mid i \geq 0\}$ is not context-free.

Proof. By contradiction. Assume that the language is context-free, and let n be the number of nonterminals in the grammar and m be the maximum length of productions. Consider the string $a^l b^l c^l$, where $l = m^{n+1}$. This string is in the language being considered and has length $> m^{n+1}$.

According to the pumping lemma, the string may be written as $uvwxy$ with $v \neq \varepsilon$ or $x \neq \varepsilon$, and all strings $uv^k wx^k y$ for every $k \geq 0$ are generated by the grammar. If v or x contains more than one type of symbol (e.g., ab or bc), then v^2 or x^2 will be unacceptable substrings (e.g., abab or bcbc). On the other hand, if *both* v and x consist of only *one* type of symbol (e.g., aa or bb or cc), the number of occurrences of the *remaining* symbol type will stay the same when the string is pumped up or down; consequently, these strings cannot be in the language generated.

Hence, the requirements of the pumping lemma cannot be met; this is a contradiction, and so the assumption that the language is context-free is not tenable.   □

EXERCISE 10.16 Prove that the language $\{ww \mid w \in \{0, 1\}^*\}$ is not a context-free language.

The language $\{a^i b^i c^i \mid i \geq 0\}$ may be expressed as the *intersection* of the languages $\{a^i b^i c^k \mid i, k \geq 0\}$ and $\{a^k b^i c^i \mid i, k \geq 0\}$, both of which *are* context-free. This example shows that the intersection of context-free languages is not necessarily a context-free language.

FACT 10.4 The intersection of a *regular* language and a context-free language is always a context-free language.

This fact may be proved by using the push-down automata discussed in Section 10.5: it is possible to *combine* a conventional state diagram for the regular language with a push-down automaton for the context-free language so that the resulting automaton accepts a string if and only if it is in *both* the regular language *and* the context-free language.

This fact may be used to prove that certain languages are *not* context-free.

EXAMPLE 10.5 The language of all strings over $\{a, b, c\}$ that have the same number of as, bs, and cs is not context-free because, if it is intersected with the regular language $a^*b^*c^*$, the result is the language $\{a^i b^i c^i \mid i \geq 0\}$, which we have already shown is *not* context-free.

EXERCISE 10.17 Prove that the *union* and the *concatenation* of any two context-free languages and the *closure* of any context-free language are all context-free languages.

EXERCISE 10.18 Prove that the *complement* of a context-free language need not be a context-free language.

10.7 Other Formalisms

10.7.1 ALTERNATIVES TO BNF

Various other notational conventions are used for productions. The ::= symbol is often replaced by $\rightarrow$, and sometimes explicit quotes are used for terminal symbols so that the "antiquoting" brackets $\langle \cdots \rangle$ are unnecessary. Sometimes typeface conventions are used to distinguish terminal and nonterminal symbols, such as uppercase for nonterminal symbols and lowercase for terminals.

10.7.2 SYNTAX DIAGRAMS

Syntax diagrams are an important alternative to BNF-like productions for describing context-free languages. The use of syntax diagrams to describe *regular* languages has already been described in Section 9.5.3. To allow description of context-free languages, it must be possible to use diagram names (as well as token symbols) as node labels. This feature provides a form of recursion (possibly indirect), which is sufficient to allow context-free languages to be defined.

A syntax diagram equivalent to the grammar of Table 10.5 is given in Figure 10.4 on page 224. The nodes labeled *Statement* refer to the diagram itself.

Figure 10.4

Statement:

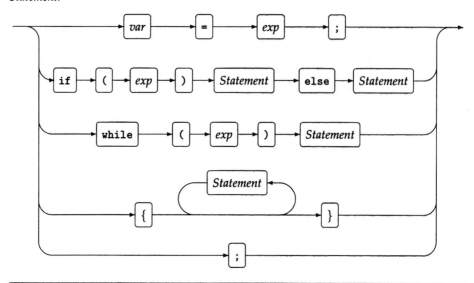

10.8 Additional Reading

Context-free languages were introduced in [Cho56], and the basic results were presented in [Cho59, BHPS61]. BNF was first described in [Bac60] and used to specify context-free aspects of the syntax of the programming language ALGOL 60 [NB+63]. The pumping lemma was first presented in [BHPS61]. The correspondence with push-down automata was proved in [Sch63, Cho62, Eve63]. For more on the theory of context-free languages, see [Gin66, HU79, MAK88].

Modern programming languages impose syntactic restrictions based on identifier scope and type compatibility. Such restrictions cannot be incorporated into context-free grammars [Flo62]. Various approaches have been used to specify such restrictions. Compiler implementers use *attributed grammars* [Knu68, WG84], in which attribute values are attached to terminal and nonterminal symbols; these may be computed both bottom-up ("synthesized attributes") and top-down ("inherited attributes") in the parse tree. Programming-language theorists specify such constraints by using systems of *inference rules*, as in logic, for "formulas" of the form $\pi \vdash X : \tau$, where X is a program phrase, π is a "context" (i.e., an assignment of types to at least the free identifiers of X, like an interface or a symbol table), and τ is the specified type of X *in that context*; see, for example, [Rey98].

REFERENCES

[Bac60]   J. W. Backus. The syntax and semantics of the proposed international algebraic language of the Zürich ACM-GAMM Conference. In *Information Processing, Proceedings of the International Conference on Information Processing, Unesco, Paris*, pages 125–31. Unesco, 1960.

[BHPS61] Y. Bar-Hillel, M. Perles, and E. Shamir. On formal properties of simple phrase structure grammars. *Zeitschrift für Phonetik, Sprachwissenschaft und Kommunikationsforschung*, 14:143–72, 1961.

[Cho56]   N. Chomsky. Three models for the description of language. *IRE Trans. on Information Theory*, 2(3):113–24, 1956.

[Cho59]   N. Chomsky. On certain formal properties of grammars. *Information and Control*, 2(2):137–67, 1959.

[Cho62]   N. Chomsky. Context-free grammar and pushdown storage. In *Quarterly Progress Report, 65*, pages 187–94. M.I.T. Research Laboratory in Electronics, 1962.

[Eve63]   J. Evey. Application of pushdown store machines. In *Proceedings of the 1963 Fall Joint Computer Conference*, pages 216–17. AFIPS Press, 1963.

[Flo62]   R. W. Floyd. On the nonexistence of a phrase structure grammar for ALGOL 60. *Comm. ACM*, 5(9):526–34, 1962.

[Gin66]   S. Ginsburg. *The Mathematical Theory of Context-Free Languages*. Addison-Wesley, 1966.

[HU79]   J. E. Hopcroft and J. D. Ullman. *Introduction to Automata Theory, Languages, and Computation*. Addison-Wesley, 1979.

[Knu68]   D. E. Knuth. Semantics of context-free languages. *Mathematical Systems Theory*, 2:127–45, 1968. Correction in Volume 5, p. 95 (1971).

[MAK88]   R. N. Moll, M. A. Arbib, and A. J. Kfoury. *An Introduction to Formal Language Theory*. Springer Verlag, 1988.

[NB+63]   P. Naur (ed.), J. W. Backus, F. L. Bauer, J. Green, C. Katz, J. McCarthy, A. J. Perlis, H. Rutishauser, K. Samelson, B. Vauquois, J. H. Wegstein, A. van Wijngaarden, and M. Woodger. Revised report on the algorithmic language ALGOL 60. *Comm. ACM*, 6(1):1–17, 1963. Also *The Computer Journal* 5:349–67, 1963, and *Numerische Mathematik* 4:420–53, 1963.

[Rey98]   J. C. Reynolds. *Theories of Programming Languages*. Cambridge University Press, 1998.

[Sch63]   M. P. Schutzenberger. On context-free languages and push-down automata. *Information and Control*, 6(3):246–64, 1963.

[WG84]   W. M. Waite and G. Goos. *Compiler Construction*. Springer Verlag, 1984.

Chapter 11

Parsing

Recognizers for context-free languages are termed *parsers*. We will assume the same interface as in Section 8.2; that is,

```
typename vocab;      /* vocabulary, augmented by EOS */
const vocab EOS;     /* end-of-string token */
vocab gettoken(void); /* returns next token */
```

where vocab is a type whose values represent all the terminal symbols, plus the "end-of-string" token EOS. Also as in Section 8.2, we require that recognizers terminate when gettoken returns EOS, producing a non-acceptance message only if the input string is *not* in the language. In practical applications, more detailed error messages would be output for incorrect input, and if the string *is* in the language, a translation of the input or a simplified representation of the parse tree would be created for further processing.

11.1 General Methods

A "brute-force" technique for parsing arbitrary context-free languages is to systematically generate strings in the language from the grammar, as discussed in Section 10.2, until either the input string is exactly matched or all further generated strings would be longer than the input. Of course, this kind of approach is extremely inefficient in time or space. The best practical parsing methods for *arbitrary* context-free grammars require time of order n^3 in the worst case, where n is the length of the input, though there are methods that are asymptotically subcubic (with very large constant factors). In practice, all these *general* methods are too inefficient for applications, such as compilers, which must be able to process long inputs very efficiently.

11.2   Deterministic Push-Down Automata

In Section 10.5, we described a way to construct a push-down automaton equivalent to any context-free grammar. Unfortunately, these automata are in general *nondeterministic* and, because they use an auxiliary stack of unbounded depth, are not implementable using the "set of states" method used for simple state diagrams in Section 8.3. Nevertheless, most context-free languages that arise in practice are in fact recognizable by *deterministic* push-down automata, and sophisticated systematic constructions of parsers based on such automata have been developed. We will not discuss these methods here, but they are an important part of any course on compilers.

11.3   Recursive Descent

In this section, we describe the basic ideas underlying a simple and relatively efficient approach to parsing known as *recursive descent*; it may be used with most context-free languages that arise in practice, provided that the developer is able to transform the grammar into a suitable form when necessary.

Here are the basic ideas.

- A recognizing function is coded for each nonterminal symbol in the grammar (except possibly those with only trivial productions, such as ⟨*empty*⟩ ::=).

- The current input token is used to decide which of several possible productions is the appropriate one to use when expanding a nonterminal.

Provided that the grammar is such that it is always possible to make the appropriate choice of production by using the current input token, the parse is determinate, and no backtracking is needed. We will study this issue in more detail after looking at some simple examples.

11.3.1   BALANCED STRINGS

Program 11.1 is a recursive-descent recognizer for the language of "balanced" strings over {0, 1}, as defined by the following BNF productions:

⟨*balanced*⟩ ::= ⟨*empty*⟩ | 0 ⟨*balanced*⟩ 1

⟨*empty*⟩ ::=

The definitions of vocab and gettoken are as in Program 8.2. Function MustBe is called when the current token is expected to be the specific token ThisToken. If it is, the next input token is read; but if not, a non-acceptance message is output and the parse is aborted by calling function exit.

Program 11.1

```
typedef enum { ZERO, ONE, EOS } vocab;

vocab gettoken(void) { ... }

vocab t;

void MustBe(vocab ThisToken)
{ ASSERT( ThisToken != EOS )
  /* verifies and then updates current token t */
  if (t != ThisToken)
  { printf("String not accepted.\n"); exit(0); }
  t = gettoken();
}

void Balanced(void)
{ switch (t)
  { case ONE:
    case EOS: /* <empty> */
      break;
    default: /* 0 <balanced> 1 */
      MustBe(ZERO);
      Balanced();
      MustBe(ONE);
  }
}

int main(void)
{ t = gettoken();
  Balanced();
  if (t != EOS) printf("String not accepted.\n");
  return 0;
}
```

The main function of the program simply initializes t and then calls
Balanced, which is expected to read one instance of ⟨*balanced*⟩. After this call,
it is verified that the current token is EOS.

Function Balanced implements the two productions for ⟨*balanced*⟩, using
the current token to choose which production is used. If the current token
is either of the tokens that may immediately *follow* a balanced string (1, represented by constant ONE, or EOS), the ⟨*empty*⟩ production is used, and if the
current token is 0 (constant ZERO), the production 0 ⟨*balanced*⟩ 1 is used. The
latter involves successively reading a 0, recognizing an "inner" balanced string
with a *recursive* call of function Balanced, and then reading a 1.

The parser is fairly efficient because it is never necessary to do any backtracking; if a production is chosen, that choice *must* be correct, or else the input
string is not in the language. The correct choice may be made because the only
token that may possibly be the *first* token of a nonempty balanced string (0) is
not one of the tokens that may immediately *follow* a balanced string (1 or EOS).

Hence, it is always possible to use the current string token to choose between the two productions, and backtracking is never necessary.

Note also that it is not necessary to store the entire string or even use a counter. In fact, the only variable defined in the program is t; yet we have proved that the language of balanced strings *cannot* be recognized by a finite-state automaton! The apparent contradiction is resolved when it is realized that the implementation of recursive function Balanced maintains an *implicit* stack that is, in effect, a counter. For this rather artificial example, a simple counter and a loop would certainly be more efficient; however, recursive descent is applicable to much more complex grammars for which ad hoc methods may not be evident.

11.3.2 STATEMENTS

Consider the grammar for C statements we gave in Table 10.5:

$\langle statement \rangle$ ::= ;
       | $\langle var \rangle = \langle exp \rangle$;
       | if ($\langle exp \rangle$) $\langle statement \rangle$ else $\langle statement \rangle$
       | while ($\langle exp \rangle$) $\langle statement \rangle$
       | { $\langle sequence \rangle$ }

$\langle sequence \rangle$ ::= $\langle empty \rangle$ | $\langle statement \rangle$ $\langle sequence \rangle$

$\langle empty \rangle$ ::=

Recursive descent parsing functions based on this grammar are given in Program 11.2.

Function Statement is structured so that the current token is used to choose among the productions for $\langle statement \rangle$. For each production, functions corresponding to the elements of the production are called successively.

Function Sequence is slightly different. First, a *declaration* of function Sequence appears before the definition of Statement; this declaration is required when a function is used before it is defined, as it is here in Statement. Then function Sequence must decide whether to follow the $\langle empty \rangle$ production. Because } is the only token that may immediately follow a $\langle sequence \rangle$ (and because a } cannot be the *initial* token of a $\langle statement \rangle$), the presence of a CLS_BRACE token in the input string may be used to choose between the productions.

The last step of Sequence is a recursive call to itself, so it is possible to simplify the function by using a while loop, as follows:

```
void Sequence(void)
{ while (t != CLS_BRACE)
    Statement();
}
```

Program 11.2

```
typedef enum
  { VAR, EXP, EQ, IF, ELSE, WHILE, OPN_BRACE, CLS_BRACE,
    OPN_PAREN, CLS_PAREN, SEMICOLON, EOS
  } vocab;

vocab gettoken(void) { ... }

vocab t;

void MustBe(vocab ThisToken) { ... }

void Sequence(void);

void Statement(void)
{ switch (t)
  { case SEMICOLON: /* ; */
      t = gettoken();
      break;
    case VAR: /* <var> = <exp> ; */
      t = gettoken();
      MustBe(EQ);
      MustBe(EXP);
      MustBe(SEMICOLON);
      break;
    case IF: /* if ( <exp> ) <statement> else <statement> */
      t = gettoken();
      MustBe(OPN_PAREN);
      MustBe(EXP);
      MustBe(CLS_PAREN);
      Statement();
      MustBe(ELSE);
      Statement();
      break;
    case WHILE: /* while ( <exp> ) <statement> */
      t = gettoken();
      MustBe(OPN_PAREN);
      MustBe(EXP);
      MustBe(CLS_PAREN);
      Statement();
      break;
    default: /* { <sequence> } */
      MustBe(OPN_BRACE);
      Sequence();
      MustBe(CLS_BRACE);
  }
}

void Sequence(void)
{ if (t == CLS_BRACE) /* <empty> */ ;
  else /* <statement> <sequence> */
  { Statement();
    Sequence();
  }
}

int main(void)
{ t = gettoken();
  Statement();
  if (t != EOS) printf("String not accepted.\n");
  return 0;
}
```

Consider now the following grammar, which specifies the syntax of the corresponding features of the programming language PASCAL:

⟨*statement*⟩ ::= ⟨*empty*⟩
          | ⟨*var*⟩ := ⟨*exp*⟩
          | IF ⟨*exp*⟩ THEN ⟨*statement*⟩ ELSE ⟨*statement*⟩
          | WHILE ⟨*exp*⟩ DO ⟨*statement*⟩
          | BEGIN ⟨*sequence*⟩ END

⟨*sequence*⟩ ::= ⟨*statement*⟩ | ⟨*statement*⟩ ; ⟨*sequence*⟩

⟨*empty*⟩   ::=

A parsing function for ⟨*statement*⟩ would be similar to that for statements in C, except that is necessary to decide whether to use the ⟨*empty*⟩ production. If the current token is one of the tokens that may immediately *follow* a statement in this fragment of PASCAL (i.e., ELSE, ;, END or EOS), the ⟨*empty*⟩ production is used; otherwise, the current token must be one of ⟨*var*⟩, IF, WHILE, or BEGIN. Because these sets of possible string tokens are *disjoint* (have no elements in common), the correct production to use may always be chosen using the current string token.

But there is a problem implementing a parsing function for the nonterminal ⟨*sequence*⟩: *both* productions start with nonterminal symbol ⟨*statement*⟩, and so there is no way to use the current string token to choose between them. The solution to this problem is simple: the property of left-distributivity of concatenation over union (Section 7.3) means that the productions

⟨*sequence*⟩ ::= ⟨*statement*⟩ | ⟨*statement*⟩ ; ⟨*sequence*⟩

are equivalent to

⟨*sequence*⟩ ::= ⟨*statement*⟩ ⟨*SequenceTail*⟩

⟨*SequenceTail*⟩ ::= ⟨*empty*⟩ | ; ⟨*sequence*⟩

where ⟨*SequenceTail*⟩ is a new nonterminal symbol. The only token that may immediately follow a ⟨*SequenceTail*⟩ is END, and the initial token of the second production is a semicolon. Consequently, these productions may be directly implemented in recursive-descent style using mutually recursive functions as follows:

```
void SequenceTail(void);

void Sequence(void)
{ Statement();
  SequenceTail();
}
```

```
void SequenceTail(void)
{ if (t == SEMICOLON)
  { t = gettoken();
    Sequence();
  }
}
```

This code may be simplified by collapsing the two functions into a single function:

```
void Sequence(void)
{ Statement();
  if (t == SEMICOLON)
  { t = gettoken();
    Sequence();
  }
}
```

But note that the last action of the function is to call itself recursively; this is more efficiently implemented as a while loop:

```
void Sequence(void)
{ Statement();
  while (t == SEMICOLON)
  { t = gettoken();
    Statement();
  }
}
```

The technique of using left-distributivity to allow recursive-descent parsing when multiple productions have identical prefixes is termed *left factoring*.

EXERCISE 11.1 Code a complete parser for PASCAL statements following the grammar given earlier.

Suppose now that we add the following production to our grammar for statements in C:

⟨*statement*⟩ ::= if (⟨*exp*⟩) ⟨*statement*⟩

This production shares a prefix with an existing production for ⟨*statement*⟩, and so we attempt to use left-factoring and replace these productions by

⟨*statement*⟩ ::= if (⟨*exp*⟩) ⟨*statement*⟩ ⟨*IfTail*⟩

⟨*IfTail*⟩ ::= ⟨*empty*⟩ | else ⟨*statement*⟩

But here there is a significant difficulty: the first token of the second production (else) may immediately follow an ⟨*IfTail*⟩, as in

if (⟨*exp*⟩) if (⟨*exp*⟩) ⟨*statement*⟩ else ⟨*statement*⟩

It would seem that a recursive-descent parser has no basis for choosing the correct production for ⟨*IfTail*⟩ if the current input token is else.

In fact, the grammar is *ambiguous*. Input of this form might be parsed as

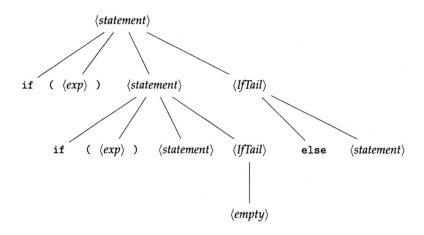

where the ⟨*empty*⟩ production is chosen for the inner ⟨*IfTail*⟩ and the `else` clause matches the *first* `if`, or as

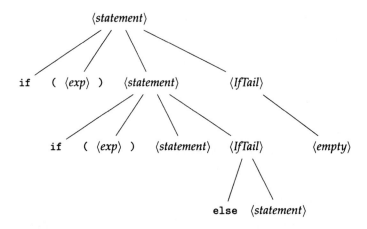

where the `else` ⟨*statement*⟩ production is used for the inner ⟨*IfTail*⟩ and the `else` clause matches the *second* `if`. Although there exist unambiguous grammars for this language, recursive-descent parsing cannot be used with them.

Fortunately, there is an ad hoc solution. If the code for parsing if statements is written as follows:

```
case IF: /* if ( <exp> ) <statement> [else <statement>] */
    t = gettoken();
    MustBe(OPN_PAREN);
    MustBe(EXP);
    MustBe(CLS_PAREN);
    Statement();
    if (t == ELSE)
    { t = gettoken();
      Statement();
    }
    break;
```

an else clause will always be matched with the nearest previous else-less if,
which is what is normally wanted and is correct for C. A programmer obtains
the other interpretation by using { ··· } brackets as follows:

$$\text{if } (\ \langle exp \rangle\ )\ \{\ \text{if }\ (\ \langle exp \rangle\ )\ \langle statement \rangle\ \}\ \text{else }\ \langle statement \rangle$$

Some programming languages avoid this problem by requiring a closing
bracket such as endif to match every if.

11.3.3 EXPRESSIONS

We now consider recursive-descent parsing of expressions. The following
grammar was given in Table 10.7:

$\langle exp \rangle ::= \langle term \rangle \mid \langle exp \rangle \langle addop \rangle \langle term \rangle$

$\langle addop \rangle ::= + \mid -$

$\langle term \rangle ::= \langle factor \rangle \mid \langle term \rangle \langle multop \rangle \langle factor \rangle$

$\langle multop \rangle ::= * \mid /$

$\langle factor \rangle ::= \langle con \rangle \mid \langle var \rangle \mid (\ \langle exp \rangle\ )$

But the use of left-recursion to define $\langle exp \rangle$ and $\langle term \rangle$ is problematic for
recursive-descent parsing. For example, any token that may be the first to-
ken of a $\langle term \rangle$ can also be the first token of an $\langle exp \rangle$; consequently, there is no
basis for choosing between the first and second productions for $\langle exp \rangle$.

This problem may be addressed by re-formulating the grammar using closure operations (as in Section 7.3.3) as follows:

⟨*exp*⟩ ::= ⟨*term*⟩ { ⟨*addop*⟩ ⟨*term*⟩ }

⟨*addop*⟩ ::= + | –

⟨*term*⟩ ::= ⟨*factor*⟩ { ⟨*multop*⟩ ⟨*factor*⟩ }

⟨*multop*⟩ ::= * | /

⟨*factor*⟩ ::= ⟨*con*⟩ | ⟨*var*⟩ | (⟨*exp*⟩)

where here the curly brackets { ⋯ } are metacharacters indicating *closure*. Strictly speaking, the phrase structures ascribed by this grammar are not those of the original; however, in practice this is not a problem because a list of (⟨*addop*⟩, ⟨*term*⟩) or (⟨*multop*⟩, ⟨*factor*⟩) pairs is understood to represent left-associated operations.

Recognizer code based on this grammar is given in Program 11.3. The closure operations are implemented by while loops in functions Term and Exp. In both cases, the tokens indicating that the loop body should be executed (⟨*multop*⟩ or ⟨*addop*⟩) cannot legitimately follow a ⟨*term*⟩ or ⟨*exp*⟩, respectively.

11.3.4 PALINDROMES

We now consider the language of palindromes over {0, 1}, as defined by the following productions:

⟨*palindrome*⟩ ::= ⟨*empty*⟩ | 0 | 1 | 0 ⟨*palindrome*⟩ 0 | 1 ⟨*palindrome*⟩ 1

⟨*empty*⟩ ::=

There are two serious problems here.

1. The empty string is generated by ⟨*palindrome*⟩, but the tokens that may immediately *follow* a ⟨*palindrome*⟩ are 0, 1, and EOS, and two of these are also *first* tokens of productions for ⟨*palindrome*⟩. Hence, a recursive-descent parser has no basis for choosing or not choosing the ⟨*empty*⟩ production.

2. Two productions both have 0 as their *first* tokens, and two other productions both have 1 as their first tokens. Hence, a recursive-descent parser has no basis for choosing between these production pairs.

Left factoring does not improve the situation, and we must conclude that we cannot parse this language using recursive descent.

Program 11.3

```c
typedef enum
{ PLUS, MINUS, TIMES, DIV, CON, VAR, OPN_PAREN, CLS_PAREN, EOS } vocab;

vocab gettoken(void); { ... }

vocab t;

void MustBe(vocab ThisToken) { ... }

void Exp(void);

void Factor(void)
/* <factor> :: <con> | <var> | ( <exp> ) */
{ switch (t)
  { case CON:
    case VAR:
      t = gettoken();
      break;
    default:
      MustBe(OPN_PAREN);
      Exp();
      MustBe(CLS_PAREN);
  }
}

void Term(void)
/* <term> ::= <factor> | <term> <multop> <factor>
   <multop ::= * | /
*/
{ Factor();
  while (t == TIMES || t == DIV)
  { t = gettoken();
    Factor();
  }
}

void Exp(void)
/* <exp> ::= <term> | <exp> <addop> <term>
   <addop ::= + | -
*/
{ Term();
  while (t == PLUS || t == MINUS)
  { t = gettoken();
    Term();
  }
}

int main(void)
{ t = gettoken();
  Exp();
  if (t != EOS) printf("String not accepted.\n");
  return 0;
}
```

On the other hand, consider the language of "centered" palindromes, as defined by the following grammar:

$\langle CenPal \rangle ::= $! $| $ 0 $\langle CenPal \rangle$ 0 $| $ 1 $\langle CenPal \rangle$ 1

The first of the two problems with $\langle palindrome \rangle$ is avoided because $\langle CenPal \rangle$ does not generate the empty string. The second problem is avoided because there is only one production for $\langle CenPal \rangle$ whose first token is 0, and similarly for 1.

EXERCISE 11.2 Code a recursive-descent parser for centered palindromes.

11.3.5   DISCUSSION

We have seen several examples of recursive-descent parsing in practice. In each case, it was necessary to ensure that, wherever there were several productions for a nonterminal, it would be possible to decide which production to choose using only the current token. In this section, we summarize the lessons of these examples in general terms. Such rules are important not only to be able to ensure that a recursive-descent parser is feasible, but also to verify that a grammar is not ambiguous, for if no alternative productions are available for expansion, the grammar must be unambiguous. It is for this reason that we may assert that *particular* grammars, for example, for expressions and statements, are *not* ambiguous, even though a *general* algorithm for testing ambiguity of context-free grammars cannot exist.

Here are two conditions that together are sufficient to allow recursive-descent parsing to be used with a conventional context-free grammar (and ensure that the grammar is unambiguous):

1. For each nonterminal $\langle N \rangle$, let $\langle N \rangle ::= \alpha_1 \mid \alpha_2 \mid \cdots \mid \alpha_n$ be all the productions for $\langle N \rangle$. It is required that

   $$first(\alpha_i) \cap first(\alpha_j) = \emptyset$$

   whenever $i \neq j$, where, for any string α, $first(\alpha)$ is the set of all initial tokens in nonempty strings derivable from α.

2. If the empty string ε is derivable from a nonterminal $\langle N \rangle$, it is required that

   $$follow \langle N \rangle \cap first \langle N \rangle = \emptyset$$

   where, for any nonterminal $\langle N \rangle$, $follow \langle N \rangle$ is the set of all initial tokens in nonempty strings that may follow $\langle N \rangle$ in any derivation, possibly including the end-of-string token EOS.

Note that the definitions of *first* and *follow* are not completely symmetric; in particular, *follow* is defined *only* for single nonterminal symbols.

In simple examples, such as those we have been considering, it is easy to determine the *first* and *follow* sets "by hand." However, for more complex grammars, fairly sophisticated algorithms must be used to allow for mutual dependencies between nonterminals and for nonterminals that may generate the empty string. The details are beyond the scope of this presentation, but they may be found in many books on compilers.

If a grammar does *not* satisfy these conditions, it may still be possible to use recursive descent if common prefixes may be left factored, or if options or closure operations may be used to re-formulate the productions. The conditions that must then be verified may be determined by expressing the use of an option or closure operation in terms of conventional context-free productions and applying the conditions stated earlier.

For example, a use of closure of the form

$$\langle N \rangle ::= \cdots \mid \alpha \: \{\beta\}$$

may be re-expressed in conventional BNF as

$$\langle N \rangle ::= \cdots \mid \alpha \: \langle Ntail \rangle$$

$$\langle Ntail \rangle ::= \langle empty \rangle \mid \beta \: \langle Ntail \rangle$$

$$\langle empty \rangle ::=$$

where $\langle Ntail \rangle$ is a new nonterminal. The conditions on the $\langle Ntail \rangle$ productions would be that $first(\beta) \cap follow\langle N \rangle = \varnothing$, and that β not generate a language containing the empty string. The corresponding recognition code would have the form

```
parse α;
while (t ∈ first(β))
{ parse β;
}
```

EXERCISE 11.3 Why, in the preceding discussion, would β generating the empty string be problematic?

Similarly, use of an option of the following form

$$\langle N \rangle ::= \cdots \mid \alpha \: [\beta]$$

may be re-expressed in conventional BNF as

$\langle N \rangle ::= \cdots \mid \alpha \; \langle Ntail \rangle$

$\langle Ntail \rangle ::= \langle empty \rangle \mid \beta$

$\langle empty \rangle ::=$

The resulting conditions are the same as those derived earlier, and the corresponding recognition code has the form

```
parse α ;
if  (t ∈ first(β) )
{ parse β;
}
```

EXERCISE 11.4 What conditions would apply to a use of *positive* closure as the last item of a production? What would be the form of the corresponding recognition code?

EXERCISE 11.5 Analyze the conditions that would apply when a use of closure or an option is not the final item in a production. What would be the form of the corresponding recognition code?

11.3.6 EXERCISES IN PARSER CONSTRUCTION

1. For each of the following grammars, construct a recursive-descent parser based on it. Use iteration in preference to recursion wherever possible. Explain in each case where a choice is made why your recognition function may make the correct choice. In each case, $\langle empty \rangle$ produces only the empty string.

   (a) $\langle paren \rangle ::= \langle empty \rangle \mid (\; \langle paren \rangle \;) \; \langle paren \rangle$

   (b) $\langle neutral \rangle ::= \langle empty \rangle \mid + \langle neg \rangle \langle neutral \rangle \mid - \langle pos \rangle \langle neutral \rangle$

   $\langle neg \rangle ::= - \mid + \langle neg \rangle \langle neg \rangle$

   $\langle pos \rangle ::= + \mid - \langle pos \rangle \langle pos \rangle$

   (c) $\langle ListStruct \rangle ::= \langle atom \rangle \mid (\; \langle sequence \rangle \;)$

   $\langle sequence \rangle ::= \langle empty \rangle \mid \langle ListStruct \rangle \langle SequenceTail \rangle$

   $\langle SequenceTail \rangle ::= \langle empty \rangle \mid , \langle ListStruct \rangle \langle SequenceTail \rangle$

   Treat $\langle atom \rangle$ as a terminal symbol.

2. Design a context-free grammar for a language of regular expressions over the (terminal) vocabulary $\{0, 1\}$, and implement a recognizer for this language. Assume the following conventions.

   • Union is expressed by +.

- Concatenation is expressed by adjacency.
- Closure is expressed by a postfix *.
- Vocabulary elements are expressed by 0 and 1.
- The language whose only element is the empty string is expressed by the character &.
- The empty language is expressed by the character @.
- Parentheses (and) may be used as usual.
- Closure has the highest precedence, and union has the lowest.

The following are examples of strings that are in the language to be recognized:

(0*(10*1)*)*	(describes strings with even parity)
0*(&+1)0*	(describes strings with at most one 1)
@	(describes the empty language)
@*	(equivalent to &)

Use iteration rather than recursion wherever possible. Explain in each case where a choice is made why your recognition functions may make the correct choice.

11.4 Additional Reading

General parsing methods are described in books on formal languages and theory of computation, such as [MAK88]. Subcubic parsing of general context-free languages is described in [Val75]. Recursive descent first developed as an ad hoc technique [Con63]; the theory was developed in [RS70, Knu71]. More advanced parsing methods are described in books on compiler techniques, such as [ASU86].

REFERENCES

[ASU86]   A. V. Aho, R. Sethi, and J. D. Ullman. *Compiler Design: Principles, Techniques, and Tools*. Addison-Wesley, 1986.

[Con63]   M. E. Conway. Design of a separable transition diagram compiler. *Comm. ACM*, 6:396–408, 1963.

[Knu71]   D. E. Knuth. Top-down syntax analysis. *Acta Informatica*, 1(2):79–110, 1971.

[MAK88]   R. N. Moll, M. A. Arbib, and A. J. Kfoury. *An Introduction to Formal Language Theory*. Springer Verlag, 1988.

[RS70]   D. J. Rosenkrantz and R. E. Stearns. Properties of deterministic top-down grammars. *Information and Control*, 17:226–56, 1970.

[Val75]   L. G. Valiant. General context-free recognition in less than cubic time. *J. Comp. Sys. Sci.*, 10:308–15, 1975.

Part D

Unimplementable Specifications

Introduction to Part D

It may not be *possible* to implement a specification. The requirements may be inconsistent, the specification may be meaningless or ill-defined, or, surprisingly, the function specified may not be *computable*. The concept of an incomputable function comes from *computability theory*, a branch of mathematical logic with particular relevance to computer science.

Chapter 12 introduces some of the key ideas of computability theory, both as motivation for subsequent study and to provide the background necessary to appreciate the significance of an incomputability claim. In particular, we will prove that some functions are not computable by *any* C program, explain why such problems are deemed to be *algorithmically unsolvable*, and list a number of unsolvable problems of practical importance involving context-free grammars.

Additional Reading

Good presentations of elementary computability theory may be found in [RS86, Sip97, Jon97, GH98, LP98, HMU01].

REFERENCES

[GH98]   R. Greenlaw and H. J. Hoover. *Fundamentals of the Theory of Computation: Principles and Practice.* Morgan Kaufmann, 1998.

[HMU01]   J. E. Hopcroft, R. Motwani, and J. D. Ullman. *Introduction to Automata Theory, Languages, and Computation.* Addison-Wesley, 2001.

[Jon97]   N. D. Jones. *Computability and Complexity from a Programming Perspective.* The MIT Press, 1997.

[LP98]   H. R. Lewis and C. H. Papadimitriou. *Elements of the Theory of Computation,* 2nd edition. Prentice Hall, 1998.

[RS86]   V. J. Rayward-Smith. *A First Course in Computability.* Blackwell Scientific Publications, 1986.

[Sip97]   M. Sipser. *Introduction to the Theory of Computation.* PWS Publishing Company, 1997.

Chapter 12

A Taste of Computability Theory

12.1   The Halting Problem

It would be very useful to have a function that could predict whether an arbitrary C function will terminate (i.e., not go into an infinite loop or recursion) when given any particular input. Is it possible to define a function that is *always* correct in such predictions?

Consider the following specification for such a function:

```
bool halts(FILE *func, FILE *arg);
/* Returns true if file func contains the definition of an
     int function with one FILE parameter, and that function
     terminates if applied to file arg; otherwise, halts
     returns false.
*/
```

FILE parameters are used to allow both the function definitions and their inputs to be of arbitrary (unbounded) size. A function satisfying this specification would certainly be useful, but we may prove that it is impossible to implement such a function in C.

Suppose that there existed a definition in C of halts that satisfied the preceding specification; we will show that this assumption leads to a contradiction. To simplify the presentation, we assume a library function copy to "rewind" file f and copy it to g, such as the following:

```
void copy(FILE *f, FILE *g)
{ rewind(f);
  for(;;)
  { int c = getc(f);
    if (c==EOF) break;
    putc(c, g);
  }
}
```

Program 12.1

```
bool halts(FILE *func, FILE *arg) { ... }

int test(FILE *f)
{ FILE *a = tmpfile();
  copy(f, a);
  if (halts(f, a)) for(;;){}
  return 0;
}

int main(void)
{ FILE *f = tmpfile();
  fprintf(f, "%s\n", "int test(FILE *f)                  " );
  fprintf(f, "%s\n", "{ FILE *a = tmpfile();             " );
  fprintf(f, "%s\n", "  copy(f, a);                      " );
  fprintf(f, "%s\n", "  if (halts(f, a)) for(;;){} " );
  fprintf(f, "%s\n", "  return 0;                        " );
  fprintf(f, "%s\n", "}                                  " );
  return test(f);
}
```

Consider Program 12.1: a function test is defined and then applied to a temporary file to which has been output an exact copy of the definition of test. Function test first copies its argument f to a new temporary file a and then calls the assumed halts function. Recall that halts is required to terminate and to return either false or true, but *neither* result would be correct.

- If halts returns false, test simply terminates and returns 0; however, this means that halts has returned an incorrect result because the call of test on its own definition has terminated.

- On the other hand, if halts returns true, test immediately begins executing the infinite loop for(;;){}, and so again halts has returned an incorrect result: test diverges if applied to a copy of its own definition.

But there is no other possibility, and so the assumption that a correct implementation of halts exists is untenable.

EXERCISE 12.1 When Professor Higgins explains this proof to Ms Doolittle, she is dubious because she recalls seeing proofs of program termination in her textbook. How may Professor Higgins resolve this apparent paradox?

EXERCISE 12.2 Is the following specification implementable?

```
bool FailSafeHalts(FILE *func, FILE *arg);
/* FailsSafeHalts always terminates; if it returns true,
   file func contains the definition of an int function
   with one FILE parameter, and that function terminates
   if applied to file arg.
*/
```

EXERCISE 12.3 Is the following specification implementable?

```
bool HaltsOnSelf(FILE *func);
/* Returns true if func contains the definition of an int
   function with one FILE parameter, and that function
   terminates if applied to a file containing its own
   definition; otherwise, halts returns false.
*/
```

12.2 The Church-Turing Thesis

In the preceding section, we proved that a specification was *not* implementable in C. Intuitively, it would seem that this is not due to any deficiency in C and that the same argument could be used with *any* nontrivial programming language. Is there any justification for this intuition? It is in fact another important insight from computability theory.

Starting in the 1930s, before any real digital computers had been constructed, logicians studied a variety of simple computational formalisms intended to capture precisely the informal notion of an "effectively computable" function. Among them are the following:

- automata that consist of a finite-state automaton with access to an auxiliary memory device, such as a floppy-disk drive; this kind of automaton is now called a *Turing machine* in honor of logician Alan Turing, who invented it in 1936*;

- a "pure" functional language similar to LISP;

- unrestricted grammars (i.e., grammars allowing productions that are not restricted to being context-free);

- a simple imperative programming language with assignable variables of type int and conventional control structures, such as conditionals and while loops;

and many others. All these simple but very different computational formalisms turned out to be equally powerful: any program (grammar, automaton) in one of the formalisms may be "compiled" into an equivalent program defining the same function in any of the other formalisms.

These results show that all the formalisms compute a "natural" and robust class of functions; furthermore, because none of the many attempts to characterize "effectively computable" functions succeeded in finding even a single such function that could not be implemented in these simple formalisms, it is now generally accepted that there is *no* "effectively computable" function on

---

*For the "auxiliary memory device," Turing in 1936 suggested a paper tape with pencil markings; for him, a "computer" was a human being following instructions.

finitary data (such as integers or finite strings over a finite alphabet) that is unimplementable in any of the computational formalisms we have briefly outlined. Even complex modern programming languages such as C++ and JAVA do not allow us to compute functions that are not also implementable in the simple formalisms invented by the logicians in the 1930s.

This identification of the *informal* notion of effectively computable functions with the precise *formal* notion of "functions computable using Turing machines" (or any of the other computational formalisms) is now known as the *Church-Turing thesis*, in honor of logicians Alonzo Church and Alan Turing, who independently proposed such identifications in 1936. Because of the reference to an *informal* notion (effectively computable function), such a thesis cannot be rigorously *proved*; nevertheless, it is universally accepted by computability theorists to be a valid identification.

The main significance of the Church-Turing thesis is that, if a function has been proved to be unimplementable in any of these "universal" computational formalisms, we must accept that it is not effectively computable at all, no matter what programming language or computer were to be used. We conclude that implementing the specification for halts is impossible, not only in C but also in any language and on any computer; it is an *algorithmically unsolvable* problem.

The practical significance of unsolvability is that it is pointless to try to devise (complete) solutions to such a problem. It may be possible to solve restricted versions or to implement an approximate fail-safe solution; but no amount of research, ingenuity, or computing power will lead to a solution of an algorithmic problem that has been proved unsolvable.

The theoretical work by the logicians also had significant "positive" practical consequences in that it influenced the design and development of the first digital computers, both in Britain and in America.

12.3 Unsolvability by Reduction

The technique used in our proof of the unimplementability of halts (applying a function to its own definition) is called *diagonalization*. Algorithmic problems may also be proved unsolvable by a technique called *reduction*. An algorithmic problem A is described as being *reducible to* another problem B if any solution of B may be used to solve A as well. On the other hand, if problem A is reducible to B and A is *unsolvable*, so is B; for if B were solvable, we could solve any instance of A using the solution for B.

For example, the problem of implementing the function HaltsOnSelf specified in Exercise 12.3 is reducible to the problem of implementing function halts because, if the latter were implementable, we could define HaltsOnSelf as follows:

```
bool HaltsOnSelf(FILE *func)
{ FILE *arg = tmpfile();
  copy(func, arg);
  return halts(func, arg);
}
```

But because `HaltsOnSelf` is unimplementable, so is `halts`.

This example might seem unimpressive; not only have we already proved that `halts` is unimplementable, but `HaltsOnSelf` is essentially a "special case" of `halts` and so it is not surprising that the former is reducible to the latter. So now consider trying to implement a function

```
bool HaltsOnEmpty(FILE *func)
```

which is to return the value of `halts(func, arg)` when `arg` is an empty file. In other words, it returns `true` if `func` is a definition of an `int` function with one file parameter, and that function terminates if applied to an empty file; otherwise, it returns `false`. It is not obvious that this is unimplementable; it might be easier to implement than `halts` because an implementation only needs to consider a particular value of `arg`. But it is possible to prove that `HaltsOnEmpty` is unimplementable because the general termination problem is reducible to this more specialized problem.

Suppose that we had an implementation of `HaltsOnEmpty`. To use this function to emulate `halts(func, arg)`, we would construct a function-definition file `FuncArg` that resembles the definition in file `func` except that the new function is to ignore its actual argument and use file `arg` as the file referenced by its formal parameter; that is, if `func` contains a function definition of the form

```
int f(FILE *a) { C }
```

where C is the body of the function definition, it should be transformed into a file `FuncArg` containing the following function definition:

```
int f(FILE *b)
{ FILE *a = tmpfile();
    fprintf(a, "%s", "arg");
    C
}
```

where *arg* is the character string in file arg. References to identifier a in C now access a locally defined temporary file a copied from arg, rather than the file supplied as the actual argument to the call. Function `FuncArg` will always have the same result, no matter what its actual argument is (including the empty file), and it terminates if and only if the function defined in `func` terminates on argument arg.

Suppose that the fairly straightforward file transformation described in the preceding discussion has been implemented by a function

```
merge(func, arg, FuncArg)
```

Then the following is an implementation of halts using the assumed function HaltsOnEmpty:

```
bool halts(FILE *func, FILE *arg)
{ FILE *FuncArg = tmpfile();
  merge(func, arg, FuncArg);
  return HaltsOnEmpty(FuncArg);
}
```

So if HaltsOnEmpty is implementable, so is halts. We have, however, previously shown that the latter is *not* implementable, so we must conclude that HaltsOnEmpty is also unimplementable.

EXERCISE 12.4 Prove by reduction that it is not possible to implement a function

```
bool HaltsOnAll(FILE *func)
```

that tests whether the function defined by func terminates on *all* files.

EXERCISE 12.5 Prove by reduction that it is not possible to implement a function

```
bool Equiv(FILE *f, FILE *g)
```

that tests whether, for *every* file input, the int functions defined in f and g *either* both fail to terminate *or* return the *same* result.

Unsolvable problems arise in many application areas. Here are several grammar-related problems of significant practical interest that have been proved unsolvable.

- Do two arbitrary context-free grammars describe the same language?
- Does an arbitrary context-free grammar describe a regular language?
- Is an arbitrary context-free grammar ambiguous?
- Does a context-free grammar describe an inherently ambiguous language (i.e., one for which there is no unambiguous grammar)?

Each of these problems may be precisely specified, but the specifications are unimplementable.

12.4 Additional Reading

Brief presentations of the key ideas of computability theory similar to those in this chapter may be found in [GL88, Har92]. Lively historical accounts of the Church-Turing thesis may be found in Part I of [Her95]. [Deu85] gives an interpretation of the Church-Turing thesis as a principle of quantum physics.

REFERENCES

[Deu85]   D. Deutsch. Quantum theory, the Church-Turing principle, and the universal quantum computer. *Proceedings of the Royal Society of London*, A 400:97–117, 1985.

[GL88]   L. Goldschlager and A. Lister. *Computer Science, a Modern Introduction*, 2nd edition. Prentice Hall International, 1988.

[Har92]   D. Harel. *Algorithmics, The Spirit of Computing*, 2nd edition. Addison-Wesley, 1992.

[Her95]   R. Herken, editor. *The Universal Turing Machine. A Half-Century Survey*, 2nd edition. Springer-Verlag, 1995.

Appendices

Appendix A

Programming Language Reference

This appendix is a compact description of the extended subset of C used for the examples in this book. It is *not* a complete description of C, much less of C++, which is an extended (some might say *over*extended) version of C for object-oriented programming. The C++ features (`class`, `public`, `private`) are used only in Part B. For complete descriptions and more explanation than we have room for here, see the Additional Reading.

A.1 Lexical Conventions

A.1.1 COMMENTS

A comment in C is introduced by the characters /* and terminated by */. In C++ (and in many implementations of C), a comment may also be introduced by the characters //, and this kind of comment is terminated by the next end-of-line. Comments do not occur within strings or character literals.

A.1.2 WHITE SPACE

Blanks, tabs, new-lines, form-feeds, and comments are known as *white space*.

A.1.3 PREPROCESSING

Before a compiler translates source code to executable code, a preprocessor performs macro expansion and file inclusion, under the control of lines beginning with a # character (possibly after some white space), as follows.

A control line of the form

```
# define I X
```

where I is an identifier (Section A.1.5) and X is arbitrary text, causes the preprocessor to replace subsequent occurrences of the identifier with X. Leading and terminating white space are stripped from X.

A control line of the form

$$\texttt{\# define } I(I_0, I_1, \ldots, I_{n-1})\ X$$

where I and the I_j are identifiers and there is no white space between I and the formal-parameter list, causes the processor to replace subsequent occurrences of $I(X_0, X_1, \ldots, X_{n-1})$ by X, but with occurrences of the macro parameters I_j in X replaced by the corresponding macro arguments X_j. Leading and terminating white space are stripped from X and from the arguments X_j.

The programs in this book assume the following macro definitions:

```
# define ASSERT(P)
# define FACT(P)
# define INVAR(P)
```

Because the macro bodies are null, calls of these macros are essentially comments.

A control line of the form

```
# include <file name>
```

causes the replacement of that line by the contents of the named file, which is searched for in a sequence of implementation-determined system directories. It is conventional to include the "headers" for standard libraries using this form.

A control line of the form

```
# include "file name"
```

causes the replacement of that line by the contents of the named file, which is searched for in a sequence of implementation-determined user directories, starting with the directory containing the source file. Included files are also preprocessed.

A control line of the form

```
# ifndef I
```

causes the preprocessor to exclude all program text until the following `# endif` line if the macro I is *not* defined. For example, the macro `__cplusplus` is defined if the processor is a C++ processor and is undefined if it is only a C processor, and so this facility may be used as in Program 3 in the Introduction to exclude a redundant definition of a `bool` type if C++ is in use.

If it is necessary to extend a control "line" over to an additional line, the last character in the line should be a backslash \ with the new-line character immediately following; the backslash and the new-line character are deleted.

A.1.4 TOKENS

After preprocessing, a program consists of a sequence of tokens. There are six classes of tokens: identifiers, keywords, constants, string literals, operators, and other separators. White space is ignored, except that some white space is needed to separate otherwise adjacent identifiers, keywords, and constants.

A.1.5 IDENTIFIERS

An identifier is a sequence of letters, digits, or the underscore character (_). The first character must be a letter or underscore. Uppercase and lowercase letters are different. It is conventional to reserve identifiers whose first character is an underscore for use by standard libraries.

A.1.6 KEYWORDS

The following identifiers are reserved for use as keywords in C:

auto	do	goto	signed	unsigned
break	double	if	sizeof	void
case	else	int	static	volatile
char	enum	long	struct	while
const	extern	register	switch	
continue	float	return	typedef	
default	for	short	union	

The following are additional keywords in C++:

and	const_cast	namespace	public	typename
and_eq	delete	new	reinterpret_cast	using
asm	dynamic_cast	not	static_cast	virtual
bitand	explicit	not_eq	template	wchar_t
bitor	export	operator	this	xor
bool	false	or	throw	xor_eq
catch	friend	or_eq	true	
class	inline	private	try	
compl	mutable	protected	typeid	

In particular, class, private, and public are *not* reserved in C and bool, false, and true *are* reserved in C++.

A.2   Basic Types and Constants

The basic data types used in this book and typical constants are given in the following table:

```
bool      false  true
char      'a'  'A'   ···    '\n'  '\\'  '\''  '\0'
int       ···  -2  -1  0  1  2  ···
float     0.   .1  3.14159  -1e2  6.625e-34  ···
```

The character designated by \0 is termed the *null* character (the NUL in the ASCII character set). The character set actually used is implementation dependent. Type bool is predefined in C++, but it may be explicitly defined in C by the following declaration of an enumerated type (Section A.5):

```
typedef enum {false, true} bool;
```

Values of types char and bool are represented by small integer values, and the representations are not necessarily unique; for example, false is represented by 0, but *any* nonzero integer value will be taken as equivalent to true by bool operations. This means that the idiom *B* == true may be inappropriate for some bool expressions *B*. It is *not* illegal in C to apply int operations to char or enum variables, or even to bool operands, or vice versa; the programs in this book generally avoid such idioms.

Only finite ranges of values are representable by variables of type int or char. The standard limits library defines the following implementation-dependent constants:

CHAR_MAX	maximum value of type char
CHAR_MIN	minimum value of type char
INT_MAX	maximum value of type int
INT_MIN	minimum value of type int

There are also constants defining the properties of float values, but we will not describe these.

Values of type int are automatically converted to type float if necessary, but there may be round-off errors if an exact representation is not possible. If necessary, values of type float are converted to type int by discarding any fraction.

An attempt to compute an int value that is too large to be represented is illegal. This is called an *overflow*. The effect of an int overflow is not defined; many implementations simply ignore them, allowing garbage results to be produced. Type int may be replaced by long int (or just long), or even long long int in some implementations, to obtain a larger range of representable integers; similarly, type float may be replaced by double, or even long double in some implementations, to obtain greater precision or range.

A.3   Strings

A string constant consists of a sequence of characters (possibly none) enclosed in double-quote marks: "...". Adjacent string constants are concatenated into a single string. After such concatenation, a null character is appended to the string to act as the string terminator. The escape sequences \n and \" for newline and double-quote characters, respectively, must be used if these characters are to be components of a string constant. A string is considered to be an array with char components. It is illegal to attempt to modify the representation of a string constant.

A.4   Variable Declarations

The basic form of a variable declaration is as follows:

- a type specifier: one of char, int, float, a defined type name (such as bool), an enumerated or structure type (Section A.5), or a class name (Section A.11), followed by

- one or more identifiers separated by commas and

- terminated with a semicolon (;) .

A declared variable may optionally be followed by = and an initializer expression that is assignment compatible with the variable; the variable is initialized to the value of the expression. If the type specifier is preceded by the qualifier const, the initial value may not subsequently be modified. If there is no explicit initializer, the initial value of a declared variable is unpredictable (i.e., garbage).

If a declared identifier is immediately followed by [K], where K is a constant expression (Section A.6.4), the identifier is defined to be an *array* whose size is determined by the value of K; the size must be positive. Some implementations of C allow the size expression K to be an *arbitrary* (not necessarily constant) int expression. The array declarator may be optionally followed by = and a list of *constant* expressions enclosed in braces and separated by commas: $\{K_0, K_1, \ldots, K_{n-1}\}$. The list may also be terminated by a comma, if desired: $\{K_0, K_1, \ldots, K_{n-1}, \}$. A char array may also be initialized by providing a string initializer of the form   "...". The number of initializers or the length of the string (plus 1 for the terminating null) must be $\leq K$ if a size expression K is specified, but the size expression may be omitted if an initializer list or string is supplied.

An n-dimensional array for $n > 1$ (i.e., an array of arrays) is declared by using n array specifiers $[K_0] [K_1] \cdots [K_{n-1}]$, optionally followed by = and a brace-enclosed and comma-separated (and possibly comma-terminated) list of constant initializer expressions. If an initializer list is provided, the *first* size specifier K_0 may be omitted; however, if K_0 is provided, the initializer list must have length $\leq$ the total number of components. Sublists may be enclosed by braces to indicate rows.

If a declared identifier is immediately *preceded* by *, the identifier is a *pointer* variable. In this book, this idiom is used only in Chapter 12 for file descriptors, as in the following:

```
FILE *f = tmpfile();
```

A.5   Enumerated and Structure Types, Defined Type Names

Enumerated types, structure types, and defined type names, as described next, may be used as type specifiers in declarations.

The construct enum{$I_0, I_1, \ldots, I_{n-1}$} (where the I_j are identifiers) defines an *enumerated type*; each identifier I_j is thereby defined to be a constant with int value j. A variable declared to be of the enumerated type should only be assigned one of the enumerated values, but not every compiler enforces this.

The construct struct{$D_0\,D_1\,\cdots\,D_{n-1}$} (where each D_j is a variable declaration) defines a *structure type*. Each variable declared to be of the structure type will have n components (called *members* or *fields*), as specified in the declarations. The variable declarations D_j may *not* have initializers, not even constant expressions; however, a list of up to n initializing constant expressions may be provided in the declaration of a struct variable.

A declaration of the form typedef T I; (where T is a type and I is an identifier) defines I to be a new name for type T. A variable declared with a type-name specifier is considered to be of the type T given in the typedef declaration.

A.6   Expressions

The basic expression forms are constants, variables, function calls, operations, and parenthesized expressions.

A.6.1   VARIABLE EXPRESSIONS

An expression is considered to be a *variable* (known as an *l-value* expression in the C literature) if it is *either*

- an identifier declared to be a variable *or*
- of the form V[E] (where V is an array) *or*
- of the form $V.I$ (where V is a structure or class object and I is one of its member variable names) *or*
- a parenthesized variable (V).

It is illegal for the value of the subscript expression E to be outside the range determined by the size of the array when it was created; however, many implementations do not check this and the effects are unpredictable.

A.6.2 FUNCTION CALLS

A function call normally consists of the identifier or class-object field selection (see Section A.11) designating the function, followed by a parenthesized (but possibly empty) list of argument expressions, separated by commas. The number of arguments must match the number expected by the function, and the corresponding types must be compatible. Function *definitions* are discussed in Section A.9.

A.6.3 OPERATIONS

The arithmetic operators are + and - and, with higher priority, *, /, and the remainder operator % (which should only be used on positive integers). Integer division discards any remainder. If all operands have type int, so does the result; otherwise, the operand values are converted to float and the result has type float.

The relational operators are <, <=, >, and >=, and, with lower priority, the equality operators == and !=. These operators all have lower priority than the arithmetic operators.

In C, assignment operations may be used as subexpressions; the programs in this book do not use this idiom. You will not get an error message if by accident you use = instead of == in an expression.

The bool operators are ! for negation, && for conjunction (i.e., and), and, with lower priority, || for disjunction (i.e., or). The latter two are evaluated "sequentially," so that the second operand is not evaluated if the value of the first operand determines the result. All these operations treat 0 as equivalent to false and any nonzero value as equivalent to true.

The sizeof operator yields the number of bytes required to store an object of the type of its operand, which may be either an expression or a parenthesized type. Note that, when s is an array parameter, sizeof(s) in the function is the size of an array reference (pointer), *not* the size of the actual array argument.

The address-of prefix operator & is needed to pass simple-variable arguments to functions by reference. In this book, this operator is used only for calls of the scanf function for formatted input (Section A.10). There is an inverse prefix operator for dereferencing (*), but it is not used in this book.

There are a number of operators that "shift" bit strings (<< and >>) or apply bool operations such as negation (~), conjunction (&), disjunction (|), and

---

Table A.1   Precedence and Associativity of Operators

( ) [ ] .	left
prefix operators: ! ~ + - sizeof & *	right
* / %	left
+ -	left
<< >>	left
< <= > >=	left
== !=	left
&	left
^	left
|	left
&&	left
||	left
? :	right

---

exclusive-or (^) "bitwise" to bit strings. In this book, these are used only in the very stylized way described in Section 6.4.

Finally, there is the following ternary (three-operand) *conditional-expression* operator:

$$B \ ? \ E_0 \ : \ E_1$$

where B normally has type bool. It is equivalent to

$$\begin{cases} E_0, & \text{if } B \ \text{!= false} \\ E_1, & \text{if } B \ \text{== false} \end{cases}$$

Only one of E_0 or E_1 is evaluated. This operator associates to the *right* and has the lowest priority of all the operators we have discussed.

Table A.1 gives the operators (in order of precedence) and their associativity.

A.6.4   CONSTANT EXPRESSIONS

In certain contexts, expressions must be evaluated during compilation; these are termed *constant expressions*. They must not contain function calls, variables, array-subscripting operations, or structure-member selections, except in operands of the sizeof operator.

A.7   Some Library Functions

In this section, we briefly describe a selection of standard-library functions that return values and do not have side effects.

A.7.1 MATHEMATICAL FUNCTIONS

Table A.2 summarizes the most useful "mathematical" functions available in the math library.

Table A.2 *Mathematical Functions*

`int abs(int i)`	absolute value of an `int`
`float fabs(float x)`	absolute value of a `float`
`int ceil(float x)`	smallest `int` not less than x
`int floor(float x)`	largest `int` not greater than x
`float sqrt(float x)`	$\sqrt{x}, x \geq 0$
`float log(float x)`	$\ln(x), x > 0$
`float log10(float x)`	$\log_{10}(x), x > 0$

A.7.2 CHARACTER FUNCTIONS

Values c of type `char` may be classified by using the `bool` functions from the ctype library given in Table A.3. Also, the char functions `toupper(c)` and `tolower(c)` convert the case of c if it is a letter and return their argument unchanged if c is not a letter.

Table A.3 *Character-Set Classification Functions*

`bool isalpha(char c)`	letter
`bool isdigit(char c)`	decimal digit
`bool isupper(char c)`	uppercase letter
`bool islower(char c)`	lowercase letter
`bool iscntrl(char c)`	control character
`bool isprint(char c)`	printing character
`bool isgraph(char c)`	printing character except space
`bool ispunct(char c)`	printing character except space or letter or digit
`bool isspace(char c)`	space, form-feed, new-line, carriage return, tab

A.7.3 STRING FUNCTIONS

The following is a selection of functions on strings defined in the `string` or stdlib libraries:

- `int strlen(const char[] s)`: length of string s, not including the terminating null (which must be present);

- `int strcmp(const char[] s, const char[] t)`: negative, 0, or positive according to whether s<t, s==t, or s>t, respectively;

- `int strncmp(const char[] s, const char[] t, int n)`:   same as strcmp, but compares at most n characters;

- `int atoi(const char[] s)`: converts string s to `int`;

- `float atof(const char[] s)`: converts string s to `float`;

- `int strspn(const char s[], const char t[])`: returns the length of the longest prefix of s consisting of characters in t;

- `int strcspn(const char s[], const char t[])`: returns the length of the longest prefix of s consisting of characters *not* in t.

A.8   Statements

Statements are executed for their effects and do not yield values.

A.8.1   BASIC STATEMENTS

An *assignment statement* consists of an *assignment*, followed by a semicolon, where an assignment is one of the following forms:

- $V = E$ where V is a variable expression and E is an expression whose value is convertible if necessary to the type of the variable;

- $V \, op = E$ (where *op* is a suitable operator), which is equivalent to $V = V \, op \, E$ except that the variable is only evaluated once;

- $V{++}$, which is equivalent to $V \mathrel{+}= 1$;

- $V{--}$, which is equivalent to $V \mathrel{-}= 1$.

Structures are assignable, but arrays (as a whole), including strings, are *not* assignable.

Assignments are actually *expressions* in C, but we do not use this idiom in this book. We have had to describe assignments (without the terminating semicolon) because they are used in the control section of the `for` loop (Section A.8.2).

A function call (Section A.6.2), followed by a semicolon is a statement. If the return type of the function is not `void`, the value returned is simply discarded.

The *null* statement consists of a semicolon by itself; it has no effect but may be used wherever a statement is needed syntactically.

A statement of the form `goto` I (where I is an identifier) transfers control to the statement labeled by identifier I (followed by a colon `:`) in the same function body. This feature is used in this book only in Exercise 8.4.

The break; and return E; (or, for a void function, just return;) statements may be used to exit loops and function bodies, respectively. In this book, we use these features only in very restricted ways.

A.8.2 CONTROL STRUCTURES

A *compound* statement or *block* statement has the general form

$$\{ D_0 \ D_1 \cdots D_{n-1} \ C_0 \ C_1 \cdots C_{m-1} \}$$

where the D_i are declarations and the C_j are statements. The identifiers declared in a D_i have the rest of the block as their scope. The same identifier may not be declared more than once in the declarations of a block except that label identifiers and the member names for each struct type are considered to inhabit "name spaces" separate from the name space of identifiers for variables, functions, type names, and enum constants. Identifiers may be redeclared in nested blocks. Initializations in the declarations are performed each time the block is executed. The body of a function definition must be a block; however, in standard C a block may not itself contain a function definition. The trivial block {} has no effect and may be used wherever a statement is required.

The if statement forms are as follows:

- if $(B)\ C$

- if $(B)\ C_0$ else C_1

where B is a bool expression and C, C_0, and C_1 are statements. In combinations of the form if (B_0) if $(B_1)C_0$ else C_1, the else matches the immediately preceding unmatched if in the same block.

There is also a switch form, which is normally used as follows:

```
switch (N)
{ case K₀:
    C₀
    break;
    ⋮
  case Kᵢ:
    Cᵢ
    break;
    ⋮
  default:
    Cₙ
}
```

where N is an integer-valued expression, the K_i are constant integer-valued expressions with distinct values, and the C_i are (sequences of) statements. Expression N is evaluated, and control transfers to the C_i that is labeled by a constant expression with the same value (or to the default-labeled statement if none of the constants have that value). After execution of C_i, control is transferred by the terminating break to the end of the switch statement. If the break is omitted, however, control "falls through" to C_{i+1}; usually, this would not be what the programmer intends. Also, any of the C_i may have *several* case labels:

> case K_{i0} :
> case K_{i1} :
> $\vdots$
> case $K_{i(m-1)}$:
> C_i
>   break;

The most basic form of *iteration* statement or *loop* has the following form:

> while (B) C

where normally B is an expression of type bool and C is a statement (possibly, but not necessarily, a compound statement). The expression is evaluated before each execution of C; the loop terminates when the expression value has become equal to false, possibly before statement C is executed at all.

The for loop form

> for $(A_0; B; A_1)$ C

is equivalent to

> A_0; while $(B)\{C$ $A_1;\}$

Here, A_0 and A_1 are assignments (i.e., assignment statements without terminating semicolons), B is normally an expression of type bool, and C is a statement. Any (or all) of A_0, B, or A_1 (but not the separating semicolons) may be omitted; if B is omitted, the condition is taken to be true.

The most common uses of the for form of loop are in the following "counting-up" and "counting-down" loops:

> for $(V=N_0; V<N_1; V++)$ C

> for $(V=N_0; V>N_1; V--)$ C

where V is a declared int variable and N_0 and N_1 are int expressions.

The following do-while form of loop is used when a loop condition is to be evaluated *after* each execution of the loop body (but not before the first execution):

> do C while (B) ;

where C is a statement (usually a block) and B is normally a `bool` expression.

The `break;` statement may be used to exit from inside a loop. In this book, only the following special case is used:

```
for(;;)
{ D
  C₀
  if (B) break;
  C₁
}
```

where D is a declaration sequence (possibly empty), B is a `bool` expression, and C_0 and C_1 are statement sequences.

A.9 Function Definitions

Here is the basic form of a *function definition*:

$$T \, I(T_0 \, I_0, \, T_1 \, I_1, \, \ldots, \, T_{n-1} \, I_{n-1}) \, C$$

where T (the return type) and the T_j (formal-parameter types) are types, I (the function name) and the I_j (the formal parameters) are identifiers, and C (the body) is a block. The formal parameters are considered to be defined in the block. If the function is intended to be used as a statement, the return type T should be `void`. The formal-parameter list may be either empty ($n = 0$) or `void` to indicate that the function does not require arguments; the enclosing parentheses are always required. A function may return a structure but may not return an array.

If the function is expected to return a value, the function body should be terminated by a statement of the form `return E;`, where E is an expression. In fact, `return` statements may be used anywhere in the function body, but this idiom is not used in this book, except in Exercise 8.4.

Parameter passing for simple variables is "by value"; that is, the value of an argument (actual parameter) is copied to a new local variable before the body is executed; assignments to the formal parameter do not affect the corresponding actual parameter.

If a formal-parameter identifier is immediately followed by an array specifier (`[K]` or `[]`), the *address* of the array is passed to the function; assignments to (components of) the formal parameter then affect the corresponding argument array. An array parameter may be preceded by the qualifier `const`; this qualification indicates that the array components will not be modified by the function. Multidimensional array parameters are treated in a similar manner.

If a formal-parameter identifier is immediately *preceded* by *, the corresponding argument must be a pointer, such as a file descriptor. The only other use of this idiom in this book is the standard scanf function (Section A.10); arguments of scanf must normally be prefixed by the & (address-of) operator.

Functions may be called recursively. If one function must call another function that has not yet been defined (perhaps because the two functions are *mutually* recursive), it is necessary to "declare" the called function, without *defining* it. A function *declaration* consists of a function *header* (type, name, formal-parameter list), followed by a semicolon (rather than a block). Examples of such declarations may be found in Programs 11.2 and 11.3.

A.10   More Library Functions

The library functions described in this section have side effects; some also return a value, though often the returned value is simply discarded.

A.10.1   INPUT AND OUTPUT

The stdio library defines a type FILE of file descriptors. The identifiers stdin, stdout, and stderr are defined to be pointers to the file descriptors for the standard input, output, and error streams, respectively. Temporary files are created by calling the following function:

```
FILE *tmpfile(void)
```

which returns a pointer to the file descriptor, as in the following initialized variable declaration:

```
FILE *f = tmpfile();
```

Here are the basic input and output functions:

- int getc(FILE *f): returns the int code for the next character in the file f or EOF (end-of-file) if there are no more characters to input;

- int getchar(void): equivalent to getc(stdin);

- int putc(char c, FILE *f): appends c to file f and returns EOF if this fails;

- int putchar(char c): equivalent to putc(c, stdout);

- int ungetc(char c, FILE *f): pushes c back into file f and returns EOF if this fails;

- void rewind(FILE *f): resets the position of file f (not stdin, stdout, or stderr) to its first component;

- void fgets(char s[], int n, FILE *f): reads at most the next n-1 characters from f into s, up to and including a new-line; the string is then terminated by a null.

The constant EOF is defined by the stdio library; this is *not* a char value, which explains why the return types for these functions are int rather than char. Only one call of ungetc is allowed before the next read from that file. The character pushed back into the file need not be the same as the one previously read.

Formatted input and output are provided by the following functions:

- int scanf(const char fmt[], ...)
- void printf(const char fmt[], ...)
- void fprintf(FILE *f, const char fmt[], ...)

Here, f points to a file, and fmt is a format string that may contain *conversion specifications* to control conversions to or from the remaining arguments, as follows:

%c	char
%i	int
%g	float
%s	char []

For scanf, initial white space (including new-lines) is skipped for each conversion-specification item (except c). The input stream is then read up to the next white space and matched against the format item; however, if a number appears between the % and the control character in the conversion specification, it is used as the *maximum* width of the field read. It is a good idea to specify a maximum field width for string input to preclude buffer overflows. A string read using the s control character does not have to be quoted. Any remaining arguments of scanf should be prefixed by the "address of" operator & if they are simple (nonarray) variables. Other characters in the format string (i.e., those not escaped by %) must match the characters found in the input stream. Scanning of the input continues until the format string is exhausted or a match fails. The int returned by a call of scanf is the number of items successfully matched and assigned (or EOF if there isn't enough input); the value returned should always be checked to verify that the input was well formed, as in the following example:

```
if (scanf("%i,%i,%i", &a, &b, &c) != 3) error("input failure");
```

For printf and fprintf, a number used between the % and the control character is used as the *minimum* field width. A string argument is output up to the terminating null character. Other characters in the format string (including escape sequences such as \n) are output directly to the output stream without conversion. The function fprintf is similar but doesn't assume stdout (the standard output stream) as the default; we use this function to send error messages to the stderr stream, such as in the definition of function error on page 7.

Note that a call of the form printf(str) or fprintf(f, str) may have unexpected results if string str happens to contain the % character. The following are safe alternatives: printf("%s", str) and fprintf(f, "%s", str) .

A.10.2 MORE STRING FUNCTIONS

The following function defined in the string library is normally executed for its effect.

> void strncat(char s[], const char t[], int n): copies at most n characters from t to s starting at the terminating null of s; then s is padded if necessary with a single null.

The two string arguments should be distinct. There are standard functions in C to just copy (rather than concatenate) strings; unfortunately, they are unsafe or inefficient. The following function

```
void strlcpy(char s[], const char t[], int n)
/* copies at most n characters from t to s,
   up to and including the terminating null
*/
{ s[0] = '\0'; strncat(s, t, n); }
```

is efficient and safe, provided n is *smaller* than the size of array s.

A.10.3 MISCELLANEOUS FUNCTIONS

The function

```
int rand(void)
```

in the stdlib library returns a pseudo-random int in the range 0 to RAND_MAX.

The function

```
void exit(int status)
```

in stdlib aborts program execution, returning control to the system environment. The status argument is interpreted in a system-dependent way, but EXIT_FAILURE indicates unsuccessful termination and EXIT_SUCCESS or 0 indicate successful termination.

The assert library provides a function or macro

```
void assert(bool p)
```

that aborts execution with an error message if p evaluates to false.

A.11 Classes

Here is the typical form of a *class declaration* in C++:

```
class I
{ private: D₀ D₁ ··· Dₙ₋₁
  public: D'₀ D'₁ ··· D'ₘ₋₁
};
```

where I is an identifier (the class name), and the D_i and D'_j are declarations and function definitions. Note the terminating semicolon.

For any object V of type I and any I'_j declared in a *public* part of the class declaration, member I'_j is accessible using the notation $V . I'_j$; however, a *private* member I_i is accessible only *inside* the class declaration. According to the C++ standard, non-static variables declared in a class declaration may *not* have initializers, not even constant expressions. Class objects may be initialized by defining a (parameterless) *constructor* function with the same function name as the class; no return type should be specified for the constructor function. The constructor function for a class is automatically called for each class object created.

A.12 Program Structure

A complete program unit (after preprocessing) consists of a sequence of declarations and function definitions, including the definition of a function called main, which is the function that is, in effect, called by the system to start execution. The scope of identifiers declared at the program level is the rest of the program. Function main returns an int to the environment as a status indication; the interpretation is implementation dependent, but 0 conventionally indicates normal termination.

It is possible to separately compile program units; this capability is not really needed for the relatively small programs discussed here, but some of the associated features, such as use of the static qualifier and header files, are described in Section 5.4.

A.13 Grammar

This section presents a context-free grammar for the language described in this appendix. The notation is Backus-Naur formalism (BNF); it is explained in Section 10.1. Note that true, false, bool, class, private, and public are treated as *identifiers* in C and as *keywords* in C++. The following metavariables are not defined here: ⟨*identifier*⟩, ⟨*constant*⟩, and ⟨*string-literal*⟩. The grammar is actually ambiguous (Section 10.4); it is explained on page 235 how the nested-if ambiguity is resolved.

A.13.1 EXPRESSIONS

⟨*primary-expression*⟩ ::= ⟨*identifier*⟩
           | ⟨*constant*⟩
           | ⟨*string-literal*⟩
           | (⟨*expression*⟩)

⟨*postfix-expression*⟩ ::= ⟨*primary-expression*⟩
           | ⟨*postfix-expression*⟩ [⟨*expression*⟩]
           | ⟨*postfix-expression*⟩ ( )
           | ⟨*postfix-expression*⟩ (⟨*expression-list*⟩)
           | ⟨*postfix-expression*⟩ . ⟨*identifier*⟩

⟨*expression-list*⟩ ::= ⟨*expression*⟩
           | ⟨*expression-list*⟩ , ⟨*expression*⟩

⟨*unary-expression*⟩ ::= ⟨*postfix-expression*⟩
           | ⟨*unary-operator*⟩ ⟨*unary-expression*⟩
           | `sizeof` ⟨*unary-expression*⟩
           | `sizeof` (⟨*type-name*⟩)

⟨*unary-operator*⟩ ::= & | * | + | - | ~ | !

⟨*multiplicative-expression*⟩ ::= ⟨*unary-expression*⟩
           | ⟨*multiplicative-expression*⟩ * ⟨*unary-expression*⟩
           | ⟨*multiplicative-expression*⟩ / ⟨*unary-expression*⟩
           | ⟨*multiplicative-expression*⟩ % ⟨*unary-expression*⟩

⟨*additive-expression*⟩ ::= ⟨*multiplicative-expression*⟩
           | ⟨*additive-expression*⟩ + ⟨*multiplicative-expression*⟩
           | ⟨*additive-expression*⟩ - ⟨*multiplicative-expression*⟩

⟨*shift-expression*⟩ ::= ⟨*additive-expression*⟩
           | ⟨*shift-expression*⟩ << ⟨*additive-expression*⟩
           | ⟨*shift-expression*⟩ >> ⟨*additive-expression*⟩

⟨*relational-expression*⟩ ::= ⟨*shift-expression*⟩
           | ⟨*relational-expression*⟩ < ⟨*shift-expression*⟩
           | ⟨*relational-expression*⟩ > ⟨*shift-expression*⟩
           | ⟨*relational-expression*⟩ <= ⟨*shift-expression*⟩
           | ⟨*relational-expression*⟩ >= ⟨*shift-expression*⟩

⟨*equality-expression*⟩ ::= ⟨*relational-expression*⟩
           | ⟨*equality-expression*⟩ == ⟨*relational-expression*⟩
           | ⟨*equality-expression*⟩ != ⟨*relational-expression*⟩

⟨*and-expression*⟩ ::= ⟨*equality-expression*⟩
           | ⟨*and-expression*⟩ & ⟨*equality-expression*⟩

⟨*exclusive-or-expression*⟩ ::= ⟨*and-expression*⟩
      | ⟨*exclusive-or-expression*⟩ ^ ⟨*and-expression*⟩

⟨*inclusive-or-expression*⟩ ::= ⟨*exclusive-or-expression*⟩
      | ⟨*inclusive-or-expression*⟩ | ⟨*exclusive-or-expression*⟩

⟨*logical-and-expression*⟩ ::= ⟨*inclusive-or-expression*⟩
      | ⟨*logical-and-expression*⟩ && ⟨*inclusive-or-expression*⟩

⟨*logical-or-expression*⟩ ::= ⟨*logical-and-expression*⟩
      | ⟨*logical-or-expression*⟩ || ⟨*logical-and-expression*⟩

⟨*expression*⟩ ::= ⟨*logical-or-expression*⟩
      | ⟨*logical-or-expression*⟩ ? ⟨*expression*⟩ : ⟨*expression*⟩

⟨*constant-expression*⟩ ::= ⟨*expression*⟩

A.13.2 STATEMENTS

⟨*statement*⟩ ::= ⟨*labeled-statement*⟩
      | ⟨*compound-statement*⟩
      | ⟨*assign-statement*⟩
      | ⟨*selection-statement*⟩
      | ⟨*iteration-statement*⟩
      | ⟨*jump-statement*⟩

⟨*labeled-statement*⟩ ::= ⟨*identifier*⟩ : ⟨*statement*⟩
      | case ⟨*constant-expression*⟩ : ⟨*statement*⟩
      | default : ⟨*statement*⟩

⟨*compound-statement*⟩ ::= { }
      | { ⟨*statement-list*⟩ }
      | { ⟨*declaration-list*⟩ }
      | { ⟨*declaration-list*⟩ ⟨*statement-list*⟩ }

⟨*declaration-list*⟩ ::= ⟨*block-declaration*⟩
      | ⟨*declaration-list*⟩ ⟨*block-declaration*⟩

⟨*statement-list*⟩ ::= ⟨*statement*⟩
      | ⟨*statement-list*⟩ ⟨*statement*⟩

⟨*assign-statement*⟩ ::= ;
      | ⟨*assignment*⟩ ;

⟨*assignment*⟩ ::= ⟨*postfix-expression*⟩ ⟨*assignment-operator*⟩ ⟨*expression*⟩
      | ⟨*postfix-expression*⟩ ++
      | ⟨*postfix-expression*⟩ --

⟨*assignment-operator*⟩ ::= = | *= | /= | %= | += | -= | <<= | >>= | &= | |= | ^=

⟨*selection-statement*⟩ ::= `if` (⟨*expression*⟩) ⟨*statement*⟩
        | `if` (⟨*expression*⟩) ⟨*statement*⟩ `else` ⟨*statement*⟩
        | `switch` (⟨*expression*⟩) ⟨*statement*⟩

⟨*iteration-statement*⟩ ::= `while` (⟨*expression*⟩) ⟨*statement*⟩
        | `do` ⟨*statement*⟩ `while` (⟨*expression*⟩) ;
        | `for` (⟨*assign-statement*⟩ ;) ⟨*statement*⟩
        | `for` (⟨*assign-statement*⟩ ⟨*expression*⟩ ;) ⟨*statement*⟩
        | `for` (⟨*assign-statement*⟩ ⟨*expression*⟩ ; ⟨*assignment*⟩) ⟨*statement*⟩

⟨*jump-statement*⟩ ::= `goto` ⟨*identifier*⟩ ;
        | `break` ;
        | `return` ;
        | `return` ⟨*expression*⟩ ;

A.13.3 DECLARATIONS

⟨*declaration*⟩ ::= ⟨*function-definition*⟩
        | ⟨*block-declaration*⟩

⟨*function-definition*⟩ ::= ⟨*declaration-specifiers*⟩ ⟨*declarator*⟩ ⟨*compound-statement*⟩
        | ⟨*declarator*⟩ ⟨*compound-statement*⟩

⟨*block-declaration*⟩ ::= ⟨*declaration-specifiers*⟩ ;
        | ⟨*declaration-specifiers*⟩ ⟨*init-declarator-list*⟩ ;

⟨*init-declarator-list*⟩ ::= ⟨*init-declarator*⟩
        | ⟨*init-declarator-list*⟩ , ⟨*init-declarator*⟩

⟨*init-declarator*⟩ ::= ⟨*declarator*⟩
        | ⟨*declarator*⟩ = ⟨*initializer*⟩

⟨*initializer*⟩ ::= ⟨*expression*⟩
        | { ⟨*initializer-list*⟩ }
        | { ⟨*initializer-list*⟩ , }

⟨*initializer-list*⟩ ::= ⟨*initializer*⟩
        | ⟨*initializer-list*⟩ , ⟨*initializer*⟩

⟨*declaration-specifiers*⟩ ::= ⟨*declaration-specifier*⟩
        | ⟨*declaration-specifier*⟩ ⟨*declaration-specifiers*⟩

⟨*declaration-specifier*⟩ ::= `const`
        | `static`
        | `typedef`
        | ⟨*type-specifier*⟩

⟨*type-specifier*⟩ ::= void
      | char
      | short
      | int
      | long
      | float
      | double
      | unsigned
      | enum { ⟨*identifier-list*⟩ }
      | struct { ⟨*member-declaration-list*⟩ }
      | class ⟨*identifier*⟩ { ⟨*member-declaration-list*⟩ }
      | ⟨*type-name*⟩

⟨*identifier-list*⟩ ::= ⟨*identifier*⟩
      | ⟨*identifier-list*⟩ , ⟨*identifier*⟩

⟨*member-declaration-list*⟩ ::= ⟨*member-declaration*⟩
      | ⟨*member-declaration-list*⟩ ⟨*member-declaration*⟩
      | private : ⟨*member-declaration-list*⟩
      | public : ⟨*member-declaration-list*⟩

⟨*member-declaration*⟩ ::= ⟨*declaration-specifiers*⟩ ⟨*member-declarator-list*⟩ ;
      | ⟨*function-definition*⟩
      | ⟨*function-definition*⟩ ;

⟨*member-declarator-list*⟩ ::= ⟨*declarator*⟩
      | ⟨*member-declarator-list*⟩ , ⟨*declarator*⟩

⟨*declarator*⟩ ::= * ⟨*direct-declarator*⟩
      | ⟨*direct-declarator*⟩

⟨*direct-declarator*⟩ ::= ⟨*identifier*⟩
      | (⟨*declarator*⟩)
      | ⟨*direct-declarator*⟩ [⟨*constant-expression*⟩]
      | ⟨*direct-declarator*⟩ [ ]
      | ⟨*direct-declarator*⟩ (⟨*parameter-list*⟩)
      | ⟨*direct-declarator*⟩ ( )

⟨*parameter-list*⟩ ::= ⟨*parameter-declaration*⟩
      | ⟨*parameter-list*⟩ , ⟨*parameter-declaration*⟩

⟨*parameter-declaration*⟩ ::= ⟨*declaration-specifiers*⟩ ⟨*declarator*⟩
      | ⟨*declaration-specifiers*⟩ ⟨*abstract-declarator*⟩
      | ⟨*declaration-specifiers*⟩

⟨*type-name*⟩ ::= ⟨*declaration-specifiers*⟩
      | ⟨*declaration-specifiers*⟩ ⟨*abstract-declarator*⟩

⟨abstract-declarator⟩ ::= *
      | ⟨direct-abstract-declarator⟩
      | * ⟨direct-abstract-declarator⟩

⟨direct-abstract-declarator⟩ ::= (⟨abstract-declarator⟩)
      | [ ]
      | [⟨constant-expression⟩]
      | ⟨direct-abstract-declarator⟩ [ ]
      | ⟨direct-abstract-declarator⟩ [⟨constant-expression⟩]
      | ( )
      | (⟨parameter-list⟩)
      | ⟨direct-abstract-declarator⟩ ( )
      | ⟨direct-abstract-declarator⟩ (⟨parameter-list⟩)

A.13.4 PROGRAMS

⟨program⟩ ::= ⟨declaration⟩
      | ⟨program⟩ ⟨declaration⟩

A.14 Additional Reading

The C programming language as of 1988 is described in detail in [KR88]. On-line textbooks are available here:

    `http://www.eskimo.com/~scs/cclass/index.html`

    `http://www.strath.ac.uk/CC/Courses/NewCcourse/ccourse.html`

The standard C libraries are described in detail here:

    `http://secure.dinkumware.com/htm_cl/index.html`

A "rationale" for the 1989 ANSI C standard may be found here:

    `http://www.lysator.liu.se/c/rat/title.html`

A context-free grammar for all of C may be found here:

    `http://www.lysator.liu.se/c/ANSI-C-grammar-y.html`

The lexical aspects are specified by (extended) regular expressions here:

    `http://www.lysator.liu.se/c/ANSI-C-grammar-l.html`

A detailed description of C++ as of 1997 and discussions of programming style in C++ may be found in [Str97].

REFERENCES

[KR88] B. W. Kernighan and D. M. Ritchie. *The C Programming Language*, 2nd edition. Prentice Hall, 1988.

[Str97] B. Stroustrup. *The C++ Programming Language*, 3rd edition. Addison-Wesley, 1997.

Appendix B

Hints for Selected Exercises

Chapter 1. Specifying Algorithms

1.2 (a) It might happen that the array segment *is* in order, and this should not be regarded as an error. (b) This statement deals with implementation (how), rather than functional behavior (what).

1.3 Allowing such changes could reduce execution time for subsequent searches, but it is conceivable that the order or multiplicity of entries might be significant to some users.

1.4 The variable should be defined locally rather than be accessible to users.

1.5 See Section 3.6.

1.8 $P == Q$ is *not* correct for P iff Q.

1.9 The quantification for j includes the case when $j = i$, which would make the entire assertion false (when $n > 0$).

1.11 (f) Here is one way to express that exactly one entry occurs more than once:
```
    Exists (i=0, i<n)(j=0; j<n) i != j && A[i] == A[j]
        && ForAll (i2=0; i2<n)(j2=0; j2<n)
            (i2 != j2 && A[i2] == A[j2]) implies A[i2] == A[i]
```

1.12 They are false and true, respectively.

1.13 It is already possible to use either !(x in A[a:b-1]) or x != A[a:b-1].

1.16 As a pre-condition, true means that there is no restriction on when the code may be used; as a post-condition, it means that the code can't be counted on to do anything in particular. As a pre-condition, false means that the code should *never* be executed; as a post-condition, it means that, for any initial state satisfying the pre-condition, the code must not terminate normally.

1.17 (a) present is false, but x is in the array. (b) x is not in the array, but present is true.

1.18 It means present == false, which is the desired property.

1.19 (c) The post-condition should be m >= x && m >= y && (m==x || m==y).

1.20 The value of x is arbitrary, and `present` is an "output" variable only; consequently, its initial value is irrelevant.

1.21 See Section 2.7.

1.22 See Exercise 2.32.

1.23 If y is to be the output variable, the post-condition should be $x = y*y$.

1.24 Generalize the solution to Exercise 1.19.

1.25 The number of distinct values in `A[0:n-1]` is $|\{x \mid x \text{ in } A[0:n-1]\}|$.

1.26 The post-condition must be strong enough to ensure that every entry in the new array is also in the original array and vice versa.

Chapter 2. Verifying Algorithms: Basic Techniques

2.7 Suppose that all the students drop out of the course and the last student to drop out tries to verify this.

2.10 What will happen if $n = 0$ and $A[0] = x$?

2.11 Consider the correctness statement `n==n {n = n-1;} n == n-1`.

2.12 If P is true initially, P will still be `true` after doing nothing.

2.13 Suppose that the value of n is 0.5.

2.14 (v) `x+1 == 1 {x = x+1;} x==1`

2.16 In the assertion `i>0 implies Exists (i=0; i<n) A[i] == x`, the first occurrence of i is free and the subsequent occurrences are bound. This "clash" between free and bound occurrences of i is, of course, bad style and should be avoided.

2.17 The *free* occurrences of i are replaced, but the *bound* occurrences are not replaced.

2.18 (a) `ForAll(x) Exists(y) y>x` ; (b) `ForAll(w) Exists(y) w<x implies w<y<x`, where w may be any fresh identifier.

2.19 (v) `x==0 {x = x+1;} x==1` because `x==0` implies `x+1==1`.

2.20 All the correctness statements are valid; for part (d), the validity follows simply because `false` implies anything, even an assertion that is always `false`.

2.22 Here is a proof tableau:

```
ASSERT(i >= 0 && y == power(x,i))
FACT(power(x,i) * x == power(x,i+1))
ASSERT(i+1>0 && y * x == power(x,i+1))
y = y * x;
ASSERT(i+1>0 && y == power(x,i+1))
i++;
ASSERT(i>0 && y == power(x,i))
```

2.24 The post-condition assertion is also the pre-condition.

2.26 The correctness statement is valid.

2.31 Show that `P && B` implies P_0, and `P && !B` implies P_1.

2.33 The inference rule has $n + 1$ premises.

2.35 $n > 0$

2.36 A special-case test for n $= 0$ is one approach; a more elegant approach is to extend the definition of Fib(n) to *negative* n and initialize f and g to Fib(0) and Fib(-1), respectively.

2.37 (b) The invariant and the loop condition do *not* imply that n-i is greater than 0. (c) The loop body does *not* always preserve the (new) invariant if n is odd. (d) The code *is* correct relative to the revised specification.

Chapter 3. Verifying Algorithms: Some Examples

3.2 Obtain the invariant from the post-condition by replacing n by i and adding a range constraint on i.

3.3 Consider the cases i $=$ n and i $\neq$ n separately.

3.4 Change the loop condition to i != n && equal.

3.6 Replace the second assertion in the post-condition by
    A[m] < A[0:m-1] && A[m] <= A[m:n-1]

3.15 Change all occurrences of 10 to 2.

3.24 What will happen if n $= 0$?

Chapter 4. Additional Verification Techniques

4.3
$$\frac{P\{A_0\}I \quad I\&\&B\{C\}R \quad R\{A_1\}I}{P\{\text{for}(A_0; B; A_1)C\}I\&\&!B}$$

4.4 Both A[i] and A[j] are set to 0.

4.6 It will be necessary to use an iteration that "counts down."

4.7 The pre-condition must become A[0] == 0 implies A[1] == 1.

4.8 Consider subscripting the arrays by $I' = I$ and $I' \neq I$ separately.

4.15 The last step of the outer-loop body may set i to 1s instead of just incrementing i.

4.19 Compare with the treatment of "array-shifting" in Section 4.2.

4.31 When $k = 0$, the rules reduce to the following sound (albeit rather useless) axiom schemes:
    false {C} Q
    P {C} true

4.33 For efficiency, consider array entries two at a time; the larger of the two entries cannot be minimal, and the smaller cannot be maximal.

4.36 The obvious solution is to find the maximal entry of every row and then determine which of these is the smallest, but a more efficient solution is possible. If a row has *any* entry greater than the current minimax, a *maximal* entry for that row cannot be smaller than the current minimax.

4.37 Consider what remains to be done after partitioning if f is in the range m:j-1, in j:i-1, or in i:n-1.

Chapter 5. Data Representation: A Case Study

5.6 The include operation would not require a search; on the other hand, the exclude operation would have to search the entire array segment currently in use in case there were more than one occurrence of the value to be excluded. This approach to implementation would be practical in an application in which the include operation was executed more often than the exclude operation and there was enough space in the array for multiple occurrences.

5.7 The advantage is that binary search could be used. On the other hand, the implementations of include and exclude would have to shift array segments right or left to preserve the ordering. This approach to implementation would be practical if membership tests were much more frequent than changes to the set.

5.8 The new operation requires e !in S as a pre-condition, but the implementation does not need to do a search.

Chapter 6. Data Representation: Additional Examples

6.1 What happens to the data representation immediately after the choice operation in the set traversals we have just considered?

6.3 The following recursive function may be used:

```
void RemoveUnacceptable(void)
{ if (!CompMetaphys.empty())
  { Entry StudentNum;
    StudentNum = CompMetaphys.choice;
    CompMetaphys.exclude(StudentNum);
    RemoveUnacceptable();
    if (acceptable(StudentNum))
      CompMetaphys.include(StudentNum);
  }
}
```

6.5 Traverse set T, either (a) adding or (b) removing its elements to or from S.

6.7 (b) Consider what should happen if remove is called more than once before another call of next.

6.8 Removing a set member is least inefficient if it is the last entry of the array segment in use.

6.9 One approach is to use a search cache and have smallest assign the index of the minimal element to the search-cache variable.

6.13 When both *A* and *B* are empty, there is *one* function from *A* to *B*, the "empty" function.

6.19 The Attr type of the SparseArray should be a SparseSet type.

6.24 Add a top variable to the interface for stacks and use the array for other stack entries (if any).

6.35 For a sparse set, consider maintaining a flag in the representation that, when `true`, exchanges the roles of `include` and `exclude` and complements the value returned by `contains`.

6.38 A sparse array of sparse sets.

Chapter 7. Basic Concepts

7.5 For part (e), strings of both even length and odd length should be accepted. The answer to part (h) is $(0 + 11)^*$.

7.8 (a) $rhs = 1 + 0L + L0$

$$= 1 \mid 0\{\, 0^i 10^j \mid i, j \geq 0 \,\} \mid \{\, 0^i 10^j \mid i, j \geq 0 \,\}0$$
$$= \{\, 0^i 10^j \mid i = j = 0 \,\} \mid \{\, 0^i 10^j \mid i > 0, j \geq 0 \,\} \mid \{\, 0^i 10^j \mid i \geq 0, j > 0 \,\}$$
$$= \{\, 0^i 10^j \mid i \geq 0, j \geq 0 \,\}$$
$$= L$$
$$= lhs$$

7.10 *Every* language satisfies the equation in part (d); but the *smallest* language is $\varnothing$.

7.11 The language defined is the closure of S (i.e., S^*).

Chapter 8. State-Transition Diagrams

8.1 (a) The following regular expression describes the language: $l(l + d + u(l + d))^*$, where $l = a + b + \cdots + z + A + B + \cdots + Z$, $d = 0 + 1 + \cdots + 9$ and $u = \_$.

8.14 (a) The transitions $s_1 \xrightarrow{\varepsilon} s_0 \xrightarrow{0} s_2$ and $s_1 \xrightarrow{\varepsilon} s_0 \xrightarrow{1} s_1$ that start with an ε transition must be replaced by new edges $s_1 \xrightarrow{0} s_2$ and $s_1 \xrightarrow{1} s_1$, respectively.

(b) See the diagram on page 195.

8.15 A transition labeled by a set of strings may be replaced by a set of transitions between the same states, each labeled by one of the elements of the set of strings. Then any transition labeled by a nonempty string may be eliminated by introducing new "intermediate" states as necessary and a sequence of transitions labeled by the individual tokens in the string. Finally any transitions labeled by ε may be eliminated as discussed in Section 8.4.

Chapter 9. Regular Languages

9.3 (a) The following describes the same language: $(1 + 01^*(0|1))(1 + 01^*(0|1))^*$.

9.5 Consider an example such that $\varepsilon \in S$.

9.7 Use the fact that this language is the complement of the language of strings with an even number of 1s.

9.9 The states of the constructed diagram should be of the form (s, t), where s is a state of the diagram for S and t is a state of the diagram for T.

9.10 Use a state-diagram construction that reverses the direction of all edges.

9.11 The language in part (b) may be described by the regular expression 0^*1^*, and so *is* regular. The other languages are *not* regular.

9.13 The pumping lemma may be used to prove that a regular language has certain properties or, by contradiction, that a language is *not* regular, but it cannot be used to show that a language *is* regular.

9.14 The "if" direction is easy: if the state diagram accepts a string of length $\geq n$, the pumping lemma applies. For the "only if" direction, the state diagram must accept a string of length $\geq n$ because there is only a finite number of strings of length $< n$. To show that a string of length $< 2n$ must be accepted, use a proof by contradiction.

Chapter 10. Context-Free Languages

10.1 The production defines the language whose only member is the empty string. The empty language may be defined by a "circular" production of the form $\langle null \rangle ::= \langle null \rangle$.

10.3 Add the production $\langle statement \rangle ::=$ do $\langle statement \rangle$ while $((\langle exp \rangle))$; .

10.4 The language $\langle neutral \rangle$ is the language of strings over the vocabulary $\{+, -\}$ with the *same* number of occurrences of + and -. The strings in the language $\langle neg \rangle$ have one more occurrence of - than +, and the strings in the language $\langle pos \rangle$ have one more occurrence of +.

10.5 Use one nonterminal corresponding to each of the states in a state diagram that recognizes the language.

10.7 Consider a string with more than one nonterminal symbol that could be expanded.

10.12 (b) The language defined by the grammar may be described by the regular expression 0^*1^*.

10.13 The grammar is ambiguous but might be satisfactory nonetheless if statement sequencing is an associative operation.

10.15 Initialize the stack with a token, say 0, to indicate "neutrality"; then use the stack to store *excess* + or - signs, as necessary.

10.16 Use a string of the form $0^i1^i0^i1^i$.

10.18 Intersection may be expressed in terms of union and complement.

Chapter 11. Parsing

11.3 The nonterminal $\langle Ntail \rangle$ could generate the empty string in more than one way, so the grammar would be ambiguous.

11.4 A positive closure of β is equivalent to $\beta\{\beta\}$.

11.5 Suppose a closure occurs in the middle of a production as follows: $\alpha\{\beta\}\gamma$. If γ does not generate the empty string, the following condition must be verified: $first(\beta) \cap first(\gamma) = \emptyset$.

Chapter 12. A Taste of Computability Theory

12.2 `FailSafeHalts` is implementable trivially: the function that always returns `false` satisfies the specification.

12.3 The same argument that showed `halts` to be unimplementable works with `HaltsOnSelf`.

12.5 Reduce `HaltsOnAll` of Exercise 12.4 to `Equiv`, using a function that ignores its argument and simply returns `true`.

Index

CPSIA information can be obtained at www.ICGtesting.com
Printed in the USA
LVOW08s1712141016

508827LV00002B/213/P